SWITCH ON YOUR MIND

SWITCH ON YOUR MIND

Accelerative learning strategies at work

Edited by
Justus Helen Lewis and Moni Lai Storz

ALLEN & UNWIN

Copyright © of this collection, Justus Helen Lewis and Moni Lai Storz 1997
Copyright © of individual pieces remains with the authors

All rights reserved. No part of this book may be reproduced or transmitted in any form or by any means, electronic or mechanical, including photocopying, recording or by any information storage and retrieval system, without prior permission in writing from the publisher.

First published in 1997 by
Allen & Unwin
9 Atchison Street
St Leonards NSW 2065
Australia
Phone: (61 2) 9901 4088
Fax: (61 2) 9906 2218
E-mail: frontdesk@allen-unwin.com.au
URL: http://www.allen-unwin.com.au

National Library of Australia
Cataloguing-in-Publication entry:

Switch on your mind: accelerative learning strategies at work.

Bibliography.
Includes index.
ISBN 1 86448 256 7.

1. Executives—Training of. 2. Learning. I. Lewis, Justus. II. Storz, Moni Lai.

658.31245

Illustrated by Jean Mulligan
Set in 10/13 pt Garamond Book and Trade Gothic by DOCUPRO, Sydney
Printed by Australian Print Group, Maryborough, Victoria

10 9 8 7 6 5 4 3 2 1

Contents

Foreword vii
Acknowledgements ix
Biographical note on contributors x

1. Introduction 1
   Justus Helen Lewis and Moni Lai Storz
2. What is accelerative learning? 15
   Justus Helen Lewis and Moni Lai Storz
3. Motivation for managers 33
   Keith Stead
4. Personality type indicators, learning styles and accelerative learning 45
   Glenda Hutchinson
5. Making sense of your communication 63
   Helen Millican
6. Accelerate your time management 79
   Lynne Wenig
7. Team building using accelerative learning 95
   Robyn Keal
8. The accelerative learning way to health and stress management 113
   Moni Lai Storz
9. Memory for managers 127
   Keith Stead
10. Memory and graphs 139
    Geoff McDonald
11. Strategic planning: An accelerative learning approach 153
    Jeffrey Lai

12 Managing for the future: Developing a whole-brain organisation 167
Justus Helen Lewis and Moni Lai Storz

13 Managing your work with accelerative learning 177
Justus Helen Lewis

Bibliography 191

Foreword
Professor David Karpin

The world in which managers operate continues to rapidly change. This is certainly the case in the Asia-Pacific region where markets are growing rapidly for an ever widening range of goods and services. As these markets have grown, competitive pressures have also increased. Today, in virtually all industries competition is global in its nature. Growth and competition have brought significant advantages to consumers. However, managers and the workforces they lead have been placed under increasing stress as they seek to cope with this complex, and changing environment. Coping with both the speed and nature of change is the major challenge facing managers as individuals and leaders within their organisations.

I recently had the privilege of leading a group of talented Australians who studied the issues and challenges facing Australian enterprises and their managers in responding to the increasingly competitive business environment. We produced a report entitled *Enterprising Nation: Renewing Australia's Managers to Meet the Challenges of the Asia-Pacific Century*. We came to the conclusion that Australian enterprises and their managers were generally not performing as well as their international counterparts. This was despite the general view that our professional and vocational education systems were more than adequate (although they can be improved).

We found that Australian managers were lacking in what has been described as the 'soft' skills. They were not good performers in important areas such as communicating, leading teams, motivating the workforce to lift performance and cross-cultural management. They did not accept that it was important to continually invest in their own, and their workforces', personal development.

Continual investment in human capital characterises the way in which high performance enterprises conduct and sustain themselves. They see the education and training of their people as a responsibility of all managers. It is not a task that can be delegated to the human resources department (although this department should provide services to assist the manager in performing the task).

Our Task Force identified five key challenges for Australia (I am sure these challenges are relevant to varying degrees to most countries). They were:

1. develop a positive enterprise culture through education and training;
2. upgrade vocational education and business support;
3. harness the talents of diversity;
4. achieve best practice management development; and
5. reform management education.

I observe that there is an increasing acceptance of the linkage between knowledge and skills and superior individual, team and organisational performance. There is a growing understanding that learning is a lifelong process, it does not end when one completes one's school or university studies.

Ideally, there should be a shared responsibility for gaining skills and knowledge between the individual and their employer. Both share in the gains of learning; both must contribute. People learn in formal and informal settings. They learn on-the-job and from other people such as superiors and mentors. They also learn from each other; sometimes individually and sometimes in groups. We must encourage learning and we must be open-minded about how we might learn.

By gaining knowledge and enhanced skills we can cope more easily with complexity, uncertainty and change. This will improve our organisation's performance and our own ability to cope with stress. Learning should also be fun. We do better what we enjoy.

This book focuses on improving the way we learn. It is practical and focuses on 'learning how to learn'. It can be used by an individual, a team or an organisation. The editors have assembled a group of talented and knowledgeable colleagues who are specialists in their own fields, but who have a common interest in improving the way managers learn. The editors have ensured that there is an integration of the various themes developed by the individual contributors in their introduction and closing chapters.

The editors and their colleagues have produced a readable and practical guide for managers who wish to improve their own, and their organisations', performance through learning.

Professor David Karpin
Monash Mt Eliza Business School
Melbourne

Acknowledgements

This book is possible because of the committed and dedicated efforts of a band of scholars and management trainers who believe that there is a better way to teach and train people to release their potential. People such as Sigrid Gassner-Roberts at Adelaide University, Bernie Neville at La Trobe University, Melbourne, Kathleen Benson formerly at the Australian Institute of Management (AIM), the members in the Accelerated Learning Society of Australia (ALSA) in Melbourne and Evelyn Low of Accelerated Learning Services, Malaysia, come readily to mind. We thank all these people for their support and belief in our ideas and our work.

To Joshua Dowse, Jo Jarrah and Karen Ward at Allen & Unwin, who have spent much time with us labouring over the book, our thanks and warm affection.

As editors of this book, we also wish to thank our contributors. They have behaved as true professionals and friends in their efforts to assist us way beyond just the writing of their articles. For that, we are more than grateful.

The practice of our ideas would not be possible if there were no 'students'. In this regard we are grateful to our clients who have spread the word about our training. In particular, we would like to thank Tony Lovell of Rohm and Haas, Australia, Doreen Ch'ng of General Motors, Asia Pacific Operations in Singapore, and Guadalupe Guajardo, Kathleen Herron and Clifton Jones of Technical Assistance for Community Services, Portland, Oregon, USA.

We also want to thank all the students we have taught (and are still teaching) at various tertiary institutions throughout the years. They number in the thousands. All of them in their own way have contributed to us as teachers.

To Professor David Karpin of Monash Mt Eliza Business School, whose commitment to management training is well known in Australia, and who took on the task of writing the foreword for this book, in spite of his busy schedule, our sincere gratitude.

To the scholars before us and whose research and writings have taught us much, our special thanks, for paving the way.

Biographical note on contributors

Glenda Hutchinson

Glenda Hutchinson is an experienced training consultant with over twenty-five years in corporate training, education and small business management. She has been a training consultant and director of Communication Connection Pty Ltd for over eight years. She conducts courses in personal development, management and leadership development, transition management, customer service, training techniques, presentation skills, communication skills and study techniques. She is a qualified administrator/accreditor of the Myers-Briggs Type Indicator and a certified practitioner of the William Bridges Managing Organisational Transition process.

Robyn Keal

Robyn Keal is a management trainer and consultant specialising in the areas of personal and professional growth. She uses accelerative learning techniques in all her work, combining it with experiential activities for team building. Working with a range of organisations, Robyn's programmes include venture training in the Australian outback and hotel resorts of Malaysia.

Jeffrey Lai

Jeffrey Lai is the Managing Director of Global Business Strategies Pty Ltd. He has an Electrical Engineering degree and a Postgraduate Diploma in Information Technology from Monash University, Australia. He has more than fifteen years experience in the computer industry working for companies such as Business Computers of Australia, Fujitsu and Olivetti Australia. Jeffrey is an experienced trainer using accelerative learning techniques and pioneered the application of accelerative learning to the teaching of computer subjects. At Global Business Strategies, Jeffrey and his team of consultants help Australian companies in developing global managers for Asia, principally through Asian languages and cultural training programmes using accelerative learning techniques. They also consult to companies on strategic planning for globalisation.

Dr Justus Lewis

Justus Lewis is a senior lecturer in the Human Resource and Quality Management section of the Nanyang Business School at Nanyang Technological University, Singapore. She has over twenty years of varied and extensive experience as a lecturer, public speaker, management trainer and consultant. Her areas of expertise include instructional design, distance education, open learning, self-access material, video and multimedia. Justus' current research interest is in the development of creative and innovative ways of using computer-mediated communication to facilitate learning. Her publications include *Get Ahead: A Life Skills Approach to Study Skills* (Oxford University Press 1995, with Yap Swi Nco).

Geoffrey McDonald

Geoffrey McDonald is a consultant, facilitator, speaker and writer. He focuses on 'Inventing the Future' through the creation of new design models. He is the author of *A Home-Office You Love* and *Beyond the Electronic Drawing Board*, both books published by Archiquar, Victoria. He is also the founding editor of the newsletter of the Accelerated Learning Society of Australia and a Master Practitioner in Neuro-Linguistic Programming (NLP). He has presented at major international design conferences, been published in four countries and holds a Master's degree in Architecture.

Helen Millican

Helen Millican was a lecturer in learning theory and teaching practice in the health sciences at La Trobe University, Australia where she used accelerative learning techniques. Currently, Helen uses the techniques to train long-term unemployed and small business people in communication strategies, management theory and occupational health and safety issues.

Dr Keith Stead

Dr Stead is a registered psychologist and senior lecturer in Educational Psychology and Science Education at Monash University, Australia. He specialises in learning skills, rapid reading techniques, motivation and memory enhancement skills. He consults to companies on motivation and memory skills using accelerative learning techniques to enable managers to cope with information overload.

Dr Moni Lai Storz

Moni Lai Storz is a senior lecturer in the Department of Anthropology and Sociology, Monash University, Australia. She is also an education and management trainer/consultant to global companies. Moni specialises in cross-cultural communication and negotiation skills, diversity management, stress management and accelerative learning techniques. She also provides a briefing service for individuals requiring information on Asian business cultures. Her pioneering of the application of accelerative learning techniques to the teaching of Mandarin Chinese is documented in her book *Mind Body Power: The Self Help Book on Accelerated Learning* (Times Books International, 1989). Her first novel, *Notes to My Sisters*, was recently published by Times Books International, Singapore.

Lynne Wenig

Lynne Wenig, managing director of CentreBrain Pty Ltd, is a process consultant, a specialist in training and development and a recognised expert on time management. She is a non-executive director of Generation Victoria, is on the board of the Old Meat Market Craft Centre and has been a commissioner for the City of Port Phillip. Lynne has an extensive client list and has worked with major Australian and South-east Asian organisations in both the private and public sectors. Earlier in her career Lynne was an academic attached to the Department of Management in the David Syme Business School, Chisholm Institute of Technology (now part of Monash University), where she was head for four years. Lynne has written textbooks and articles for business and professional journals and her most recent book, *The A to Z of Time Management*, was published in Australia by Allen & Unwin and in South-east Asia by Heinemann.

Introduction
Justus Helen Lewis and Moni Lai Storz

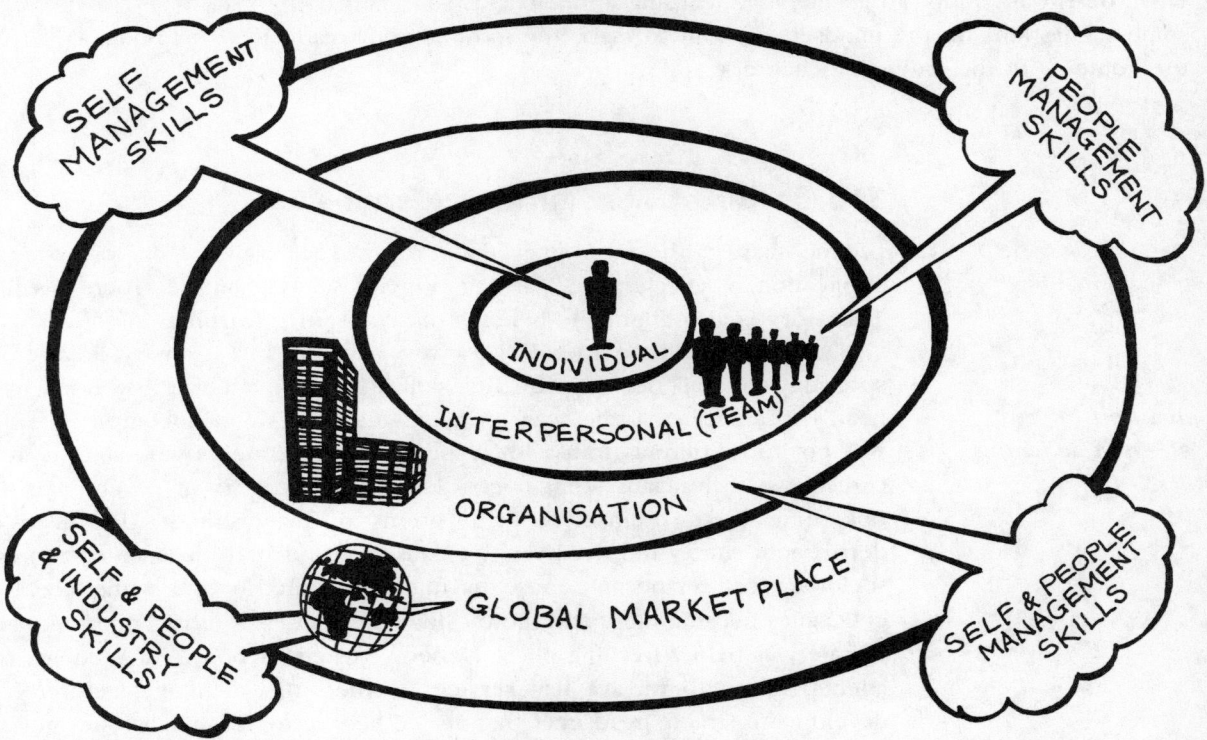

In this chapter

- The power of accelerative learning
- Managing change with accelerative learning
- How to read this book
- The sources of accelerative learning theory
- About the chapters . . .
- Enjoy the change
- Why accelerative learning works
- Transform your lifestyle and your work

Overview

This chapter introduces you to:

- why you should adopt an accelerative learning approach to work;
- some suggestions on the mindset to adopt to make the most of your reading of this book;
- the contents of the individual chapters.

The power of accelerative learning

Let me share with you a story that I know very well, a story of how the application of accelerative learning principles has changed a person's life. This story is also about the benefits of accelerative learning.

Application of accelerative learning principles

Once upon a time there was a very capable but ordinary lecturer in sociology. Like all her departmental colleagues, she was very stressed by a head of department who was promoted to his level of incompetence. He was not too different from a lot of heads of departments who started their careers as 'technicians'—engineers, doctors, sociologists or psychologists—but then found themselves in positions of management. Her head of department simply did not have the skills for good staff management. So our sociology lecturer became more and more frustrated by her workplace. Her colleagues became more and more estranged from each other and workplace morale was below freezing point. Nobody trusted anybody. The students (or clients) began to receive bad service. By then, the sociology lecturer had developed migraine headaches that visited her weekly, then daily. She smoked a packet of cigarettes a day and lived on coffee; her ulcers flourished. The sociology lecturer began to hide from her students or, when she couldn't, she disliked them. Then one night she had a dream. She was back in a makeshift classroom in a country far, far away and there were little children all round. A glowing light surrounded these children. As the light grew whiter and brighter, the sociology lecturer saw herself making a promise that she would always teach in the best possible way to release all the gifts these children had brought with them from the angels above. Then the light disappeared. She woke up.

Dr Lozanov

There must be a better way, she said to herself. And there was. Soon after that, this sociology lecturer was introduced to a man who told her about the work of Dr Lozanov. She undertook a research project to test out the ideas of accelerative learning by setting up two different tutorial groups. One was taught by herself in the traditional way, as she had always taught sociology. The other was also taught by herself, but with accelerative learning techniques. The results were astoundingly different. The students in the accelerative learning class enjoyed themselves more, operated as a team and had more creative ideas. The class taught with accelerative learning principles also scored higher marks in the examination. The sociology lecturer, convinced of the value of accelerative learning methodology, started to apply the philosophy of accelerative learning to her work and her life. She gave up smoking by using accelerative learning techniques of relaxation and positive suggestions to access the power of her subconscious mind. She became more relaxed, and her mind was calmer. In this state, she communicated better with her students and colleagues. Things and people started to change in a more positive way for her. The spiral of success began. Feeling so good about herself, she completed her first book on accelerative learning and then a novel. Both were published. The book on accelerative learning was sold out in the first six months in Asia alone. It has now been reprinted for the third time.

The potential for creativity, the birthright of everyone, was realised for her. She was so thrilled and excited about her performance, based on her discovery about accelerative learning, that she was highly motivated to share her ideas with others. She designed a management programme on stress and health management and took it to Asia. That saw the beginning of her consultancy and training business in the Asia-Pacific Rim. Meanwhile, back home in Australia, she began to package sociology into cross-cultural training programmes for global executives who were moving into Asia to work. These programmes became her highly successful 'Asia Business Cultures' series, offered in Australia and on the North American continent for global executives. This sociology lecturer discovered to her delight that the more she did, the more she could do. So she lived happily ever after, teaching at the university and travelling around the Asia-Pacific region training people in using accelerative learning to enhance themselves, their teams and their organisations.

Potential for creativity, the birthright of everyone

This story demonstrates that the benefits of accelerative learning are both personal and professional. In order to be effective in our occupation, be it a housewife or a trainer, we first need to be effective as a human being. Successful human beings make effective workers. Accelerative learning or whole-brain approaches enable the person to be an effective individual in the workplace.

Benefits of accelerative learning are both personal and professional

Managing change with accelerative learning

This book is a response to many of the issues that face managers as we move into the next century. As trainers and managers, we have found that there is no longer one right answer: the changes that confront us are simply too rapid and constant in our lives. Our experiences and our discussions with many others in a similar position reinforce this one fact: unless we find new ways of absorbing information and using it creatively, and begin to do this at an increasingly faster pace, we and the organisations we belong to will not survive. Ultimately, the final challenge for us as managers is to learn how to be authentic human beings by developing ourselves and helping to develop those with whom we work. In short, we are engaged in learning, changing and adapting.

The final challenge for us as managers is to learn how to be authentic human beings

This book recognises that managers need to acquire the skills of learning how to learn or they will be left behind. These skills demand both our mind-brain and our body. They require a commitment to change, for learning is about changing—in attitudes, emotions, knowledge, skills and lifestyle. The philosophy of this book is that accelerative learning principles provide us with the best tools for doing this. When we master these tools, the benefits are many.

How to read this book

So how does one acquire these tools and how will reading this book assist you to 'switch on your brain'? You want to improve your own performance in some way, if you are reading this book—you want to be more creative with your ideas, achieve more with your time, realise some of your more cherished aspirations. At the same time, as you read, you may find that you hear the chatter of internal dialogue: 'This is just too Pollyanna-ish to be credible.'

Internal dialogue

'Well, maybe, but the human mind is certainly capable of some of the most amazing things.'

'No doubt, but these things are unlikely to happen to me.'

'Why not?'

'Well, how *do* I actually apply all this stuff?'

These are all valid responses. The accelerative learning approach is not a magic panacea which will instantly change your life. Like any other learning process, it must be systematically implemented over time. But it does provide an attitude to our experience and a set of strategies and techniques for dealing with life situations which the authors have found to be effective for themselves. Like anything else worthwhile, it requires us to apply the techniques and strategies deliberately and systematically over a period of time in order to reap the maximum benefits. And different people will go about doing this in different ways and achieve different results.

But where do you start? And how do you know which strategies are going to be best for you? Chapter 13 describes a 'five minutes per day' approach which you may like to try. However, it will also help to put yourself into the right frame of mind as you read through the earlier chapters, whether you prefer to read them in sequence or dip into those that interest you most. Here are some suggestions.

Which strategies are going to be best for you?

- Before you start to read, take a couple of moments to remember that you are a unique individual. There is no one quite the same as you. Ask yourself what kind of a person you are. This does not necessarily mean in terms of the Myers-Briggs indicator, one of the several personality description tools that are available. It often helps to concentrate on simpler, more obvious things. Are you the kind of person who usually feels better after vigorous exercise, for example? Or does sitting quietly in a rocking chair with some good music do more for you? Are you a morning rooster who can jump out of bed and jump into your routine, or a night owl who gets going in the late evening? Are you the kind of person who can't stand an untidy house and must get the dirty dishes washed up immediately, or can you tolerate a fairly high degree of disorder around you so long as you feel you are achieving something worthwhile? Or—more likely—do some of these things apply some of the time in some situations, but not in others?

- When you have some idea of the kind of person you are, you can work from your strengths. Thinking about this will focus your reading to notice those techniques and suggestions which will be most relevant to *you*. These are the things that you instinctively know will benefit you. By applying and implementing more of them, you develop habits that will reinforce and develop your strengths. It is easier to build habits that give us satisfaction, and this is a good basis from which to start.

Work from your strengths

Extend your repertoire of successful behaviour

Try out some of the behaviour patterns of other people

Surprise yourself with some creative new behaviours

- At the same time, be open to the possibility that you can extend your repertoire of successful behaviour. For example, accelerative learning places great emphasis on the visualisation of the end result. This is a proven method used widely by athletes to assist them to achieve peak performance. Some people seem to have very clear visual images. Other people seem to have blurred images or even none at all. It can be an interesting exercise to ask a few friends about the images or lack of images that they regularly experience. If you are the kind of person who doesn't have much in the way of visual imagery, ask yourself whether your imagination is orchestrated by talking to yourself about what you are going to do and how you will go about doing it, or perhaps by feeling what it will be like to have achieved your goals. Whichever way your imagination works, you probably assume that everyone else experiences the same thing—not so! Life can be richer if you try out some of the behaviour patterns of other people. They just might click for you or give you a handle on another way of being more effective. One of the writers of this chapter has found that this strategy of trying on other people's behaviour has worked extremely well for her. For example, although she was familiar with the idea that some people have idetic imaginations (they can imagine accurately whole scenes or pages from a book), she assumed that this was something one either had or didn't have and 'knew' she definitely didn't have it! Then she attended a Neuro-Linguistic Programming (NLP) course (see next section) and learnt that there were enormous differences in the type and quality of other people's visual imagery. A lot of other people reported specific vibrant, coloured images while hers were abstract, blurry and black and white. At that point she decided that she would think in colour and organise her mental imagery more efficiently; to her surprise, she was able to do so and has continued to think in colour ever since. So, surprise yourself with some creative new behaviours.

The sources of accelerative learning theory

The founding father of accelerative learning, or 'Suggestopedia' (see Chapter 2), is Dr Georgie Lozanov, a Bulgarian psychotherapist and medical scientist. The heart of his ideas can be found in the psychology and physiology of the mind-brain, the subconscious mind as pioneered in the writings of Sigmund Freud and Carl Jung: the theory of suggestions and multi-sensory learning.

Sources of accelerative learning theory

Accelerative learning today is a large, eclectic bundle of ideas and approaches which have extended the pioneering work of Lozanov. One strand comprises whole-brain approaches with their emphasis on the integration of left- and right-brain learning techniques. Neuro-Linguistic Programming (NLP) is another strand, included by some trainers as a closely related approach to accelerative learning. In fact, any approach which brings into focus the 'right' side of our brain has been loosely termed accelerative learning. For example, the focus on feelings, senses, imagination and intuition which is part of the Myers-Briggs instrument can also be associated with accelerative learning. So can developments in cognitive psychology, such as the seven intelligences work of Howard Gardner. In summary, any approach that looks at learning, change and performance and places emphasis on the integration of the body and mind-brain with an implicit or explicit aim of realising human potential can be seen as a form of accelerative learning.

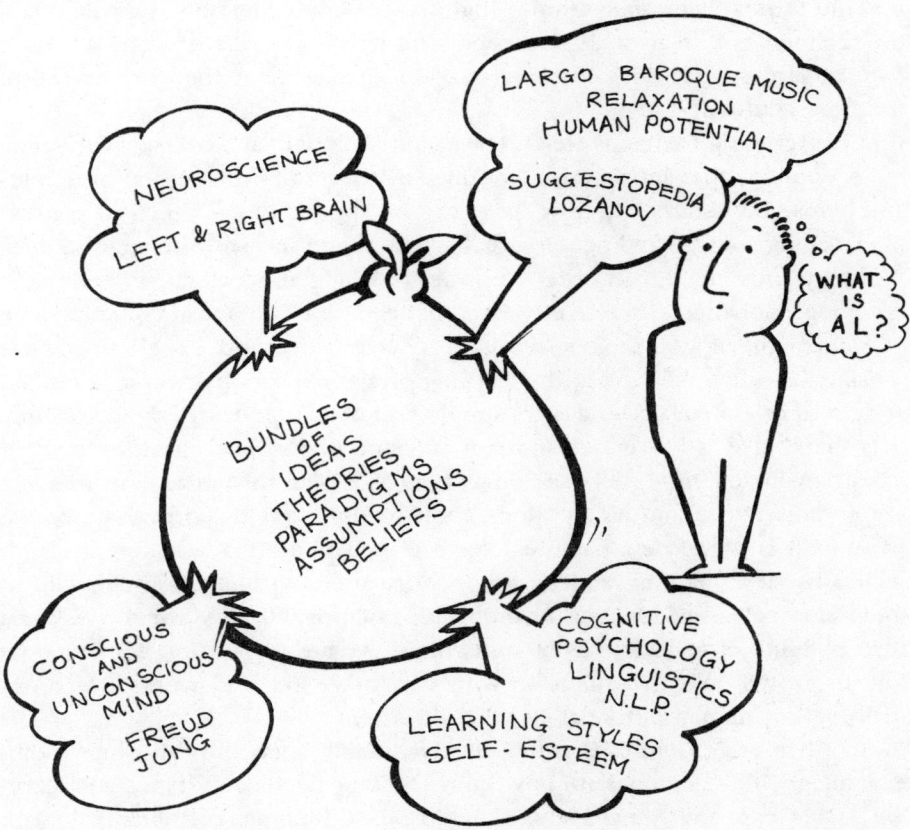

About the chapters . . .

This book is written by authors with a passion for accelerative learning. They have found that accelerative learning approaches work for them in their roles as supervisors/managers and educators/trainers. Taking these whole-brain principles as a framework, these authors have shared their ideas from their own specialised fields to help managers empower themselves in the workplace. Some critical areas in which managers need skills include identifying the potential of their workforce, motivating their people to perform at their best, dealing with stress, managing time, using their memories, communicating with others and building teams, and business planning. These are all traditional people-management skills that managers have to master. By putting each of these in the framework of accelerative learning principles, we believe that you will be given a fresh look at what you are doing. The empowerment of self and others that comes from using the accelerative learning paradigm and the techniques that go with it to cope with new and global changes are their own reward. Accelerative learning is also a management tool for survival in the next century.

Chapter 2

Chapter 2, by Dr Justus Helen Lewis and Dr Moni Lai Storz, sets the scene by explaining what accelerative learning is. It describes the central principles and helps you understand how these can be applied in the practical context of managing yourself and people, creating teams and surviving in organisations. We wrote this chapter in order to make it clear that accelerative learning is not about individual discrete elements that can be taken out of context. Some of them can, of course, but we can achieve more and experience more satisfaction when we look at the learning process in a global way as a unified system. Accelerative learning is not simply a set of techniques for rapid learning. It is that, but it is also much more. It is also a philosophy, an attitude taken towards yourself and others as human beings. Within this attitude or mindset are certain values and assumptions about people and the organisations we work in. It is therefore a paradigm, for it gives you a set of assumptions with which to view learning and human performance. Within this philosophical mindset, accelerative learning, or the whole-brain paradigm, views the task and responsibility of managers as being twofold: we are responsible for our own human growth and that of those with whom we live and work. It is about realising our human potential and that of others.

In Chapter 3, Glenda Hutchinson gives many anecdotes and interesting examples which demonstrate how knowledge of personality types and learning styles can assist managers. Hutchinson, a training consultant, is well qualified to write about personality type indicators, learning styles and accelerative learning. She has been deeply involved with the Accelerative Learning Society of Australia for many years and was its hard-working secretary for a year. During that time, her work in accelerative learning using the Myers-Briggs indicator was well known. In recent years, the Myers-Briggs indicator has been widely used as a management tool. As it is multi-dimensional and focuses on the right side as well as the left side of the brain, this indicator is compatible with accelerative learning principles which stress whole-brain learning.

Chapter 3

Chapter 4 examines an important topic for managers: motivation of self and others. Dr Keith Stead, a psychologist at Monash University, has spent many years teaching the subject, as well as training managers in it. He focuses on the role that feelings play in the process of motivating ourselves and others. Feelings are very important in the accelerative learning model, but they are often neglected in management literature. There could be many reasons for this. Possibly the main one is to do with the notion that feelings cannot be trusted. They are seen by many as irrational and non-scientific. Feelings reside in the right brain hemisphere where the subconscious and the intuition are also found. By accessing feelings through the use of positive suggestions—or what Dr Stead calls affirmations—it is easier to motivate ourselves and others. Under conditions of relaxation, our subconscious functions better and thus these suggestions are inclined to work more efficiently.

Chapter 4

Chapter 5, by Dr Moni Lai Storz, a sociologist at Monash University, is on the management of health and stress. The accelerative learning model has an important theoretical component to do with relaxation. It is under conditions of relaxation that the human mind-brain and body perform at their peak. An unhealthy and stressed manager is an unproductive person. This has been well documented in many people's lives, as well in many studies on the subject. Stress management experts globally concur that stress management education is vital to all managers, regardless of culture.

Chapter 5

We have used the framework of accelerative learning to train managers about stress and health, as we believe that this topic in particular requires them to commit themselves totally. Stress management is about life management: when we do not handle our stress well, we tend to fail. Behind every successful manager is an effective stress management programme. Managers will find that applying accelerative learning principles to the management of stress is both easy and fun—twin principles intrinsic to this learning model. When a stress management programme is neither easy nor fun, it will not work. By using the power of your subconscious, you will find that the ideas derived from accelerative learning principles in this chapter will work for you—that is, if you want them to.

Chapter 6

Chapter 6, written by Lynne Wenig, a well-known management consultant in Australia and author of the *The A to Z of Time Management,* is a succinct, fun piece on how to be more effective in relation to the second most important resource managers have: time. Time management and stress are closely related, as every manager knows. Wenig examines time management in a profoundly novel way, compared with the more traditional approach. Using the principles of accelerative learning, time is examined from a whole-brain model. Wenig looks closely at what a lot of people don't know: that there is a left-brain approach and there is also a right-brain approach to managing our time. When we are not aware of the way our brain relates to time in the world, we may be using the wrong side for the right time, or the right side for the wrong time. The integrated brain approach to time management can accelerate your use of time.

Chapter 7

Once your health, stress and time management skills are under control, Chapter 7, by Dr Keith Stead, takes you to the delights of memory enhancement. Many managers have admitted to us that their battle with the information explosion is a losing one because of bad memory. Inevitably, as the conversation goes on, we discover that they are in despair chiefly because they have accepted that their memories are bad. Almost in the same breath, they also tell us that they have no idea what memory is all about—thus the need for this chapter on memory skills.

Chapter 8

Side by side with his chapter is another written by Geoff McDonald, an architect who loves accelerative learning so much that he became the editor for the Accelerative Learning Society of Australia's newsletter for two years. In Chapter 8, McDonald talks about the relationship between graphs and memory. This is useful for managers, especially those who have to use graphics a great deal in their area of expertise. Equally importantly, McDonald shows us how to use our memory to recall graphs. Remembering that graphs are really pictures, the process of recalling them is a challenge, much like trying to remember Chinese ideographs.

Chapter 9

No book for managers can be complete without at least one chapter on communications. Helen Millican, senior lecturer in La Trobe University's School of Nursing, has spent much of her time doing research and writing as well as teaching using Neuro-Linguistic Programming. The NLP model shares similarities with accelerative learning in many respects. Essentially, the accelerative learning model is a communications model; so is NLP. In Chapter 9, Millican discusses how you can become a better communicator by understanding and using some of the principles and techniques that are common in these two models of communication.

Chapter 10 on team building was written by Robyn Keal, a trainer with her own consulting business. It deals with a topic critical to managers' success: the process of creating an effective team. Keal draws on many familiar concepts about team building, putting them together into a unique, integrated whole that is easy and fun to implement. Her chapter makes team building a truly holistic, creative process that results in synergy.

Having acquired the knowledge and skills for their own self- and professional development, managers can apply some of these to a very important area in their organisation: that of strategic planning. In Chapter 11, Jeff Lai, a consultant in global business strategies, discusses strategic planning using accelerative learning principles. Essentially, strategic planning requires creative thinking, a right-brain function, not just logical thinking (left-brain) skills. Generating ideas—the best ideas from your team—demands that managers use techniques which combine the totality of the mind-brain. This means maximising the use of both sides of your brain and those of others. The creative impulse, the Eureka factor, the flash of insight and the aha! feeling reside in the right side of the brain. By drawing out the intuitive potential of people engaged in planning, managers can lead a more creative team and increase their success in strategic planning. Planning demands skills drawn from an integrated mind and body—the ability to think holistically is crucial. The thrust of this chapter is that business planning has to take place in a creative, energy-giving work environment. By focusing on one critical stage of the total process of strategic planning, that of business planning, Lai enlightens us by showing how SWOT can be done in a holistic way that seeks to bring out the creative potential of the managers.

Chapter 12, Managing for the future: Developing a whole-brain organisation, by Dr Justus Helen Lewis and Dr Moni Lai Storz, offers managers some suggestions for coping with the changing needs of organisations within the global marketplace and the challenges these changes pose. The threads of the previous chapters are drawn together and examples given of how accelerative learning principles can be implemented in organisations. Left-brain and right-brain organisations are identified and strategies suggested for bringing about whole-brain organisations.

Chapter 13, by Dr Justus Helen Lewis, currently teaching Business Communication at Nanyang Technological University, weaves the diverse strands from the preceding chapters into a suggested blueprint—a way in which you can progressively switch on your brain to create your own unique accelerative learning lifestyle. It is based on what Lewis calls the 'five-minute principle of learning': if you can do something over a period of time, regularly and with enjoyment, for even five minutes, you stand a very strong chance of developing a positive addiction to that activity—and this, of course, is what accelerative learning is about. This chapter provides a series of suggested five-minute activities for daily use, based on the content of the previous chapters.

Enjoy the change

A synergistic union

As an accelerative learning practitioner, you will find that life takes on a different guise insofar as many things that used to be hard work can become effortless when you consistently implement the suggested strategies. Using your mind and body together creates a synergistic union that makes things easier. You may find yourself becoming healthier once you incorporate accelerative principles into your lifestyle. This is a side-effect that has been noted by many students taught using accelerative learning principles. When you picture yourself being fitter mentally and physically, you may be surprised to find that life suddenly looks more colourful. The joy of living returns as you realise more and more of your potential each day. You can be true and authentic as an individual. This is effective self-management.

Energy generates energy

Picture a person at work who is managing herself well. She bounces into her office, enthusiastic about projects, cheerful in the face of difficulties and problems. She communicates clearly to her colleagues, honouring their gifts and knowing their weaknesses. She is a valued team member simply because she injects energy into others: energy generates energy. To manage herself well, she has acquired the ability to motivate herself as well as to manage her time and control her stress levels. This self-management is a necessary condition for working with others effectively as a team. When there is good teamwork, the benefits to the organisation are enormous.

Learning a whole-brain process

As this example shows, the interpersonal benefits created by accelerative principles can have a ripple effect throughout the organisation, because it is people who shape the corporate culture. Accelerative learning principles, because they are based on a holistic paradigm, tend to make people feel good about themselves—mind-brain and body. People who feel like this find it easier to make others feel the same, thus resulting in more caring organisations. Caring organisations are places that make learning a whole-brain process, as it must include feelings (the heart) and the intellect (the head). Such organisations are effective because they are created by effective people. The two—people and organisations—are linked in real synergy.

It is our conviction that the benefits of accelerative learning principles can be all-encompassing, from an individual level to that of the whole organisation. This book was written on the basis of conviction. When something is good and it works, we want to share it!

Why accelerative learning works

The reason why accelerative learning works is straightforward and simple. It relies on a pre-given factor: human potential, something which is universal. By tapping into the power of the subconscious mind, which is a force that is in every person, changes are set in motion for the release of the potential inherent in us all. The power of the subconscious mind is like electricity: you cannot see electricity as such but its effects are powerful. If a child were to ask you 'What is electricity?' you would have difficulty in showing her. However, you will surely tell the child not to stick her fingers into an electric socket. Likewise with the power of the subconscious: you cannot see it, but the results are tangible enough—and often surprising.

Transform your lifestyle and your work

You, too, can transform your lifestyle and your work and release the potential that is your birthright. The rest of this book offers advice on how accelerative learning can work for you. It is easy, fun and liberating. Try it!

Recapping the key points

- Accelerative learning strategies are supported by research.
- We need to find new ways of absorbing relevant information and using it creatively. Accelerative learning principles provide us with tools to do this.
- Like implementing any other change, adopting a deliberate and systematic approach will reap maximum benefits.
- Work from your strengths and then extend your repertoire.

- Allow yourself to be surprised by your creative new behaviours.
- Accelerative learning theory crosses subject boundaries and integrates their findings in a holistic way.
- Harnessing and harmonising the mind and the body creates synergy and releases the potential in us all.
- Change is inevitable so we might as well find ways of enjoying it!

What is accelerative learning?

Justus Helen Lewis and Moni Lai Storz

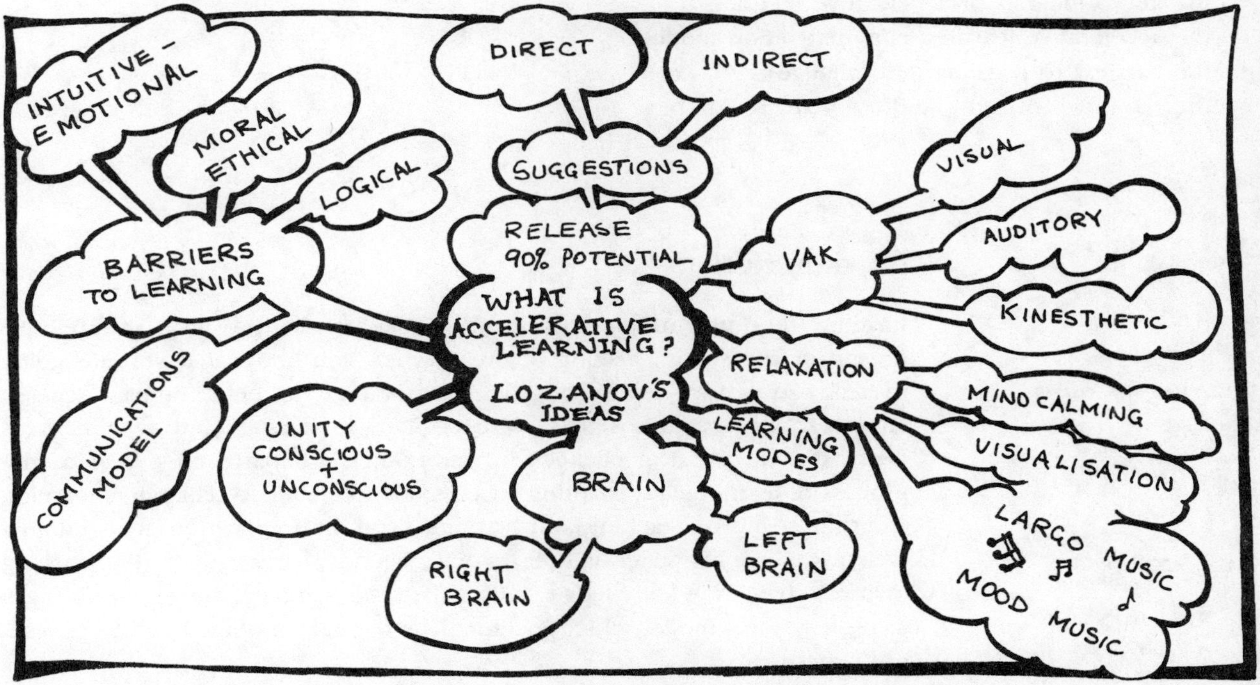

In this chapter

- Introduction
- Lozanov's principles of learning
  - the conscious and the unconscious
  - direct and indirect suggestion
  - relaxation
- The accelerative learning communication model
- Barriers to learning
  - The logical barrier
  - The intuitive-emotional barrier
  - The moral-ethical barrier
- Accelerative learning and brain research
- This is how you do it

'Life is like a ten speed bicycle: most of us have gears we never use.'
Charles M. Schulz

Overview

This chapter explains:

- the key principles of accelerative learning;
- the accelerative learning communication model;
- the barriers to learning (and change);
- the relevance of right- and left-brain research.

Introduction

Imagine the flutter of anticipation when you are about to meet an attractive person or the sinking feeling of dread when you know that you are going to hear bad news. These feelings are a natural part of being human. Accelerative learning recognises that these changes in feelings and awareness, as well as some physical changes in our bodies, are part and parcel of the process of learning and adapting successfully to change. Accelerative learning is an approach to teaching and learning—and, by implication, to communication in general—which is holistic and systemic. It recognises that learning involves changes in knowledge, skills and attitudes and explains these changes using a systems model which includes our mental, emotional and physiological processes.

The implications of this for managers are enormous. Managing the processes of change in an organisation involves managing not only one's own learning to adapt to change, but also the learning of one's associates and employees. Organisations themselves need to learn how to learn. According to Senge, one of the leading exponents of business management, a business that sees itself as a learning organisation is one that 'enhances the capacity to create, rather than one that merely adapts and survives'. Managers who understand and apply the principles of accelerative learning to themselves and to their organisations can expect to reap the benefits in terms of reduced stress, greater productivity, higher job satisfaction and more creative adaptation to change.

This chapter explains the key principles involved in accelerative learning, starting with its founding father, the Bulgarian psychotherapist and medical scientist, Dr Georgie Lozanov.

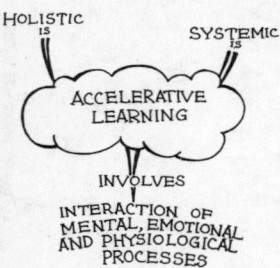

Learning involves changes

Dr Georgie Lozanov

What is accelerative learning?

> Lozanov's highly researched and specific approach to applying accelerative learning principles to teaching and learning is called Suggestopedia. The name, Suggestopedia, refers to one of the central theoretical underpinnings of the theory, the power of suggestion—both direct and indirect—to set in motion our unconscious mental processes, and hence the central role of suggestion in communication in general.

Suggestopedia

Lozanov starts from the premise that conventional ways of teaching and learning do not take into account the untapped potential and reserves of the unconscious. Reserves are 'all those possibilities, known or still unknown, which are not a customary phenomenon for the average individual under given time and places' (Lozanov, 1978).

It is difficult to prove that the unconscious exists in terms of showing it to you empirically, like a table or chair. Instead, it is more like the power of electricity. You can't see it, but the results flowing from it are extremely powerful.

Lozanov includes all human potential in his definition of reserves of the unconscious and considers that the average person may be using only about 10 per cent of their potential. He is particularly interested in hypermnesia (super memory), the involuntary control of the body demonstrated in such things as psychogenic (mind-induced) anesthesia and the ability of the body to heal itself. He believes that all human beings have a vast repertoire of stored capacities, talents and knowledge and this is the 90 per cent potential waiting to be released in all of us.

Reserves of the unconscious

90 per cent potential

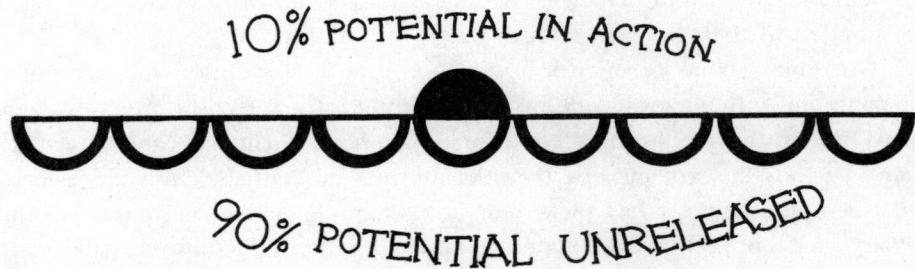

These potential capacities and talents can be released chiefly through unconscious mental activity. Suggestions, both direct and indirect, play a key role in setting unconscious mental activity in motion.

Lozanov's principles of learning

Unity of the conscious and the unconscious

Because human beings are integrated wholes, the conscious and unconscious always operate together in a partnership in everything we do. Our conscious mind is like the tip of an iceberg: the submerged part of the iceberg is the unconscious mind. Every time we remember something, we bring part of the unconscious into consciousness.

Unity of the conscious and the unconscious

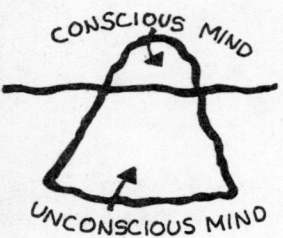

Imagine yourself walking along a busy street and a poster catching your eye. You stop, scratch your head and whistle a tune for no apparent reason. You wonder why it suddenly popped into your mind. Then you realise that you are looking at a poster advertising a holiday tour. You recall that the tune was played regularly in the hotel where you spent a most enjoyable holiday. Unconsciously you have made the connection between the poster and the tune.

The cues that our unconscious picks up can influence our behaviour more than those things of which we are consciously aware. In one frequently mentioned case, a group of psychology students decided to play a joke on their psychology professor. Every time the professor moved to a certain corner the students looked wide awake and attentive. Every time he moved away, they fidgeted, yawned and looked at their watches. By the end of the class, the professor had stayed put in the corner to which the students had driven him by subtle changes in their behaviour. His unconscious had responded to their non-verbal cues.

Our unconscious can perform complex feats of perception and decision-making and influence our actions. For example, at a selection interview we may find we have a strong feeling for or against a particular candidate that can't entirely be explained by considering their credentials. The chances are that our unconscious has picked up cues that the conscious mind is not aware of. Months or weeks later, we find our intuitions confirmed and can find a rational justification for our earlier feeling. The importance of the unconscious is a well-documented phenomenon and it plays a crucial role in accelerative learning when combined with the use of suggestion and relaxation.

We learn through direct and indirect suggestion at both conscious and unconscious levels

'What you are speaks so loudly that I cannot hear what you say.'
Ralph Waldo Emerson

Suggestion is the key to tapping the stored reserves of human potential. When we use the term 'suggestion' in connection with accelerative learning, we are using it as a technical term. It refers in general to all the processes of influence used in communication, either with others or with ourselves. More specifically, in applications of accelerative learning, suggestion refers to certain types of indirect suggestion. Suggestion in general, however, may be direct or indirect, verbal or non-verbal.

Direct and indirect suggestion

For example, in the traditional approach to teaching, a teacher tells students what they need to know, using words—either spoken or written—as the principal medium of communication. This is an example of direct verbal suggestion.

Translated into the business world, a conventional induction programme for new employees may involve a short lecture and a folder of material to read. This is direct verbal suggestion. Most people recognise that this tends not to be very motivating. When you understand the principles of accelerative learning, you can see why. It doesn't take into account many of the other 'suggestions' that are around. If the general behaviour of the organisation reflects high morale and commitment, these indirect suggestions may be far more motivating. They may even encourage the newcomer to listen to the lecture and read the material. If, however, the general behaviour reflects clock-watching and lack of interest, it is less likely that the verbal direct 'suggestions' will be attended to. These other factors are equally part of the organisation's communication process and the quality of these non-verbal, indirect suggestions will have a considerable influence on how 'suggestively' the direct, verbal 'suggestions' will be interpreted.

Much of our conscious focus tends to be on direct, verbal suggestions—on what we are told to do. However, when we decide to stop at a red traffic light or cross the road with the 'green man', we are consciously responding to direct, non-verbal 'suggestions'.

Recent studies of communication have highlighted the importance of non-verbal communication, and there is now a flood of books on the market dealing with body language and its interpretation. Body language exemplifies indirect, non-verbal suggestion. The burgeoning image industry is another example of a recently developed field which focuses on the influence of

Non-verbal communication

non-verbal suggestion in our day-to-day communication. Although this is nothing new (managers have always known that the interviewee who turns up in clean, well-pressed clothes with a recent haircut will have an edge over the slovenly presented), the attempt to understand why this is so and to use this understanding to empower people certainly is.

One way of looking at suggestion is as a continuum that has, at one end, direct, conscious, verbal and non-verbal suggestions, and at the other end, indirect and unconscious suggestions. Because we are unaware, most of the time, of the suggestions that are being made to us, indirect and unconscious suggestions can be extremely powerful. For example, we may tell our subordinates that we have an 'open door' policy. This is the verbal, direct suggestion. Consciously, we recognise the value of good relationships on the job.

Unconsciously, however, we are less convinced, so we find ourselves instructing the secretary to insist on everyone making an appointment, which may mean a delay of up to a week. This behaviour is the indirect, non-verbal suggestion to our team. Conscious and unconscious suggestions are in conflict—not only for us, but for our employees. They hear our words and they also experience the secretary's insistence on an appointment. Guess which message wins out in their minds.

In applications of accelerative learning, 'suggestion' usually refers to hinting and intimating in an indirect way. For example, if you want to improve productivity in your department, you have two options. You can issue a memo and inform everyone that greater productivity is required, or you can use 'indirection'. You can practise 'management by wandering about', take an interest in what your staff are doing, catch people in the act of doing the right thing, and praise them on the spot, as advocated by the One Minute Manager.

Suggestion continuum

CONSCIOUS EXPLICIT DIRECT SUGGESTION
↑
THE SUGGESTIVE CONTINUUM
↓
UNCONSCIOUS IMPLICIT INDIRECT SUGGESTION

> Suggestion, as discussed above, can take a wide variety of forms. The history of the use of suggestion also goes back a long way and spans many cultures. We know, for instance, that some Australian Aborigines practise bone-pointing. Bone-pointing can lead to illness and even the death of the person at whom the bone is pointed. In a modern context, many doctors recognise that patients' attitudes towards their illnesses and their will to live can substantially affect the outcomes of a disease.
>
> In pre-scientific societies, there is strong evidence that the power of suggestion has always been used. In the Indian Ayurveda and in the ancient Chinese systems of medicine and philosophy, the power of

> mind over body is closely related to the power of suggestion. In the Chinese martial arts, the training of both mind and body seeks to establish practitioners' mastery of their environment.
>
> Suggestion is part and parcel of the process of the socialisation of children. Suggestions by parents, teachers and friends affect the development of children's self-esteem, identity and self-concept. So if we are constantly told we are stupid, the chances of us thinking of ourselves as stupid people are high. We may think we can't do maths and this becomes a self-fulfilling prophecy.
>
> Good novelists and playwrights use 'indirection' extensively. They do not say that a person is good or bad: they show it through the character's words and actions and use these to elicit the appropriate responses from their readers and audience.

Since suggestion is always present in any communication, why not become more aware of it and use it to release the remaining 90 per cent of our untapped potential?

Relaxation

Relaxation is the third of Lozanov's principles of learning. This is the key which empowers suggestions to activate the potential of our unconscious minds. Relaxation enables us to let go and experience ourselves as free-floating beings. By letting go, we release more of our unconscious mind power. For example, how often have you tried in vain to remember a person's name? Later on, when you have 'given up', and may be taking a shower, the name comes back to you. In accelerative learning terms, the explanation is that, although your conscious mind has let go, your unconscious is still working on the problem. When you relax sufficiently and empty your conscious mind of some of its preoccupations, your unconscious has a chance to 'speak' to you.

Of course, we can't empty our minds of preoccupations all the time, but we can cultivate our ability to relax at will and keep a certain relaxed alertness that encourages the retention and recall of important information.

The process of suggestion works best when we are physically and mentally relaxed. Suggestive messages, either given to ourselves or given by

Relaxation

others, enter our unconscious more quickly and produce maximum results when we are free of stress. We learn with joy, interest, enthusiasm and increased motivation.

Accelerative learning uses an integrated approach to relaxation, including physical, mental and breathing exercises, and the use of music. Since total relaxation involves all our senses—sight, hearing, smell, touch and taste—the more all these senses are harmoniously and simultaneously integrated, the more body and mind become relaxed, thus releasing more mental and physical energy. Used properly in a teaching situation, the different methods of relaxation combine with the teacher's suggestions to activate the unconscious resulting in hypermnesia (super memory) and rapid learning.

The accelerative learning communication model

Accelerative learning communication model

As a manager you are constantly engaged in the process of communication, whether directly or indirectly, using the spoken or written word, or by the workplace practices that you encourage or discourage. By definition, a communication is interpersonal: it involves at least two people.

The accelerative learning approach to communication recognises that when two people communicate, messages go from one to the other in a four-way system. Because our conscious and unconscious minds are two aspects of a unitary system, both are involved when we communicate.

For example, Sharon is introduced to John at a party. She sees him as well-dressed and good-looking. He sees her as vivacious and well-informed. This is Sharon's conscious awareness interacting with John's conscious awareness. But for each of them, their conscious mind is also interacting with the other person's unconscious mind. John's unconscious is registering interest in Sharon and, although he is not aware of it, he is standing closer and his body stance is mirroring hers. Sharon is aware of this, however, and her conscious mind registers it. Unconsciously, she goes on the defensive and John's conscious mind registers that she seems to be paying less attention than she was a minute ago. They continue to talk, however, and as they relax with another drink, both their unconscious minds communicate rapport to each other as they unconsciously mirror each other's body language, their conscious minds intent on the conversation.

4-WAY COMMUNICATION

CONSCIOUS

UNCONSCIOUS

CONSCIOUS ←→ CONSCIOUS

CONSCIOUS ←→ UNCONSCIOUS

UNCONSCIOUS ←→ CONSCIOUS

UNCONSCIOUS ←→ UNCONSCIOUS

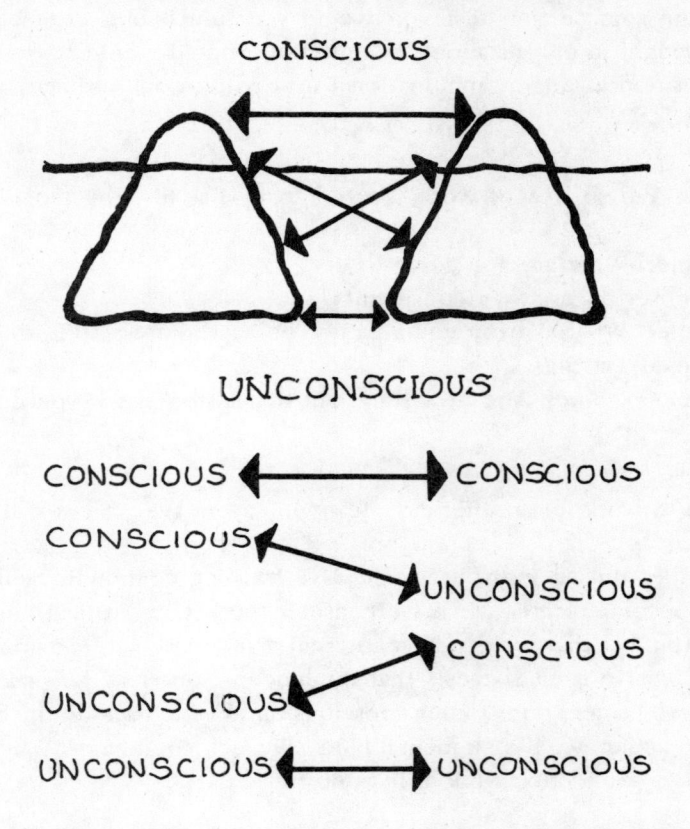

The communication model also applies to communication with ourselves. We communicate with ourselves both consciously and unconsciously. The suggestion factor is always there, and the unconscious is always busy picking up cues.

How many of us have experienced the situation of moving to a new home in the same city and then, the first time we go out for the night, finding to our surprise that we have driven back to the front door of our previous home?

One of our relatives had an interesting experience of her unconscious mind at work. One evening, a friend remarked: 'I always know it's you coming. You give a little cough just as you open the gate.' In this instance, the conscious mind recognised the familiar front gate and the unconscious mind communicated with a cough to the friend.

Internal dialogue

How often have you experienced an internal dialogue that holds you back from taking some action that you would very much like to take. Visualise yourself caught in mid-air about this question. Should you leave your current secure position in a large multinational firm and go out and start your own business?

First voice: I'm so sick of work. The company has lost the plot. It's time I got out.
Second voice: What are you going to do?
First voice: Set up my own consultancy.
Second voice: What are you going to live on as you are setting up?
First voice: My savings.
Second voice: Oh yes. And how long will that last? What if you don't make it?

So you go to work for another day. Meanwhile, your two voices will continue the dialogue.

How does this fit into the accelerative learning communications model? This will become clearer when we consider the barriers to learning. For the moment, the fact that we can have internal dialogue which sometimes never seems to resolve itself suggests that our unconscious may be making some very powerful suggestions to our conscious mind which inhibit the conscious mind from acting. We have a mental block. We lack confidence. Why do some people have confidence while others do not?

Barriers to learning

We don't accept every suggestion made to us. This is just as well. If our unconscious and conscious minds were willing to accept every suggestion, we would be exposing ourselves to all sorts of dangers. If I suggest to you that you can jump into a pool and swim to the other side, then you will rightly reject my suggestion if you cannot swim. Fortunately, human beings have a number of 'filtering' mechanisms which are part of our mostly unconscious functioning. These filters are of various kinds. Some of them are part of the framework that enables us to make sense of experience and talk about it with other people. Other filters prevent us from accepting suggestions that would be injurious to us in some way, like jumping into the deep end if we can't swim.

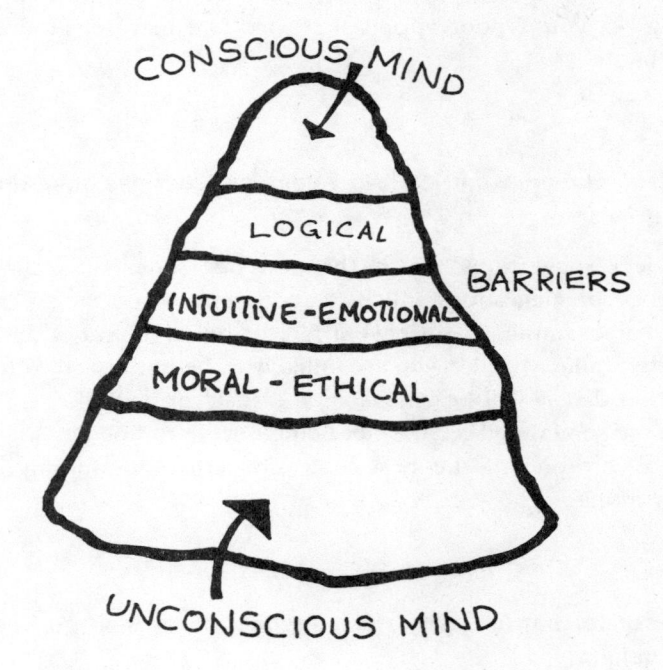

```
        CONSCIOUS MIND
              ↓
         ╱─────────╲
        ╱  LOGICAL  ╲
       ╱─────────────╲   BARRIERS
      ╱ INTUITIVE-EMOTIONAL ╲
     ╱───────────────────────╲
    ╱     MORAL - ETHICAL     ╲
   ╱───────────────────────────╲
              ↑
        UNCONSCIOUS MIND
```

> Lozanov identified three types of barriers to learning:
>
> - logical;
> - intuitive-emotional; and
> - moral-ethical.
>
> Since these barriers are part of our protective mechanism, incoming suggestions must harmonise with them in order to be accepted. 'The more a suggestion harmonises with the logical requirements of the personality, the intuitive-emotional and moral-ethical components of the personality, the quicker and easier is the suggestion realised.' (Lozanov, 1978)

Barriers to learning

Logical barrier

The logical barrier: We reject illogical suggestions

We naturally reject suggestions which seem illogical to us. For example, if you have performed well throughout the year with no adverse feedback and your boss gives you a poor appraisal report, you may reject this as being unfair and biased.

Intuitive-emotional barrier

The intuitive-emotional barrier: We reject suggestions that are threatening to us

We also reject suggestions which threaten our sense of security or our self-confidence, or suggestions which run counter to our strong feelings about something. For example, if you have a fear of being on water and someone recommends a holiday cruise, you are unlikely to be impressed. You will resist the suggestion that it will be enjoyable and that you will like it. The uneasy feeling that we sometimes get, despite being unable to find any logical reason for it, is possibly one of the best indications that our intuitive-emotional barrier is working.

Moral-ethical barrier

The moral-ethical barrier: We reject suggestions which go against our moral beliefs

We also reject suggestions which run counter to our sense of values, particularly if these values are based on religious or cultural beliefs of long standing. For example, you will be unlikely to continue to read this book if you feel that it violates your values in some way.

The unconscious mind is a bit like a computer. The operating system it runs on is programmed to accept what it sees as being in our best interests. Hence it screens out anything that it sees as illogical, emotionally threatening or against our deeper values. Unfortunately, there are some 'bugs' in the operating system too. These bugs have been introduced at various stages in our lives.

For example, we may firmly believe 'No pain, no gain' because parents and teachers emphasised this philosophy when we were young. Consequently, we see learning as something that is difficult and that has always been a struggle with little result. It may be that you had a rotten teacher who punished you every time you made a mistake. To this day, one of us hates dealing with numbers because she had a terrible teacher who used to send her out of class for every mistake she made. If your experience is similar, you will have to 'debug' your mental operating system through a process of desuggestion.

Another common mental 'bug' has to do with your self-concept. If you have been constantly told you are stupid, you may already have internalised a view of yourself as stupid. You may believe you have reached your present position only through a series of 'flukes'. You may have little confidence in your ability to learn.

Self-concept

So, although our conscious and unconscious minds are a unity and our unconscious is in one sense 'always on our side', seeking what it *sees* to be the best for us, it is not always the best judge of what *is* the best. It is a bit like a very loving but uneducated parent who, when her child leaves home and studies information technology, can't accept that this subject will lead to a worthwhile career. It wasn't around when she went to school.

The three anti-suggestive barriers intertwine and mutually interact. Since they are protective mechanisms, they cannot be destroyed totally and we would not wish them to be. We can, however, re-educate them by using the power of suggestion.

This can be done by critically examining our assumptions about ourselves and our ability to learn. Having identified some of the limiting beliefs we have about our own learning, we can learn to put ourselves into a state of relaxed alertness where, through suggestion, we can implant more positive beliefs about ourselves. By 'debugging' our mental programs, we can achieve more mental energy and learn with enjoyment and enthusiasm. The positive suggestions we make to ourselves can supplant the negative ones.

Throughout this book you will be given a multitude of 'suggestions' as to how you can apply the accelerative learning principles explained above to your personal and professional life as a manager. You will be shown how you can use the power of 'indirection', or indirect suggestion, through relaxation, to tap into your potential. You will have the opportunity to listen to the voices of a number of different experts in their fields, telling you how you can learn to be more in control of your time, your memory, your learning and your planning for the future.

Many studies have been undertaken to investigate the power of suggestion. One of these, in the mid-1980s, was of two groups of school children. Each group contained an equal representation of confident and less confident children. The difference between the groups was that one group of children believed that their intelligence was fixed. The other children believed that intelligence could be increased with practice. Both groups of children were given a series of problems of increasing difficulty. Initially the confident children forged ahead. When the more difficult problems appeared, however, the children who believed that their intelligence was fixed gave up, apparently believing that they had reached the limits of their intelligence! Even the most confident ones in this group lost their confidence as they encountered initial failure. Those who believed that intelligence could be increased, on the other hand, viewed the more difficult problems as a challenge that they could conquer with greater application. They persevered and were successful. Such is the power of the belief that there is an enormous area of untapped potential awaiting release in all of us.

Accelerative learning and brain research

Unused potential

Recent brain research supports the belief that we all have a degree of unused potential. The more we learn about the brain, the more we realise there is to know and the more possibilities open up to us. People workers, like teachers and managers, can use this knowledge to better understand themselves and the people they work with.

Brain dominance

> One of the areas which has been particularly influential in teaching, and is equally applicable in management situations, is research into brain dominance. Psychologists and other scientists have conducted experiments which show that there are two sides or hemispheres of the brain, and that each has its own way of doing things.
>
> The left hemisphere is used for speaking, reading, writing and analysing. It is the logical, rational, serious, idea-linking side and the side that helps us to reason. The left hemisphere is interested in facts and knowledge, structure and organisation.
>
> The right hemisphere is for holistic and artistic thinking. It is illogical, irrational and playful. It enables us to recognise similarities and differences, to have insight, to visualise. It deals with spontaneity, feelings and intuition.
>
> Research shows that almost everyone has a preferred or dominant side—the side they use most often. Right-brain dominant people like

> trying new things, and prefer excitement and change in their lives. The more unpredictable something is, the happier the right-brain person is. Left-brain dominant people prefer logic and order. Happiness for them is predictability.

Understanding the principle of brain dominance (which side of the brain we tend to prefer to use) helps us to understand ourselves and others better. From a practical viewpoint, we are more likely to accept suggestions that are in line with our own preferred brain dominance patterns. If we are left-brain dominant and like to live in a neat, predictable and orderly environment, we may have an emotional barrier to adopting a 'management by wandering around' approach, which would be more in tune with a right-brained person—unless, of course, we see the wandering around as a way of ensuring that other people are as neat, predictable and orderly as ourselves!

As we progress through this book we will see how both the principles of suggestion—the barriers to learning and the principle of brain dominance—continue to emerge again and again to explain some of the challenges commonly encountered by managers. They also enable us to focus on ways in which people can be both more comfortable and creative in today's working environment.

This is how you do it

Here are some suggestions for applying the principles discussed in a practical way.

- Adopt the belief that you, like every one of us, has 90 per cent unrealised potential.
- Develop a systematic action plan which uses both direct and indirect suggestion for some area of your professional or personal life.
- Experiment with the use of music to achieve a state of relaxed alertness.

Ninety per cent potential?

Rome wasn't built in a day! And neither is the application of accelerative learning. More than likely you will find you have a 'logical barrier' to believing that we all have 90 per cent unrealised potential. Well, for practical purposes, it doesn't really matter whether it's 90 per cent or 9 per cent. The point is, can you accept that you personally may be able to learn, develop and solve a few problems that up until now have eluded you? The only way to test it is to try it.

Begin in a way which does not violate your own logical barrier. What about suggesting to yourself: 'I have at least 1 per cent more potential than I am currently using. I wonder in what interesting area my unconscious will choose to allow me to experience this.' Write this—or whatever is acceptable to you—on a card or in your diary, or some other place where you will come across it regularly. Be prepared to notice any changes in your life.

Develop a systematic action plan that uses both direct and indirect suggestion

Maybe you have to give presentations from time to time and would like to develop some computer-generated transparencies for these presentations. However, you haven't seen yourself (up until now) as computer-literate and feel that you wouldn't be able to do this. This is an example of a logical and an emotional barrier. You haven't done it in the past, so the 'bug' in your thinking argues that you won't be able to do it now (logical barrier). Also, using a computer makes you feel inadequate (emotional barrier).

Start by noticing the lack of logic in your unconscious. Affirm that major reasons for not making computer-generated transparencies in the past were lack of opportunity and not giving yourself time to sit down and play with the program. Now you have the opportunity for a new challenge and you are the kind of person who enjoys a challenge, aren't you? You would not have read this far if you did not enjoy a challenge. Also, playing with the computer can be fun. After all, other people can enjoy this fun activity so you can too. So give yourself time and encouragement on a regular basis and notice any changes in your thinking and behaviour.

Experiment with the use of music to achieve a state of relaxed alertness

Listening to certain types of music, especially slow (largo) music which has approximately 60 beats per minute, has the effect of slowing down the heartbeat from its normal rate (approximately 70 beats per minute). This physiological change is reflected in a feeling of relaxed alertness, accompanied by more integrated brain activity. In layman's terms, it is easier to concentrate and learn. Listening to music also gives you pleasure, and these pleasurable feelings make the access to your subconscious more efficient. Experiment with playing some slow music quietly in the background when you have a lot of reading to do quickly, and need to remember the key points. A word of caution: it is probably better not to listen to songs. You are wanting to remember the words in your reading and the words in the songs may interfere with your processing of the words you are reading.

Music

Recapping the key points

- Learning occurs on both the conscious and unconscious level.
- All communication involves suggestion.
- Learning is most effective when it occurs in a state of relaxed alertness and enjoyment.
- Learning will be resisted if it violates our logical, emotional or ethical values.
- Learning that taps into our unused potential occurs when we remove the negative barriers in our beliefs.
- Learning is easier and more meaningful when we make use of our natural brain dominance.
- Learning is most effective when it involves both sides of the brain.

Motivation for managers
Keith Stead

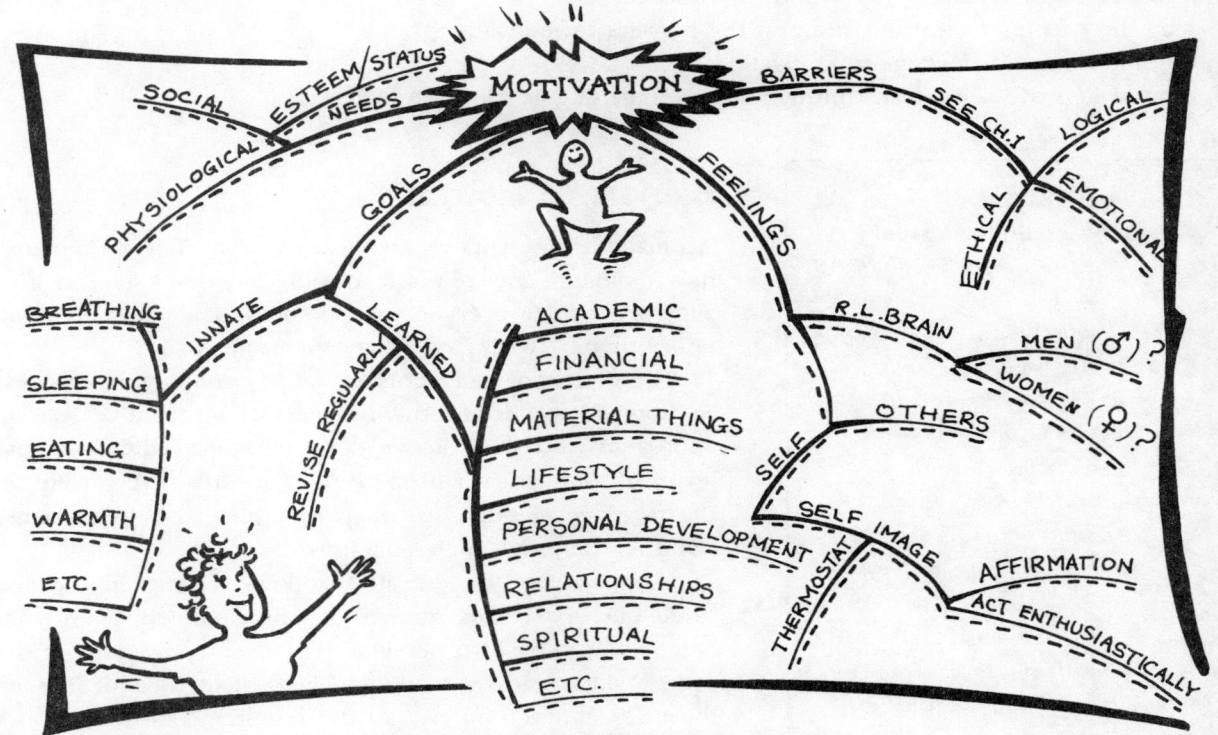

In this chapter

- Barriers to motivation
- Motivation and feelings
- Motivation and self-image
- Motivation and suggestions
- Motivation and needs
- Motivation, accelerative learning and goal-setting
- This is how you do it

Whether you think you can, or whether you think you can't, you're right.

Overview

This chapter explains:

- how accelerative learning applies to motivation;
- why the barriers to learning are also the barriers to motivation;
- the importance of feelings in motivation; and
- how to improve self-esteem through suggestion using accelerative learning.

If you think you're beaten, you are
If you think you daren't, you don't
If you'd like to win but think
you can't
It's almost certain you won't.
If you think you'll lose, you're lost
For out in the world we find
Success begins with an
individual's will
It's all in the state of mind.
Life's battles don't always go
To the stronger or faster person
But sooner or later the person
who wins
Is the person who thinks s/he can
Anon

Barriers to motivation

Barriers to motivation

'So many of my workers aren't motivated! They do the absolute minimum. They're not involved! They don't see that if we all work harder everyone will benefit. They need a bomb under them! I wish I could get them motivated.'

These sorts of comments are all too common in business. So how do we handle them using the accelerative learning approach? And how do we cope ourselves when our own levels of enthusiasm and motivation are low? We can invoke the three accelerative learning principles to help us understand and improve such situations.

Many of these 'unmotivated workers' are very highly motivated out of working hours. They have endless energy and creativity in their own pursuits. They even apply some of that energy and creativity to finding innovative ways of bending the rules and getting around the requirements of the workplace.

Why can they tap into their potential in these situations and not at work? One reason is that they feel more in control of their situation in their outside pursuits, and therefore are more relaxed and have more freedom to experiment. No one is breathing down their necks and about to criticise them. Outside of work, they feel reasonably relaxed and in control. In the work environment, however—for a number of reasons—they go on the defensive. In accelerative learning terms, they put up a variety of logical, emotional and ethical barriers which prevent them from becoming involved in their work to any significant extent. Many of these are familiar: 'We tried that before and it didn't work out' (logical barrier); 'You surely don't expect us to do that!' (emotional); 'That's not the way we do things around here' (ethical).

By applying the accelerative learning principles discussed in Chapter 1, we can more easily motivate ourselves, motivate others and, most importantly, motivate others to motivate themselves—the greatest skill any manager can acquire.

Motivation and feelings

Feelings are the main engine that drives motivation. The bottom line is that, in the long run, we only do willingly (that is, with self-motivation) what we *want* to do. Self-motivation is essentially to do with *feelings*. Facts are important and we need to make decisions based on facts, but if we don't feel like carrying out a particular line of action despite all the facts that indicate that we should, we are unlikely to carry out that action. This is the *emotional barrier* in action!

Consider the situation where you bring home some work you think you should do, but end up watching TV instead. Your feelings are more powerful in this situation than your logic. Incidentally, TV commercials are designed to change our behaviour, but reflect for a moment on those which really do work. Commercials which give us only a list of facts or so-called 'benefits' don't usually alter our behaviour. The effective ones are those which involve our *feelings* in some way.

Accelerative learning recognises that the whole person is involved in learning. In terms of brain functioning, both the left and right hemispheres are used in all effective behaviour. When we collect various facts to present to a board meeting, we are using our left hemisphere. But when we are appealing to our fellow board members for agreement with our proposal, feelings—and hence the right hemisphere and other parts of the mid-brain that control how we feel—are also involved.

The message for us, as managers, is that we need to recognise and accept the feelings of our work team as much as we need to recognise and accept their logic. If we are seeking to alter other people's behaviours, then we need to ensure that their feelings are given due recognition in any proposal we make.

It is useful to note that, in Western societies, women are often more in touch, with their right-brain functioning than are men, so are often more effective in motivating men! Their holistic functioning gives them the edge over those who prefer to use only their left hemispheres!

Values and the corresponding ethical barriers also play a part in deter-

Feelings

Women are often more in touch, with their right-brain functioning mining how motivated people will feel, particularly if we have people from different cultural backgrounds in our team. If what we propose runs counter to what they hold as a deep-seated value, we will run into conflict and disagreement.

Understanding these three barriers to learning—the logical, the emotional and the ethical—and proposing solutions and outcomes which do not conflict with them, assists us in negotiating with those around us. When people's genuine concerns are met in this way, they are more likely to listen receptively to our proposals.

Motivation and self-image

Unconscious messages

Before we leave this discussion of the barriers to motivation—and remembering that the accelerative learning communication model takes into account unconscious communication—let's stop for a moment and consider what some of the unconscious messages at work may be. 'You are not important.' 'Equipment needs more attention than human beings.' 'If you make any comment, it will be construed as criticism of the management and won't be listened to.' 'Being seen in the right place is more important than doing the job.' If a workplace is unconsciously giving out messages like these, it is scarcely surprising that most of the people who work there are likely to put up all sorts of logical, emotional and ethical barriers to being involved in their work. It is a way of protecting their self-image.

> A person with high self-esteem:
>
> - feels confident;
> - respects others;
> - enjoys having fun;
> - has a sense of humour;
> - takes risks and has a go;
> - is able to help other people;
> - trusts him/herself and others;
> - makes his/her own decisions;
> - is able to love and receive love;
> - is real with him/herself and with other people;

- feels OK and feels others are OK too;
- feels he/she can cope in most situations;
- succeeds in most things he/she attempts;
- takes responsibility for mistakes and successes.

Techniques

There are a number of techniques which we can use personally to overcome the barriers to motivation and to encourage others to feel more motivated. One of these is to take care of our self-image and make plenty of suggestions to ourselves, both direct and indirect, which reaffirm and reinforce our sense of human worth and self-esteem.

The way we see ourselves, and also the way we talk to ourselves about our lives, is another avenue of direct and indirect suggestions between our conscious and unconscious selves. The unconscious is usually very literal in its interpretation. If we continually tell ourselves that we are tired and we do not enjoy our work, we can scarcely be surprised when the morning finds us reluctant to get out of bed and face the day. Of course, it is a different situation if we are experiencing an excessive amount of stress—Chapter 5, dealing with health and stress management, will address this.

If we see ourselves as confident, capable and in control, that is the way we will behave. However, if we see ourselves as lacking in confidence and ability, and perceive the world as stacked against us, we will have difficulty behaving other than defensively. We will not feel that we have control over our lives. The way we *see* ourselves affects the way we *talk* to ourselves and the way we *feel* about ourselves.

We will discuss this in greater detail in Chapter 9, dealing with communication. For the moment, it is worth reflecting that, as managers, we have different learning preferences and these affect our ability to motivate and be motivated. Seeing, hearing and feeling are three basic preferences. If we are very visual, we may feel more motivated to adopt a new idea when someone gives us 'the big picture' or 'the vision statement'. We may put a lot of energy into 'showing' people what we mean. This works well a lot of the time. But some of us have a more auditory inclination. We like to be 'told' and 'informed'. We feel upset if someone suddenly 'shows' us what has been accomplished. We want them to 'explain' it to us first and reassure us that they are 'in tune' with our ideas. Yet others of us are more kinesthetic. We like to feel we 'have a handle' on the situation, that we have 'leverage'. We prefer if someone 'runs an idea past us' before showing us how it will look in practice.

Accelerative learning, taking on board insights from Neuro-Linguistic Programming, suggests that, as managers, we may motivate and be motivated more effectively if we develop flexibility in our use of language. By using different language patterns which appeal to the visual, the auditory and the kinesthetic amongst us, we raise our 'motivation quotient'.

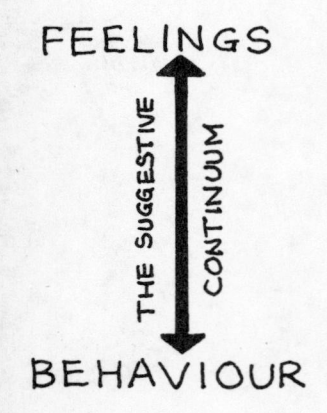

Motivation and suggestions

The relationship between feelings and behaviour is part of the *suggestive continuum* discussed in Chapter 2. When we feel fit and healthy, our conscious feeling of wellbeing communicates suggestively to our unconscious. Unconsciously, we put a spring in our step and a smile on our face. We may only become aware of this if someone else comments on it. Conversely, our behaviour can influence our feelings. By consciously straightening our back and walking more briskly, we suggest to our feelings that all is well and, more often than not, our feelings respond to the suggestion and we *do* feel better than before.

Because our feelings and our behaviour are part of the one interactive holistic system, our feelings about ourselves and the self-image we carry around with us can act rather like a thermostat. A thermostat on the wall in a room ensures that the temperature remains fairly close to a pre-set level by turning on and off the heating/cooling system as the temperature drops or climbs. In a similar fashion, most of us have a pre-set feeling level or self-image that automatically keeps our emotional thermostat on an even keel. We generally continue to feel much the same way about ourselves as we have always felt unless we are faced with some major change in our circumstances. We tell ourselves that we are not the kind of person who does x, y and z. As we saw in Chapter 2, however, the way we feel about ourselves incorporates many barriers to learning that we have acquired at an early age. One consequence of this may be that we do not feel motivated to take advantage of changed situations that come our way. Because of our previously acquired barriers—'bugs' in our operating systems—we view many of the changes that happen to us as problems rather than as opportunities, as difficulties rather than challenges.

Returning to our image of the thermostat, we may find, on closer investigation, that we are living at a most uncomfortable emotional temperature. We have too many negative feelings and not enough positive beliefs about

FEELINGS ↕ BEHAVIOUR
THE SUGGESTIVE CONTINUUM

Self-image

ourselves to feel truly motivated to perform at our best when we are challenged. We need to adjust the thermostat of our feelings to improve our performance, free up more of our unconscious potential and eliminate the unnecessary barriers that limit our self-motivation.

There are several ways in which we can do this. For example, have you ever had a touch of flu but an important contract depended on you being able to present your ideas competently and confidently? You acted enthusiastically and as if you were feeling well, confident and in total control. After a few minutes, you 'forgot' you had the flu until after the presentation. This is an example of a situation where we directly suggest to ourselves by our behaviour that we can do the job. And our feelings follow on. Professional presenters (such as TV newsreaders, actors, politicians, teachers) have this down to a fine art!

Rogers and Hammerstein recognised the power of suggestion very clearly:

> *Whenever I feel afraid*
> *I hold my head erect*
> *And whistle a happy tune*
> *So no one will suspect*
> *I'm afraid . . .*
> *The result of this deception*
> *Is very strange to tell*
> *For when I fool the people I fear*
> *I fool myself as well.*
> Rogers and Hammerstein, The King and I

Power of suggestion

That lyric reminds us of another important aspect: that, as long as we are working in the company of others—even if we are not communicating consciously to them—we are communicating unconsciously. So beware! Your behaviour affects not only your own feelings, but the feelings of those around you. By deliberately suspending attention to our feelings and getting on with the desired behaviour, we not only motivate ourselves, we also encourage others to do likewise.

Motivation and needs

Because human beings exist as a systemic interaction of mental, emotional and physiological processes, motivation can be greatly affected by the extent to which any part of our system is functioning at a reduced level. Have you ever received advice about not broaching a new proposal to your boss in the hour immediately preceding lunch? Many people find it harder to concentrate at that point in the day because their stomachs are beginning to feel hungry.

Maslow's hierarchy of needs

> Maslow suggested that everyone has a hierarchy of needs which affect motivation, starting with the most basic, the physiological. A person on the verge of death by starvation will have little motivation to develop self-esteem. Once a lower order need has been met, a person will be motivated to achieve the next highest order need.

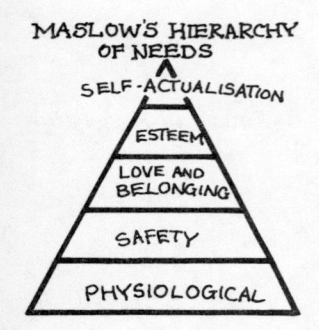

MASLOW'S HIERARCHY OF NEEDS
- SELF-ACTUALISATION
- ESTEEM
- LOVE AND BELONGING
- SAFETY
- PHYSIOLOGICAL

We need to ensure that our employees' basic physiological needs are met (for example, that the environment is not too hot or cold or draughty; that they have adequate breaks and access to nourishing food), then attend to their security and safety needs (for example, ensuring that the computer screen is not emitting harmful electromagnetic rays; or that they are not endangering their health by continuous poor seating arrangements), then meet their belonging and social needs (for example, they do not feel rejected because of race, gender, creed, etc.). Only then can the higher order needs for esteem and status—those that relate to the motivational issues of concern to most managers—be addressed appropriately.

Motivation, accelerative learning and goal-setting

Goals are outcomes we want to achieve for ourselves or our company. Goals give us a sense of direction.

Goals

> Some goals are innate while others are learned.
> - *Innate goals.* Examples of these are finding air, food, water, shelter, warmth, company. Essentially these are the 'needs' we must have in order to survive and are those found on the bottom two layers of Maslow's pyramid.
> - *Learned goals.* These are influenced by personal circumstances

> and experiences. For example, in some societies it is important to learn how to climb coconut palms. In other societies it is important to know how to operate a computer and a video recorder.
>
> Goal-setting can be seen as a form of direct self-suggestion. By setting ourselves goals, we are implying that we can achieve more than we already have, that we have undeveloped potential.

Goals, too, have to filter through our logical, emotional and ethical barriers. If we think a goal is too ambitious for us, our unconscious will reject it on logical grounds. That is one reason why it is often preferable to set smaller goals: 'The journey of a thousand miles begins with a single step.' By satisfactorily achieving a smaller goal, we not only avoid our own logical barriers, we also lower our emotional barriers when we feel good about our achievements and are thus encouraged to take the next step.

All human beings need goals. Individuals who apparently have met all their goals may become listless, unmotivated and unproductive. This is often so of very successful people (sportspeople, artists, career-oriented executives) who, when they've achieved their long-term goal, feel life has lost its meaning and there's only one way to go—down.

Why is this? In the accelerative learning framework of thinking, despite their considerable achievements, they are unconsciously dominated by a limited view of what is possible for them. They do not accept that, with all their successes, there may yet be 90 per cent of their potential still waiting to be explored. Invariably, these people have set only one or two goals. To be constantly motivated, a range of goals is needed in a variety of areas—for example, career, social, financial, personal development, religion, health, material things, travel.

As we journey through life different goals emerge. Goals do change—this is to be anticipated—and we still need to spend time reflecting (another variation of suggestion) on where we want to be and where we want our company to be in one year's time, five years' time and so on.

This is how you do it

You may like to try some of the following suggestions:

- If you are an auditory person and enjoy words, use direct self-suggestion to improve your self-image.
- If you are a visual person and find it easy to see how things will look, use creative imagination and visual imagery.
- If you are a kinesthetic person who likes to get a feel for a new situation, use mental simulation.
- Identify some of the barriers to motivation in your company.

We need to recognise that our actions, thoughts and feelings are usually consistent with each other. For example, when we're not feeling too well, other people often soon notice this because of our actions (we move more slowly than usual or we've a pained expression on our face).

Therefore, because our feelings directly influence our behaviour, we need to know how to alter our feelings if they are making it difficult for us to be self-motivated. To do this, three particular strategies are very useful, particularly when used in concert:

1. Focus on behaviour: get on with the behaviour required—just do it! e.g. You've got to make that important telephone call which has been bothering you. Accept your feelings are negative, but just pick up the telephone and make the call and get on with it! Not only do feelings affect behaviour, but behaviour also affects feelings. You'll be surprised how quickly your initial feelings will change once you start doing whatever is required to be done!
2. Focus on thoughts: are they negative? Change them! Use positive self-talk (affirmations), e.g. you find yourself thinking, 'I'll make a mess of this presentation.' Rip such thoughts out of your mind and replace them with, 'I'm feeling confident; this will go well!'
3. Focus on feelings: okay, they're negative. Start with pretending to be enthusiastic (a particularly useful feeling). By acting enthusiastically, you will soon find the charade soon becomes real—you actually do become enthusiastic. That is, your feelings become positive, and you're on your way.

Recapping the key points

- Motivation is about feelings.
- We feel more motivated when our self-esteem is high.

- We feel more motivated when we are enjoying ourselves.
- Other people feel more motivated by us when they sense that we believe in them and their potential.
- Effective motivators use language skilfully.
- We feel more motivated when we have a variety of goals.
- We feel more motivated when we review our goals regularly.

Personality type indicators, learning styles and accelerative learning

Glenda Hutchinson

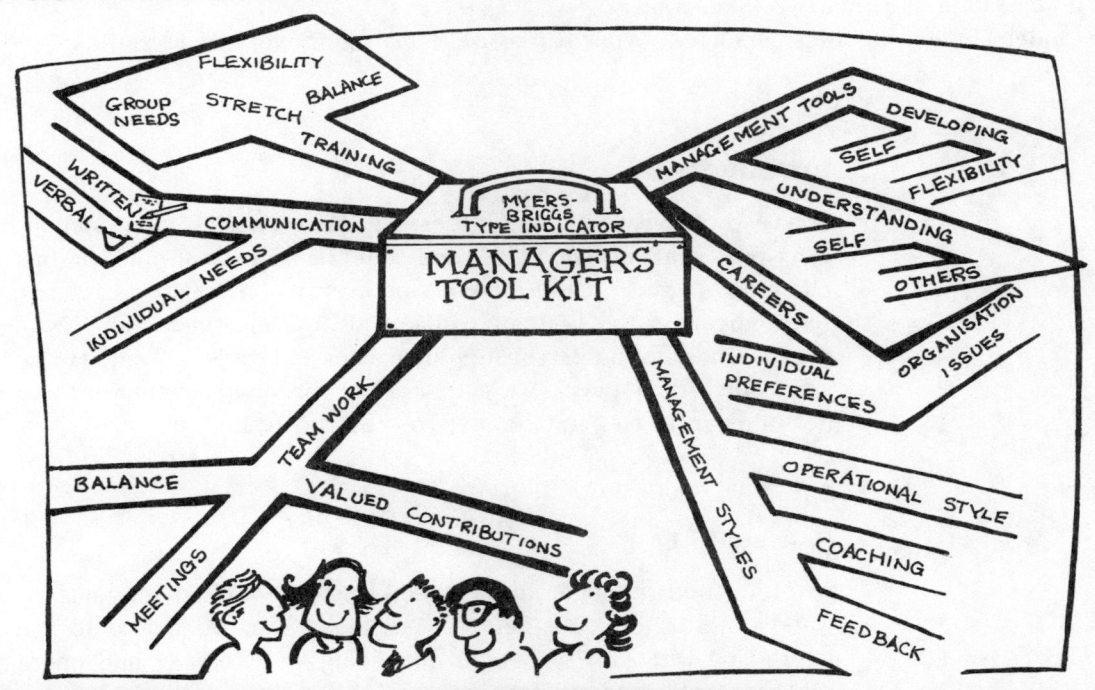

In this chapter

- Introduction
- Use of personality type indicators
- Management tools applications: this is how you do it
- Summary

'Let a thousand flowers bloom.'
Chinese saying

Overview

This chapter explains:

- how personality type and learning style indicators relate to accelerative learning;
- how managers can use personality type indicators with accelerative learning to improve communication and understanding in their work situations;
- how understanding different personality types can assist in managing workplace conflict.

Introduction

You've probably heard the expression, 'You can pick your friends but you can't pick your relatives.' The same could be said about our workmates. Very rarely do we get to choose them. And even when we do, we're supposed to select them on the basis of work needs, qualifications and previous work performance, not on personal opinion, likes and dislikes. Even managers don't get to pick their peers. We get to select the people who work for us, but not other managers and certainly not our bosses!

Case study 1

Case study 1

A retail shop manager hired a new person with an outgoing nature to work in the shop. The person was thought to be suited to the job of interacting with lots of people and being very friendly and energised by the constant contact with people.

The existing staff members were more interested in the operational aspects of the business than the customer interface side of things. So there was wisdom in the selection of the new team member. They needed someone who wasn't like them and liked being around people a lot, rather than spending time in the workroom or on the computer.

The new person loved to talk a lot and started to annoy the other two, who liked to work alone. When customers weren't in the shop, the new person preferred to keep busy by talking to the others. Because of these differences in the needs and preferences of the people involved, it wasn't long before some conflict started to emerge.

The others kept more flexible hours and often worked a few minutes late after closing. The new person was out the door at closing time, keeping to a very precise time frame, and also arrived on time and stuck to agreed times for breaks.

Basically the new person jumped into things, assuming that friendly intent would ensure inclusion in the group. The others were much slower to respond and liked to take their time to get to know people. They felt the new person was a bit pushy and therefore withdrew even more. Of course, the new person then became even 'friendlier' and tried even harder to be accepted . . . and on it went.

This is a classic example of how conflict arises when people with different personalities are not having their needs met. It also neatly illustrates some of the principles on which accelerative learning is based. The new person was unconscious of—some might say insensitive to—the effects of the intrusive behaviour on the rest of the group. The existing staff members, because their preferred style of working was very different from that of the newcomer, intuitively rejected the newcomer's 'pushy' behaviour. Because these factors were largely unconscious, they were rationalised at a conscious level as 'This person doesn't fit in' on the one side and 'I need to try harder' on the other side. So, each side consciously tried harder, repeating the very things that gave rise to the conflict in the first place. And so the situation escalated . . .

Use of personality type indicators can improve understanding

So what is the solution to this situation? Recent research into personality type indicators supports the accelerative learning model by providing a way of becoming consciously aware of many of the factors which influence our preferred style of behaviour. This enables us to review the logical, intuitive and ethical barriers which we may have to accepting other people's styles. By understanding our own style better, we can use our strengths and work on improving our flexibility and use of other styles. This assists us to take more control of our own behaviour and be more accepting and respectful of the behavioural styles of others.

Personality type indicators

There are many personality type indicators currently available. Probably the best known and one of the most widely used is the Myers-Briggs Type Indicator (MBI)*. There has also been, along similar lines, research into different learning styles and a number of different instruments are available to assess people's learning preferences. This is not the place to discuss in detail the relative merits of these many tools. Perhaps one of the best ways of looking at them is to view them as providing a variety of roadmaps for understanding the strengths and different perspectives of others. They also validate these differences by clarifying the need for different skills, opinions and methods. They are helpful to us in understanding ourselves and others and enabling us to make informed decisions and choices.

The Myers-Briggs Type Indicator (MBTI)

The Myers-Briggs Type Indicator (MBTI) is a personality indicator that seeks to uncover a person's natural preferences. It deals with recognising similarities and differences in people and validating these differences by understanding the strengths of each type and what their contributions are to their work, family life, community, relationships, etc.

MBTI offers insights into work and career preferences, different organisation structure—their benefits and pitfalls, different management and communication styles and training or instructing styles when working with employees.

The MBTI is a sixteen-type personality profile instrument. It was started in the United States in the mid-1940s by Katherine Briggs, later joined by her daughter, Isabel Briggs Myers. In her early research, Katherine Briggs discovered Carl Gustav Jung's work on personality types and was so impressed with it that she took his model of typology, researched it and developed it even further. Together, she and her daughter developed a questionnaire which is constantly updated and validated to determine the sixteen personality types. It is currently used in many countries throughout the world—the United States, Canada, Japan, Australia and some European countries.

* Myers-Briggs Type Indicator and MBTI are registered trademarks of Consulting Psychologists Press, Inc.

> It is a non-judgmental instrument in that it seeks to explain and understand the differences in people. By showing the need for differing opinions and perspectives, and a variety of skills and qualities, it defuses some of the conflict and opens the door to more acceptance and tolerance of other ways of doing things.
>
> To have an in-depth understanding of the MBTI, a questionnaire needs to be completed and scored by a qualified administrator. Then the results are discussed. However, I find many people have a pretty good sense of some of their preferences, even without completing the questionnaire. Since we're not doing the MBTI here, our purpose is to help you gain some insights into the issues around personality typology, thereby creating more understanding and empathy towards others and getting rid of some of the judgments you may have collected.

Can you remember a time when you were in a strange city, armed with several tourist maps? Some of them listed only the main shopping centres and cultural highlights, leaving out vast tracts of the city, which was presumably of little interest to the tourist: others were 'not to scale' but nevertheless indicated what destinations could most readily be reached from any particular point. After some trial and error, you probably decided which map suited you best and made the most use of that, reserving one or two of the others for more specialised use. The map is not the territory and just as there are many different maps, all relating to the same territory but highlighting different aspects, so there are many different instruments which highlight the territory of human beings and enable us to make informed choices relating to our personal and professional development, rather than relying exclusively on local knowledge and informed guesswork.

An example: The Myers-Briggs Type Indicator (MBTI) learning styles

The MBTI recognises four main learning styles:

1 Intuitive thinkers—people who need theory, overlying principles, the big picture, challenging ideas, new solutions and applications;
2 Sensing thinkers—people who need facts and figures, evidence, practical applications, a chance to solve problems and make decisions, clear agendas and schedules;

3 Intuitive feelers—people who need discussion, use of imagination, personal meaning, interaction with other people and the opportunity to discuss the concepts;
4 Sensing feelers—people who need information to be well-organised, clearly presented, sensible and practical while paying attention to the needs of the people involved—respectful of those involved, their opinions, positions, input.

If you would like to know more about the MBTI learning styles or some of the other popular learning styles instruments, there are a number of references listed in the bibliography at the end of this book.

There is no right or wrong type

There is no right or wrong type—only different types and different qualities. This is why personality type indicators and learning style instruments are so useful as management tools—they simply acknowledge the needs of individuals and treat them appropriately. They can give us insight into many aspects of our lives and are particularly useful when these steps are followed:

1 Understand yourself first.
2 Then understand others' behaviour.
3 Next use the indicator or instrument to:
 - develop your own strengths; and
 - work on gaining flexibility in the areas in which you are not so strong.

Management tool applications: this is how you do it

Managers can use personality type indicators in conjunction with accelerative learning principles to gain insights into many aspects of their roles, including:

- work and career preferences;
- the benefits and pitfalls of different organisation structures;
- different management styles;
- teamwork;
- communication styles;
- giving instructions; and
- achieving training outcomes.

Work and career preferences

Although people are generally able to work in all sorts of jobs, performing a wide range of activities, career issues relating to work preferences centre on three areas:

1 satisfaction;
2 competency;
3 stress.

Work preferences

Different types of people are often attracted to particular jobs and, because of their personality type, experience greater satisfaction in their work and less stress overall in the work environment. They are naturally energised by the work, are often more creative and describe themselves as more interested in what they do, say they find the work more interesting and generally experience a feeling of confidence and well-being.

The following true story of a successful two-day intervention illustrates how this flexibility, using accelerative learning techniques in conjunction with the MBTI, operates in practice. In this accelerative learning environment, an understanding of personality types clarified the source of an employer–employee conflict and enabled strategies to be put in place for the long-term benefit of both the employee and employer.

Case study 2

A consultant was called into an organisation to provide some coaching to a person who, according to the manager, was not working in an appropriate way.

The first thing that leapt out, on talking with the employee, was that she was in a job that required skills she didn't have. However, she had interviewed very well. That was how she got the job—she thought on her feet quickly and responded confidently.

The job required a high level of organisational ability, precise keeping of records, tolerance of constant interruptions, a pleasant telephone manner, patience and skill at working under pressure while remaining cool and detached. It also required an ability to prioritise in a changeable environment and work to deadlines. A tall order!

Here's what happened, step by step.

a	Completion of the MBTI to have a mutually understood framework for understanding the conflict and frustrations of the situation.	My client and I discussed her type and reached agreements on what this meant to her in her current job. It became very clear to her that she wasn't suited to it, but enjoyed the buzz of getting selected.
b	Determine what the person liked about the job and what she didn't like and why and how that related to the MBTI.	She liked the full-time employment, the environment and some of the people. She didn't like the actual work much, but realised she could learn a lot of valuable skills by staying in the job. She was unclear about what else she wanted to do and she didn't want to leave the job.

c   Decide whether the person wanted to continue in the job and, if so, why. What were the reasons for continuing?

She decided to stay and work at developing the skills required in the job. She knew it would be difficult, but decided it was worth the effort because she would use them even when she left. Plus she was getting paid to learn them! During this time she would decide what else she wanted to do in the long term.

d   Decide on what strategies to put in place, based on the decision in (c) above.

Once the decision to stay was made, she worked on time-management techniques and practised some communication techniques; stress management strategies were discussed and rehearsed and a schedule was drawn up that was real and practical. At this stage, the bonus and reasons for staying were reinforced as well as the anticipated pitfalls and lows that would be part of the process. This way they became part of the strategy.

The accelerative learning techniques used during the two days included:

- a relaxed and private environment;
- blending of theory and practice;
- use of stories, analogies, metaphors;
- relaxation techniques and visualisations.

Using both accelerative learning and the MBTI helped create a quicker result for the client with long-term benefits.

Organisation structures

Organisation styles

It is important to point out that, even when a person is working in the 'right' job, the environment or political culture of the workplace may not meet their needs or may distract them from the work itself. The organisation itself will therefore have a great impact on the individual. Different organisation structures will affect the way people feel about their competency in their work. This highlights the need to pay attention to individual differences in the workplace and create flexibility in work conditions and operating procedures.

The phrase 'I love my job—if only they'd let me do it instead of interfering all the time' is a common expression heard from many people. Appreciating the nature of personality type differences can help managers to understand these different needs and find suitable ways of dealing with them, rather than blaming people for poor work performance. By gaining insight into varying needs, people may be enabled to make changes in their career plans without a sense of failure, while still meeting the demands of the organisation, customers and fellow staff members.

The flexibility required to meet the needs of individual staff and the demands of the organisation and customers can contribute to achieving better work performance and reduced stress in the workplace.

Management styles: Counselling and feedback

Styles of management

Different personality types may have distinctive styles of management, each with its pluses and minuses. Certain environments require different styles of management and a change in situation may require a change in style. Because staff are dependent on the manager for direction, information, performance appraisal, guidance, support and training, the issues involved in management styles are complex and critical. As each person—even those of the same personality type—is distinctly individual, it is unreasonable to assume that each person can be treated the same and be happy with that treatment. Excellent management skills involve being tuned into the individual needs of people, treating them respectfully and paying attention to the current development needs of each person.

Thus counselling and feedback techniques become very important for a manager. Their skill at interacting with each staff member on an individual basis forms the crux of their effectiveness in managing a team. The process described above could just as easily be used by a manager with a member of his or her staff, rather than calling in a consultant.

Teamwork

It is critical that all members of a team are worthwhile contributors to the team output. It is also important that they are seen to be worthwhile contributors by other members of the team. In order for this to happen, the team has to work harmoniously together, respecting the input of the other members and trusting the manager to support them in their work endeavours.

Acknowledgement of different personality types and learning styles can operate like a window, helping people to 'see' the differences in contributions as worthwhile and valuable in an open and non-threatening way. It also explains why some people clash, by showing the totally different perspectives they have. With this understanding, the way is paved for greater acceptance of the other's perspective by showing the contribution that the person makes. A classic situation in which conflict can emerge is at meetings.

Case study 3

Harry and Jean always arrive on time, ready to start at the agreed time, paper and pens in hand, reports ready to be discussed, deadlines met.

Mary and Tom frequently arrive late, and even when they arrive on time they still need to leave again to get something they forgot. They take phone calls during the meeting and often don't have projects for which they are responsible finished on time. Harry and Jean consider them to be irresponsible and immature.

On the other hand, Mary and Tom are the ideas people and have frequently been the ones responsible for finding unusual solutions in times of trouble. They seem to be able to come up with new and innovative ideas when the rest of the team is stumped. They just get bored with daily details and paperwork.

The dilemma here is that a company needs the skills of *all* these people in order to operate efficiently and stay up to date. Harry and Jean are the operational people, good with paperwork, on time, reliable and steady. Mary and Tom, however, give the business new life, look for new opportunities, create new products, sell their ideas to customers effectively. Each has something to learn from the other while still doing what they do best. Each can benefit from appreciating the skills of the other and learning how to do some of the things the other does.

For Mary and Tom, getting paperwork in on time will mean that Jean and Harry can get their job done on time. People will get paid on time, receive the information they need, have brochures printed when they are needed, without causing stress to others. Perhaps Harry and Jean can praise Mary and Tom more for their new ideas, rather than grumbling and complaining about the extra work it makes for them or saying, 'We've never done that before, why now?' Each person needs to move a little closer to the other to understand their perspective, rather than criticising it.

The effective manager will understand this and facilitate the process of helping others understand as well.

Communication styles

The growth of research into personality style indicators and learning styles is one of the factors that very clearly highlights the impact of our communication style on others. Organisations experience confusion, delays, expensive mistakes and conflict when the channels of communication are unclear. Issues of preferred communication methods, such as written versus oral or formal versus informal may need to be acknowledged and dealt with in an open, positive way, explaining the need for different methods, when to use them, the effect on others, the organisation's preferred method and other associated factors.

For example, some people prefer to communicate through memos and other written or electronic systems. For those who prefer face-to-face communication, this can be very frustrating, as they feel they never quite know what the other person is thinking. They miss being able to see all the non-verbal signals such as facial expressions and hand movements.

Case study 4

A manager (Bill) in a large organisation, who called me in as a consultant, wanted to find out what his staff thought about the new procedures that had been implemented recently. The new procedures were part of a change to make the organisation more responsive to customer needs and to appear to be more 'personal'. Bill had decided to send around a questionnaire/survey to find out what his staff thought about the changes.

I suggested he talk to his people personally to find out what they really thought. I also suggested he talk to them individually and prepare questions in advance to prompt the discussion, but not rely on them totally. An informal approach would encourage people to talk honestly and openly and provide valuable feedback. It would also demonstrate his commitment to both the opinions of his people and the success of the organisation in creating change. But equally importantly he would be demonstrating the desired changes in his interaction with them—by being personal and responsive to their needs as internal customers.

Bill's preference to send around a survey was quite typical of his 'type', which prefers to have information on paper rather than uncovering it through discussions. When this was pointed out to him, he realised he needed to step out of his preference and do something different, if he was to get the best result possible. He sought help from another manager, Hugh, who had quite a different style—a very personal, informal approach to his staff. Hugh helped him to prepare for this new experience and gave him some coaching along the way.

No doubt Bill will be able to help Hugh someday, because although Hugh likes to talk to people face to face and is very good at it, he has trouble writing reports and that is something Bill is very good at. So we can all learn from each other.

Giving instructions

All managers are trainers and teachers at some time. As managers, we have to explain things to our employees, outline new rules and regulations, conduct meetings, instruct them in completing forms, present new ideas and concepts to them and coach them in writing various business papers, such as plans, proposals, procedures and reports.

As managers, it is our job to teach our people new techniques so they can grow and develop. In many companies, this is built into a formal system called the Performance Appraisal System or some other similar name. Whether it is formal or not, it is still a critical part of every manager's job.

The training room

In a training environment, knowledge of different learning styles and preferred ways of learning is particularly useful for helping trainers to develop course information in a suitable way for participants. For example, some 'types' prefer to learn through activities—a real hands-on approach. By understanding the types of people attending a training course and the kinds of business they work in, it is possible to prepare the course structure, topics and handouts to suit their needs and preferred learning styles.

For example, if I were training a group of highly technical people in interpersonal communications skills, I would:

- prepare a clear agenda outlining what will be covered in the allotted time, including breaks;
- stick to the agenda, making only minor changes to the timing of handouts

of facts, figures and statistics because technical people generally like to have more concrete information and more detail;
- prepare overhead transparencies to support and display the factual information;
- organise activities that allow and encourage participants to discuss the information in depth and solve problems;
- supply copies of articles for them to read at their leisure, after the course, as well as some to read on the course;
- prepare lots of course notes.

I would also plan activities outside of their comfort zones to help them develop new skills and levels of understanding. However, in doing this, I would be aware that discussion of perceived personal issues may be uncomfortable for some of them, so I would spend less time on that and provide time for personal reflection by using written exercises to guide them through the process.

I would take a completely different approach if I were training sales people in interpersonal communication skills. Sales people tend to prefer lots of activity, group discussion, plenty of movement and new ideas and challenges. In preparing for their course I would:

- use games to introduce new ideas and concepts on communication;
- allow more time for group discussion because they generally love to talk about things together. In fact, getting them to be quiet is a challenge!
- keep facts and figures to a minimum, as too many tend to bore them;
- use overhead transparencies with cartoons and interesting captions to make a point.

I would also plan some reflective exercises with written directions to follow, but would allow less time for this than for the first group. This exercise will be less appealing to sales people, so—although it is a useful exercise for helping them develop new skills—it will need to occupy less time.

Summary

The four main MBTI learning styles are a good starting point for your understanding of how personality types and learning styles affect the ways in which people work and interact with each other. Understanding them is useful so that, as managers, we can allow people to work within their comfort zones, yet also stretch themselves sometimes to learn in new and different ways. When these techniques are used in meetings and with individuals, the messages are delivered in a way that makes sense to the individual.

Why? This will increase their learning and development, help them to find other ways of getting their job done more efficiently and effectively and enable them to work with others with less conflict and more respect.

Case study 1 continued

Case study 1 continued

So, back to our conflict outlined at the beginning of this chapter. How do we resolve it?

First of all, the new person needs to know that he is accepted by the other two employees. They need to tell him that he is good at what he does and that the customers really seem to like him. The new person will enjoy telling them 'stories' about the customers, the funny little things that happen as part of the day-to-life in a shop. It is important that they listen to these stories, both to support him and also to know what is going on in the shopfront.

Secondly, the new person also needs to respect the other employees' need for concentration and privacy. When they say they need some quiet time to work on a particular job, this needs to be respected by the new person. Perhaps they can make time for short breaks and arrange time at lunch to talk and 'catch up'—shop talk.

Thirdly, if the new person likes to get away on the dot at closing time, and if the work is done and customers are attended to properly, then perhaps that's fine. If the others want to stay, that's their choice. It's important to discuss the issue with all concerned and find out what the reasons are for leaving promptly or staying late and then decide on appropriate actions. The assumption that staying late demonstrates commitment may be false. There are many ways of demonstrating commitment and, for some people, this may be by arriving and leaving on time.

You may have noticed that the solution to this conflict is not a simple 'do this and then do that'. It takes time, commitment and the acceptance of others. The solution was written on the second page of this chapter:

1 Understand yourself.
2 Understand others.
3 Develop yourself and gain flexibility.

No model or theory will ever solve all our problems. At best they will be useful tools, if applied at the appropriate time and in the appropriate place. Personality type indicators and learning style instruments, used with accelerative learning techniques, have the potential to be very useful and valuable tools—a must in every manager's tool kit!

Recapping the key points

- People learn more effectively when their individual differences are respected and the changes involved do not violate their logical, emotional and ethical barriers.
- The use of personality type indicators and learning style inventories assists us to acknowledge and respect individual differences.
- The benefits of using personality indicators as management tools include:
  - appreciating the skills and contributions of others;
  - allowing for open discussions, rather than blaming, argumentative sessions;
  - providing a basis for complimenting others on their achievements in a genuine way;
  - providing a framework for planning, based on the needs of the people involved and the organisation as a whole;
  - developing insights into areas of personal growth;
  - providing a framework for objectively viewing an issue or relationship. Once this perspective is taken, new insights may emerge and more appropriate actions then follow.

Making sense of your communication
Helen Millican

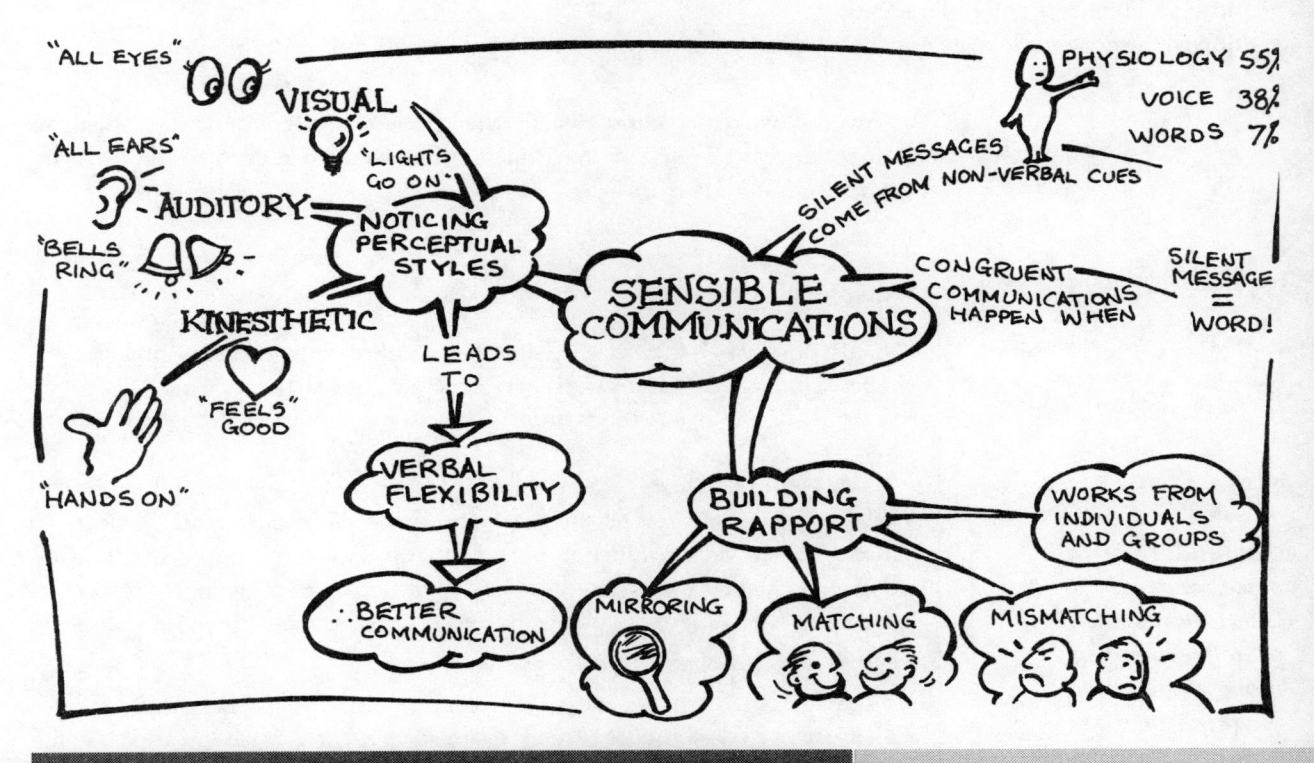

In this chapter

- Building rapport with one person
- Building rapport with a group
- Identifying perceptual styles
  - Visual perceptual style (V)
  - Auditory perceptual style (A)
  - Auditory (internal dialogue) perceptual style (Aid)
  - Kinesthetic perceptual style (K)
- This is how you do it
- Communication congruence

Overview

This chapter explains:
- how to build rapport;
- how to identify perceptual styles;
- how to use perceptual styles to improve your rapport and communication.

How do we really know what other people mean when they speak to us? How can we be sure we have made ourselves clear, even to people who seem really different from us?

> **Silent messages**
>
> In his book *Silent Messages*, Dr Albert Mehrebian describes how we receive messages from other people. He believes that we do this in three main ways, and the words spoken by them are at the bottom of his list.
>
> Dr Mehrebian states that the quality of the voice, and the intonation and speed of delivery, tell us more about the meaning of the message than the words. And more important than this are the non-verbal and non-vocal aspects of communication which we receive from the person's physiology, body posture, gestures and even their breathing patterns.
>
> **Amount of message received from:**
>
> | | |
> |---|---|
> | Physiology | 55% |
> | Voice | 38% |
> | Words | 7% |
>
> Table 5.1 Message grid
>
> This model of communication is very useful as a place to begin thinking about our communication patterns. It highlights how important it is to make sure that our spoken words are backed up with congruent or consistent gestures and vocal tonality, because these make up 93 per cent of our communication.

'The quality of the voice, and the intonation and speed of delivery tell us more about the meaning of the message than the actual words.'
Dr Mehrebian

'Congruent gestures and vocal tonality make up 93 per cent of our communication.'

In what ways can we begin to work with this model?

> **NLP and communication**
>
> Neuro-Linguistic Programming (NLP), first developed in the 1970s by Richard Bandler and John Grinder, provides us with a set of techniques based on observations of strategies used by excellent communicators. Bandler and Grinder identified several ways in which we use our five senses to communicate with others, particularly the visual, auditory and kinesthetic senses. Learning about this helps us to understand our primary style of communication and to appreciate a range of other styles of thinking and communicating which exist amongst our work colleagues, friends and family. This understanding is invaluable for improving communications at work, in the training room, at meetings, in sports and at home.

Visual
Auditory
Kinesthetic

In this chapter we will consider how we can use our sensory perceptions and processes to align our physiology, voice and words and to communicate our messages more clearly. But first, let's find out how to build rapport with other people so that we can receive their messages more clearly.

Building rapport with one person

Television interviewers and interviewees often adopt similar postures unconsciously when they are in agreement. But when one of them is being antagonistic, their body postures usually become mismatched. Friends adopt physiological rapport very easily. Similarly, children will often imitate their parents' postures during play or at the dinner table. And the closest physiological rapport of all happens between lovers.

If messages are mostly received from physiology and voice, what can we do to pick up another person's message and meaning more clearly? Building physiological rapport will help us to do this.

The first step is for us to match or model the other person's physiology, such as their breathing patterns, hand and facial gestures, amount of eye contact and voice tone or pitch, speed of speech and choice of words. This process is rather like becoming a mirror image of the other person.

Rapport-building exercise

An interesting exercise to try out is to subtly match or mirror someone's physiology during a conversation. Notice how this affects the flow of information. Then, when the conversation has become easy and comfortable, gently change something about your posture, breathing, eye contact or voice and speech. Now notice what the other person does in response to your changes. Notice also how this mismatching feels to you. Is it as comfortable as the matching process? If you are doing this with a friend, discuss what you notice about each other's conversation, and whether your attention level varied at any stage.

During this process, you will mostly likely notice that it is more comfortable to be 'in rapport' or matching another person's physiology. At this time the conversation seems to flow and there is a feeling of ease between you, especially once you have become accustomed to the matching process and can return your main attention to the conversation.

Building physiological rapport is an easy process and mostly happens naturally and unconsciously when we wish to communicate with someone. Now that you have become aware of this process consciously, you will start to notice when it does or does not happen, and you will be able to utilise it whenever communication is not going so smoothly, or when you feel that you cannot understand what someone is saying. By matching physiology, you will begin to match the other person's model of the world, and to increase your ability to see inside it a little more clearly. You learn to stand in the other person's shoes for a while, and to see things through new eyes.

Notice when matching physiology occurs naturally

When you use your whole neurophysiology in the communication process, not just your ears, you can more easily perceive the other person's real meaning and message. And, because they feel they have your full attention and interest, they are more likely to relax, so the conversation can flow more easily.

This is a wonderful tool for successful business negotiations and training. But often these forms of communication involve groups of people. So how can we build rapport with more than one person—with a group of very different people?

Stand in the other person's shoes

Building rapport with a group

With one person we are going for sameness with their physiology, voice and choice of words. Even with a small group, we can still match physiologies and language to a certain extent. But what about with a large group of people? There are obvious difficulties here.

A strategy that has worked for me has been to invite everyone in the meeting or training group to do the same thing. For example, everyone can stand and shake hands or bow to those around them at the beginning of a meeting. Sharing such simple physical greeting activities begins to build a level of physiological rapport amongst the group.

Invite everyone to do the same thing

In addition, structure the meeting to begin with some other opening processes or rituals. You might pose a beginning question to which everyone in the room makes a brief verbal response or contributes a comment for the flipchart or whiteboard. Other ice-breaking exercises could include everyone introducing themselves to one another, naming their organisation, stating their perceptions of their role at the meeting and explaining what expertise they bring to the meeting.

Begin with some rituals

Further physiological rapport will be achieved if, at this point, all members acknowledge each introduction verbally (e.g. by saying 'thank you') or by clapping. Opening rituals may also provide members with the opportunity to state their perceptions of the focus or purpose of the meeting—what they expect to get out of it, to clarify time frames, and to include agenda items or questions that they wish to have addressed.

If your meeting is in-house or less formal, you may feel comfortable beginning each session with everyone having the opportunity to make a brief opening statement, which may be related to the business at hand but may also be a comment on other issues which might be bothering them at that time, such as a hassle at home or that the car is illegally parked.

If your meeting is for longer than one hour, build in refreshment breaks. When you resume the meeting, begin with a brief shared activity to restore and build on the physiological rapport established amongst the group. You will find that these processes are worthwhile, as the communication channels seem to open up and the work is dealt with more easily and quickly.

Two rules to follow here are:

Everyone should contribute

1. Everyone should contribute or be involved in some way. This means that you should structure the meeting in such a way that this happens easily and naturally.

Everyone's contribution should be acknowledged positively

2. Everyone's opening contribution should be accepted in its entirety and acknowledged positively. At this point, you need to ensure that they 'have the floor' and everyone's attention for a brief time.

This process sets up a context where members quickly learn that their contributions are valuable and acceptable; they are therefore more likely to continue to participate fully. Full participation ensures that the business will be moved along more quickly, and if necessary members may clarify their opening statements later.

In a training session, the processes used are very similar to those used in meetings. If the training group is too big for everyone to 'have the floor' briefly at the beginning, then arrange for people to introduce themselves in small groups of three or four and to identify their expectations of the training session. These expectations can then be shared with the larger group. The whole of this opening ritual need only take about ten minutes, yet can potentially save hours. It can help you to identify and target the requirements of the group and to facilitate group rapport and active, cooperative work and learning.

It is also useful to start with shared activities such as:

- physical stretches for spines and bodies;
- writing lists of personal issues (such as shopping and phone call reminders) and putting them aside somewhere until after the session when the trainees can get back to them;
- asking trainees to identify their existing knowledge, beliefs and attitudes about a topic and to share this with one or two others in the room.

Start with shared activities

These processes enable the mind and body to be alert and attentive, and enhance memory by drawing on associations from prior learning. But, most importantly, they are activities which are shared and so create rapport in the training room.

We have now considered ways in which we can build rapport with one or more persons by matching their activities, physiologies, voice qualities and word choices, in order to improve our chances of receiving their messages clearly. Rapport-building will also enhance our ability to communicate clearly.

Rapport building enhances your ability to communicate clearly

How else can we use our senses to improve the clarity and congruence of our own communication?

Perceptual styles

Visual (V) information comes from what we see. We gain auditory (A) input from what we hear and kinesthetic (K) input from what we feel, touch, taste and smell. In addition, NLP identifies another form of auditory input which is like an internal dialogue (Aid) and this involves the processes of talking to oneself and of doing calculations and figure work in our heads.

Even though we each have the physiology for all these forms of sensory input, most of us have a preferred or primary physiology through which we perceive our own version of the world. This input form or perceptual style will tend to predominate whenever we recall incidents, solve problems or communicate with others.

Most of us have a preferred physiology

If we are communicating and working with others with the same perceptual style as ourself, it is usually easy to achieve clear communication. But what happens when we work with someone who has a different style?

To address this question, we need to first identify our own primary perceptual style. Can you find yourself in the following descriptions?

Identifying perceptual styles

Visual perceptual style (V)

People with a visual perceptual style tend to find that they learn most quickly by watching a demonstration, reading some instructions or seeing a chart, diagram or drawing of a task before tackling it. Visual people are very aware of the aesthetic shapes, colours and movements in the world around them. They like to have tidy, colour-coordinated environments with things of beauty, especially paintings, adorning their offices and homes. The colour-coordinated theme is often carried through into their smart clothes. Artwork is hung high on their walls, as this brings the paintings into the visual portion of their line of sight (see diagram below). You might notice that visual people tend to look up when recalling information because they are literally seeing a picture of it in their 'mind's eye' before they tell you about it.

When a visual person gets a new idea, they will often describe it as 'having a flash or a vision', 'getting a bright idea' or 'the lights going on'. They will 'preview information', 'watch for a clear picture', 'draw some guidelines' and then 'frame a written proposal'. If you look, you will see that the visual person's language is full of pictorial words and images.

Auditory perceptual style (A)

If you give people with an auditory perceptual style a set of written or diagrammatical instructions they may find it very difficult to do the job. But if you *tell* them about a project and *talk them* through the steps, they are able to follow the instructions more easily.

Auditory people tend to adopt listening postures with their heads and eyes to the side, hands to their ears as if listening on the telephone. Their voices often have mellow and middle tonality, and they make good radio announcers. They often have a wide collection of music at home, possibly even a sound system in every room.

When an auditory person gets a new idea they would say that 'bells rang', 'cymbals chimed' and it 'had a pure tone to it'. They will 'listen for the resonance and rhythm' of a new project, try to create 'harmony' amongst the elements, and then 'orchestrate a response'. If you tune into auditory people, you will hear yourself listening to lots of words about sounds.

Auditory (internal dialogue) perceptual style (Aid)

This perceptual style is a form of auditory perception. In this case, however, these people talk to themselves about what they are experiencing. It is normal for all of us to have some internal dialogue at certain times. Sometimes it can sound like the voice of authority such as our teachers or parents who are saying critical things about us. If we choose, we can change the tone of this self-talk to make it less disturbing.

Aid people, however, process most of their sensory perceptions through what they would say to themselves about what they are experiencing. When you communicate with this group it might be useful to use phrases like 'What would you say to yourself if (an event) was to happen?' or 'Tell me what story you might have about that (an experience)?'

We can change the tone of our self-talk and make it less disturbing

Kinesthetic perceptual style (K)

Kinesthetic people find they can learn most easily by trying things out and 'getting their hands dirty'. Looking and talking may not help them so much. They like to *handle* equipment and *get a feel* for how it might work. These people definitely read the instructions only as a last resort!

Kinesthetics are not usually too concerned with appearances, but often have very comfortable clothes and home furnishings, with an emphasis on textures and soft-to-the-touch fabrics. They tend to be very grounded in their bodies, with their feet placed firmly on the earth. Kinesthetic people will often look down to check their feeling state before deciding to take action.

Kinesthetic people will 'get a buzz', 'feel right' and have 'a gut response' to a new idea. They will want 'to come to grips' with a problem, 'step through it' and 'carve out new pathways' as they 'walk' their way to a solution. As you process their communication, you will fall over large numbers of acting and feeling words.

Did you find yourself in any of the above descriptions? Did one seem to mean more to you than others? And did you recognise some people at home or at work? Does the similarity or dissimilarity between your style and that of those others explain some of the ease or difficulty you might have encountered when attempting to communicate with those people?

In the above descriptions, you may have recognised aspects of more than one style in your learning and communication repertoires. Using an analogy from the computer world, we all have the necessary 'hardware' for all forms of sensory perception. However, the 'software' we choose to work with can vary considerably. Some of us will be using several varieties of software simultaneously for most purposes, and some of us will use one set of software for one purpose and a different set for another.

There are no right or wrong styles of perception: all are valid and useful. Certainly, the more flexible we can become in using our own perceptual neurology, the more likely we will be able to communicate with others with different styles, for this is where our communication difficulties often lie. It is easy to imagine, for example, the frustration a kinesthetic person might feel when trying to build rapport with a visual person. Have you had such an experience?

There are no right or wrong styles of perception

This is how you do it

Work with your strengths while you take more notice of those sensory inputs which you have tended to ignore until now. This means catering to your own style of learning input, and adding gradually to your repertoire.

Now, as you recognise more precisely what styles other people might be using, you can fine tune your matching skills to mirror others' styles more accurately and build rapport easily and quickly.

If you are working with a group, you can safely assume that all three perceptual styles will be present. This means you need to ensure that all the sensory styles are covered and present information visually, auditorily and kinesthetically. This takes practice. You can add sensory aspects to your training or business presentations gradually, as you become more accomplished and comfortable with a variety of styles.

Some exercises in extending your VAK communication repertoire are included below. Practise them with a friend or colleague so that you can enjoy the process and get valuable feedback along the way.

Work with your strengths

Fine tune your matching skills

If you are working with a group you can safely assume that all three perceptual styles are present

VAK exercise 1: Verbal flexibility

Part A: Add as many visual, auditory and kinesthetic words as you can to the lists below. An essential element of good communication is an extensive and flexible vocabulary, so add more words to those provided below if you can.

Visual	Auditory	Kinesthetic
picture	listen	hold
look	shout	grip
bright	loud	warm
peer	tone	smooth
draw	ring	exciting

Did you find that one list was harder to expand than the others? Most people do.

Part B: Work with two friends or colleagues to practise your verbal flexibility by telling stories using the three different sensory styles. For example, if Moira began with a story about a holiday at the beach using visual language, she would describe the sunny shimmering skies, the green glistening seas and the yellow ripples of the sand. After one or two minutes, Fred would continue the story using auditory language and tell about the sounds of the gulls screeching loudly, the gentle whisper of the waves on the sand, and the rasping sound of the sand on his shoes. After another one or two minutes, John would pick up the story with information about the feeling of the cold water sliding off his legs as he walked at the edge of the water, the smell of the seaweed, and a sense of contentment and relaxation as he enjoyed the seaside holiday.

Continue around the circle until each person has talked for a few minutes in each sensory style. The point here is not to focus on the story but on verbalising as many different words in each sensory style as possible. As with the written exercise, you may find that one of the sensory styles is harder for you than others, and this may or may not be the same as the one you discovered in the previous activity.

VAK exercise 2: Presentations

Part A: List all the types of visual, auditory and kinesthetic approaches you can imagine using for a training session or business presentation. Refer to the message grid in Table 5.1 at the start of the chapter.

- *Visual* could include colourful flipcharts, video, slides, overhead transparencies, diagrams, use of the whiteboard and the movements and gestures of the presenter.
- *Auditory* might include the versatile use of your voice, having participants discuss issues, gentle music in the background during the session and lively music during the breaks, use of audiotapes to replay interviews and radio discussions, clapping or other noisy activities for the group members.
- *Kinesthetic* may include activities which induce good feelings like debriefing the day before beginning work, neck and shoulder massages, telling jokes or highlighting the humorous aspects of a topic. Kinesthetic also includes opportunities to handle equipment and practise new skills, to pull something apart and to rebuild it.

How many other approaches can you come up with?

Part B: Now look at some of your existing presentations or training sessions and identify the elements which are visual, auditory or kinesthetic.

Have you covered all three aspects? Remember you do not have to VAK every single part. But you do need to provide visual, auditory and kinesthetic stimuli at different stages of the session. If you have an aspect not covered—and usually this will be an area of sensory input which is not your preferred style—consider which VAK activities from your list could be added to enhance the clarity of your presentation. Remember that an activity or game usually incorporates all three VAK aspects of learning and, therefore, may have the most impact in terms of depth and breadth of learning and understanding.

The VAK model is an excellent model for developing a presentation. It encourages you to focus on the sensory-based *processes* of communication as well as the *content*. Using a VAK approach will make your presentations more dynamic and interesting, and will enhance the understanding and retention rates of your audience.

When I began teaching, I tended to present material in a similar way to the one in which I had been taught myself. It took me time to begin to gradually incorporate more creative VAK elements into my training and presenting. This worked best if I added small things at a time. It was less stressful, and also allowed me to check the response of the group to see if what I had done was really effective. If I had changed too much at a time, it would have been difficult to refine each aspect and correct what was not working. As with many things in life, a slow, steady pace will produce results faster than trying to change everything at once.

Communication congruence

We have now turned full circle to the message grid in Table 5.1. We have seen how the identification of the visual, auditory and kinesthetic styles of perception can enhance our ability to build physiological, vocal and word rapport between ourselves and others. We have considered how to add to our communication repertoire with more flexible VAK words and strategies.

The final step is to practise increasing our congruence as communicators. Congruence is the consistence which is achieved by matching our physiology and vocal qualities with our actual words. What I mean here is that the non-verbal 93 per cent of the message grid supports and gives meaning to the words we use, and that this meaning is what we intended to convey.

Practise increasing your congruence

My experience is that congruence needs to be practised with a friend who will give you honest feedback. Learning is about observing people who are excellent at something and identifying the elements of their approach in order to model and learn from them. If one person can do something well, it is possible for any of us to learn how to do the same by studying their approaches closely.

Congruence exercise 1: Observing excellent communicators

Choose some excellent communicators from television or film and obtain video clips of their speeches. Watch these videos repeatedly with a friend to identify what they do to create congruence and believability. What is it about their approach that makes them so persuasive? What are their gestures and physiology telling you? How are they using their voices? And what words are they choosing to get their message across? Good communicators might include John F. Kennedy, Martin Luther King—even Adolph Hitler, who was very persuasive!

Congruence exercise 2: Practise congruence without the words

With an honest friend or colleague, practise saying a meaningless statement while conveying feelings of happiness, sadness or anger. Choose a phrase like 'The sky is blue' or 'I like noodles', and say these words while conveying one of the three feelings. Try not to use gross movements, but notice how your physiology and vocal qualities change as you convey a feeling state behind the words. The words themselves are not the issue here.

Ask your friend to tell you if they know what feeling you are conveying and more than this, whether they can feel the same thing.

Now change roles and have your friend say the words 'with feeling'. Notice how it feels to you when congruence amongst physiology, vocal qualities and feeling state occurs. You seem to 'just know' what is meant. It is like magic. Be honest, kind and yet challenging to each other as you practise becoming more powerful communicators.

Once you have your physiology and vocal qualities really congruent with your feeling state, several things will happen. Other people will be able to receive the full meaning of your message because they will feel it within themselves. Practising at this will further extend your behavioural repertoire and help you to gain confidence in speaking with conviction. This approach is very powerful, and is one of the techniques that works for excellent speakers.

And finally . . .

This chapter has suggested many new strategies to enhance our communication abilities. These ideas are just a beginning to improving the clarity of our communication. These ways of communicating can be very persuasive and need to be used with integrity. Therefore use these methods only with the best interests of all parties in the communication relationship in mind.

Meanwhile, you have—and always will have—much more than these strategies to enhance your communication. You have the depth of your character, your principles and your personality to enhance interactions with your fellow human beings.

Recapping the key points

- The non-verbal aspects of communication convey more of the meaning of a message than do the words.
- Much of the time we may be only vaguely aware of these non-verbal aspects, such as stance, breathing, voice quality. When we become aware of them in ourselves and others, we can build rapport by learning to mirror the other person's non-verbal behaviour.
- Group rapport can be developed by inviting everyone in the group to do the same thing!
- Developing group rapport is particularly important at the start of any training session.
- People's perceptual styles vary: some people are predominantly visual, others auditory, others kinesthetic. Others do a lot of talking to themselves. Rapport can be built by adopting the same perceptual language as the person you are addressing.
- All styles of perception are valid and useful.
- We can all improve our communication with others by making a series of small changes and checking to see how effective these are.
- When our verbal and non-verbal messages are in agreement, we are clearer and more persuasive to the people around us.

Accelerate your time management
Lynne Wenig

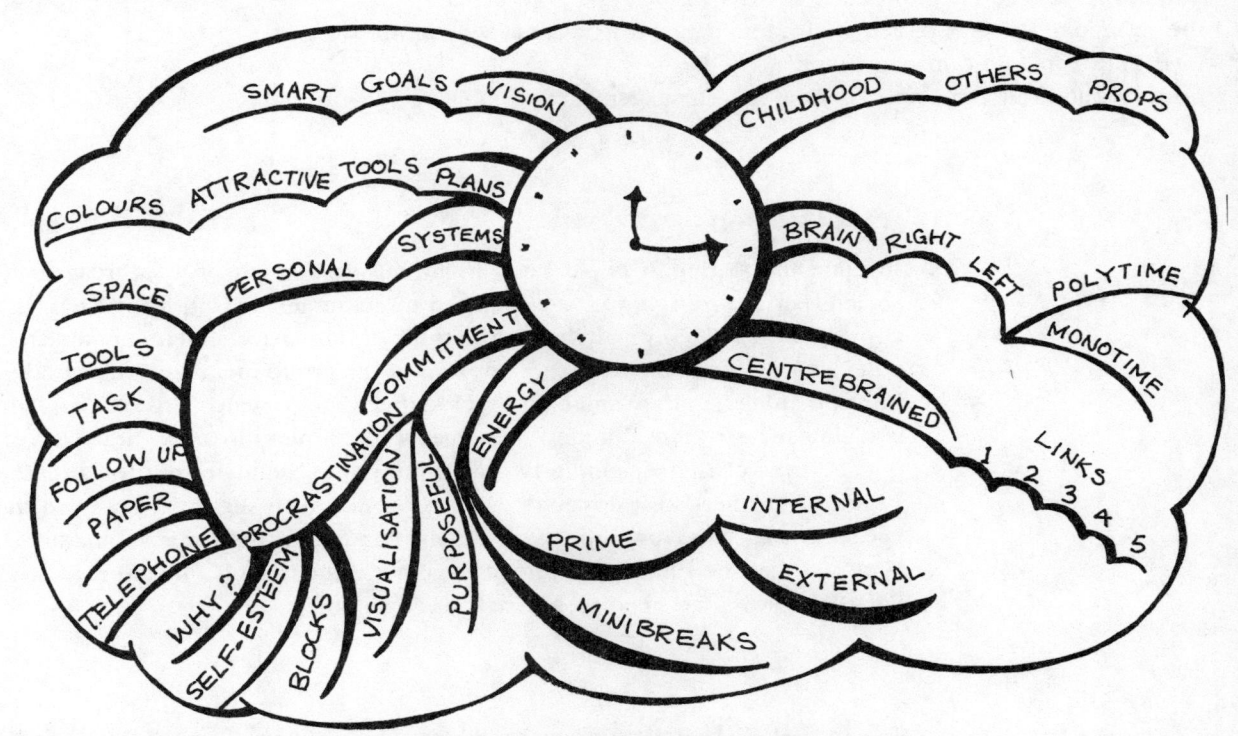

In this chapter

- Early conditioning
- Becoming 'centrebrained'
- This is how you do it
  - The 'five time zone' concept
  - The centring process
  - Developing zone one: Vision and goals
  - Developing zone two: Plans
  - Developing zone three: Personal organisation systems (pos)
  - Developing zone four: Commitment
  - Developing zone five: Energy

'For everything there is a time and a season under the sun.'
Ecclesiastes

Overview

This chapter explains:

- why some people have difficulty being on time;
- the influence of right or left brain dominance on time management;
- 'five time zone' time management;
- how visualisation can improve your time management.

Introduction

Imagine the setting. It could be a Friday business lunch or a Saturday night social. Half a dozen people are engaged in some general chit-chat when the conversation suddenly switches to the topic of time management. Immediately you can sense excitement in three or four of the group members. Their bodies become animated, they smile and look expectantly towards the speaker. You can almost hear them thinking, 'Aha, maybe I can pick up a few new tricks'.

The eyes of the remaining two or three group members roll towards the ceiling. Their heads tilt downwards. Their bodies turn slightly away from the speaker. Legs cross or uncross restlessly. For them, this topic is anathema. Why is it that the subject of 'time management' elicits such a mixed response? For the answer, we need to go backwards in time.

Early conditioning

Since you were old enough to understand even the most vague meaning of the word, much of your world has been governed by time. 'It's *time* to get up', says a parent. Once you are 'up', the day begins to go forward from one time phase to another. By the time you are old enough to go to preschool, at about age three, a daily time pattern has been established. You know that there is a *time* to eat breakfast, a *time* to go to kinder, a *time* to play, a *time* to have a bath, a *time* to go to bed. This is 'other'-driven time, as parents, teachers and older brothers and sisters direct you through the day.

To increase your awareness of time even more, and instil in you a sense of responsibility for utilising your time, you will soon be introduced to the first 'time prop'. This prop is known as the clock. We now begin to learn how to 'tell time'. Can you recall your keen sense of satisfaction when you eventually found out what it meant when the big hand was in one place and the little hand in another?

Once the 'others' were confident that you knew how to 'tell time', they were ready to introduce some additional 'props'—the wristwatch and the alarm clock. This added a new dimension to your concept of time. You were now able to regulate your own life without the 'others'. You knew how to be 'on time'.

But wait a minute! Despite this knowledge of how to tell time, the use of an alarm clock and a wristwatch, some children just never seem to be *on time*. They are not deliberately late. It is more that they seem to get caught up in things which, to them, are more important than being *on time*. This capacity to *not be on time* does not always disappear when children become teenagers, as has been well documented.

And what happens once we are gainfully employed adults? We apparently know enough about life, commitment, planning, hiring and firing to make it our business to be *on time*, to make our scheduled appointments, to meet our deadlines. Or do we? And if not, why not, when your livelihood is at stake and the boss applies some pressure? You know what to do, you know how to do it, you just can't seem to do it *on time*.

Monochronic and polychronic time

Recent brain research provides some answers. The right and left hemispheres of the brain (see Chapter 2) also influence how we see and use time. The left brain thinks and works in *monochronic time*. This is objective time which can be externally measured in specific units such as days, hours, minutes, seconds. If you want to know how much time it will take before a printing machine will print fifty pages, and the manual says the machine prints at ten pages a minute, the answer can be objectively observed. It is straightforward and monochronic. Once the operator has set the machine to 'go', you have five minutes before you can collect your papers.

If, however, you want to know how long it will take to make a person a skilled machine operator, the answer is more complex. We are now dealing with *polychronic*, or subjective, time. Such time cannot easily be measured because it varies enormously from one individual to another. People with a strong preference for the right

> brain tend to see work in subjective terms. When their boss asks them how long it will take to complete a task, they feel uncomfortable and shy away from a time commitment. Their right brain is saying, 'How do I know how long it will take? What if I get a new idea? What if my intuition tells me to change something halfway through? How can I measure this in precise times?'

Unfortunately, most organisations (and most bosses) think about, see and place a value on work in monochronic terms. If there is a meeting to be held at 9.30 a.m., you are expected to be there, whether you are in the middle of a right-brain breakthrough for a new product or not. The important thing for the 'system' is that you turn up at the meeting—*on time*. The same 'rule' applies to social events. If you have a lunch appointment with friends for 12.30 p.m., they want to feel relaxed and confident knowing that you will be there at or about 12.30 p.m.

Becoming 'centrebrained'

Work with time, not against it

So how do you cope with a healthy need for subjective, polychronic, self-imposed time and at the same time fit in with the monochronic and objective time measures placed on us by society, organisations and bosses? Doing so means finding your centre or balance. I call this becoming *'centrebrained'* because it involves blending and integrating the left and right hemispheres of your brain. It means balancing outside, traditional time-management pressures with your own rhythm and inner needs, and learning to work *with* time, not against it. It is developing an 'inside out' philosophy and approach to time. You can accelerate this process by adopting some or all of the following suggestions.

This is how you do it

The 'five time zone' concept

You are probably familiar with the idea of living a balanced life to enable you to function more effectively. We can apply the idea of balance to accelerate our ability to manage our time.

Think of this new way of managing time in terms of finding a balanced way to work within five basic 'time zones'. The five basic zones are:

1 visions;
2 plans;
3 personal organisation systems;
4 commitment;
5 energy.

Imagine your time as a series of links in a beautiful daisy chain. The links are made up of five different components, arranged in a variety of uniquely satisfying ways. Each of these components is a 'time zone'. How you string your chain together is up to you. As you become more 'centrebrained', you will become more adept at stringing the links together as you move more comfortably within each zone. If any zone is out of balance, the link becomes weak and your chain is at risk of breaking. Once you have centred these zones, the concepts will flow naturally on to your other time management needs.

> **Centring**
>
> - Look inwards.
> - Identify the person you choose to be.
> - Set goals.
> - Plan the steps.
> - Create personal organisation systems.
> - Develop commitment.
> - Overcome procrastination.
> - Radiate energy.

The centring process

- The centring process starts when you *look inward*. It means that you identify the person you choose to be.
- Doing this enables you to forge the first and strongest link in your chain, your visions. Once you have identified your visions you can use them to guide your goal setting.
- From there you can proceed to plan the steps which will help you achieve them.
- To assist in carrying out your plan, some *personal organisation systems* will be necessary.
- When you develop the commitment to overcoming procrastination, and finding enough energy, your chain will be complete.

> **My visions and goals . . .**
>
> - What is most important to me?
> - What would I like to do if there were no limitations?
> - What things in my life would I like to be different?
> - My visions for myself are . . .

Developing zone one: Vision and goals

Begin within *zone one*, by getting in touch with the things which are meaningful for you. Free yourself up for some holistic, right-brain activity.

Start by placing a piece of paper and some coloured pencils or pens in a handy position where you can reach them. Then perform some gentle exercise for five minutes. Stretch, bend and jog in place. Put some relaxing music on quietly in the background. Sit in a comfortable chair, close your eyes, and do some mind-calming deep breathing. Inhale to a count of two, hold for four counts, then exhale for two. As you gradually relax, imagine yourself lying in a soft place—a shady lawn, some sand on a beach, a fluffy cloud, a soft mattress—and as you are lying in this relaxing place, let your mind wander freely, thinking about what you would like to be, what you would like to achieve. Feel free of all constraints. Don't let negative, 'I can't', left-brain thoughts intrude.

Visions and goals

Search for visions, not tasks. These visions will be guided by your personal standards and values, and the direction you want to take. Consider what you would like to be able to do that you are not doing now, or what things in your life you would like to be different. After a minute or so, try to focus your mind on the two or three visions that feel the strongest for you—the ones which are most important. Once your visions have crystallised, open your eyes, pick up a writing implement and begin recording them. You can use words or pictures, or both, to capture the spirit of your visions.

Next you need to do some thinking to create goals from your visions and action steps from your goals. This requires being centrebrained. Your right hemisphere is needed to help conceive the goals and action steps; the left hemisphere is needed to record your ideas and turn it all into manageable action.

For example, if one of your visions is that you want to be the best provider of customer service in your industry, then your first goal might be to decrease the number of customer complaints by at least 50 per cent by the end of the financial year. This is a time-manageable goal. It meets the SMART criteria for goal setting.

SMART goals are
Specific
Measurable
Attainable
Relevant
Time framed

For a goal to meet the SMART criteria, it must be:

- specific—the statement is clear and anyone reading it would know exactly what you mean;
- measurable, as a 50 per cent decrease is specified;
- attainable, within your experience and your resources;
- relevant, because it is an important part of your job;
- time framed, with the end of the financial year as your deadline.

Goal setting should always be tested against the SMART criteria. The time frames you have established will give you a perspective on priorities which you will need to consider as you do your planning.

If all your goals are long-term goals, you will probably want to set some smaller goals with a shorter time frame. Using the customer service example, having already established your long-term goal, a shorter term goal might be to have all frontline staff undertake a customer service training program.

My current most important goals are . . .

Before you move into your next time zone, it helps to have one final look at each of your goals. Take a brightly coloured pen or marker and identify those goals which are high-payoff with a circle or a highlight. This last review will tell you what you want to proceed with, and will suggest an order.

Developing zone two: Plans

Having established your goals, you now can move into zone two, plans. You can *have* a vision and *set* a goal, but you can't *do* either of them. A plan is needed to turn visions and goals into action. Planning is a logical, organised process which calls strongly on your left-brain skills. Writing things down and using some form of planning 'tool' are keys to successful planning. If you are strongly right-brained, you may not find this easy. You may, for example, write things down and then forget to look at what you have written. You may have an expensive diary but forget to take it out of the briefcase in the morning. You may find that you never seem to have time to plan at all.

The planning tools I enjoy using are . . .

Planning tools

Finding a planning tool that works for you is the first step towards good planning. Many of the traditional planners and diaries on the market do not hit a creative nerve and act as 'turn offs' for right-brain dominant people.

They are dull, colourless and lifeless. Try some imaginative approaches to recording your plan. Search for a diary or planner that you find attractive. Look for bright colours, attractive page layout, different shapes which appeal to your right brain. Alternatively, you might choose to look for a bound book with blank pages that you find interesting and would like to own and design your own page arrangement using geometric or other shapes or images.

If you are forever losing things, using a bound book for planning may well help. Alternatively, draw up your plan on flipchart paper, with coloured felt pens, and tape it to the wall. Don't always stick to blue or black ink or pencil. Try writing plans for different projects in different colours. Use coloured 'flags', dots or symbols. The *way* you record your plan is not important, the *plan* is.

My high-payoff activities are . . .

My priorities are . . .

When you have recorded your plan, review it. Plan for high-payoff and low-payoff activities, for high and low priorities. Then find a simple way to draw your eye's attention to the payoffs and priorities.

Developing zone three: Personal organisation systems (pos)

My action plan to develop my pos
1.
2.
3.
4.
5.

Zone three encompasses your personal organisation system. Being centre-brained will help. Your right brain will come up with creative ideas for systems; your left brain needs to go into overdrive to turn these ideas into practical solutions. Your planning tool, of course, is the first part of your system. But that is only one part. Organising your desk, your follow-ups, your paperwork, your physical environment are all part of your system. Here are some useful tips to help your personal organisation system:

1. *Work space.* Create an interesting and relaxing work space for yourself. Hang coloured pictures, have a flowering plant, bring in some attractive 'toys' which make you feel good. You spend an extraordinary amount of time in your work area. Why not make it as pleasant and comfortable as possible?

2 *Basic tools*. Have an organised briefcase with duplicates of your basic tools (pens, paper, paper clips, etc.) to avoid excessive transfer of materials from desk to briefcase and back again. If you are strongly right-brained, select tools which are colourful and different. If you want a Mickey Mouse pen, go for it!

3 *Task organisation*. Group similar tasks together, but limit the time you spend on each group. Forty to fifty minutes in any hour is enough. If you need to continue that task, have a ten- to twenty-minute break doing something completely different, preferably something relaxing. Each time you complete a task, you will become faster and better at doing it. If you have several letters to write, accounts to pay or journal articles to read, put them together into one time block and complete the group. Right-brain dominant people get excitement by always doing new things and they need to practise strong self-control to 'group'. The self-imposed time limit helps.

4 *Follow up*. Devise a good follow-up system—one that works for *you*. The stronger your right-brain preference, the harder it will be to find the 'right' system. If you are computer competent, there are many software packages which have features to help you follow up. For example, Windows has a reminder note speciality which pops into the screen when you start your program each day. You can find systems with alarms and other reminder capabilities, so check out the latest packages. Many organisations have purchased computer systems with an 'in-built' follow-up feature.

The most basic system is a quick note jotted on the desk calendar. Use special sections in your planner, or set up extra follow-up files in your four-drawer cabinet. Try using index cards. Coloured cards can be designated for different purposes—for example, yellow for customers, blue for projects, etc.

5 *Paper handling*. Learn to handle each piece of paper once only. That sounds like an old refrain, but do you follow the practice? Using the 'measles method' can stimulate the right brain and help get you into this habit. Sort your papers with a pencil in your hand. Each time you read a piece of paper, mark a small pencil dot in one of the corners. When your papers start to break out in measles, you know you are not following a basic rule of paper management.

6 *Telephone calls*. Start hearing telephone calls as potential connections and customers rather than as time wasters. Interruptions aren't necessarily all bad. Whether internal or external, it is always a customer calling.

Give up playing telephone tag. Organise both your incoming and your outgoing call systems. For your outgoing calls, plan and group. Don't make sporadic calls throughout the day. Find a convenient time (for you and the receiver of your call) and make them in a series. Leave a *very specific* message about call-back time so your return calls are also grouped.

Take a log of your incoming calls for a week and work out what strategies you can employ to cut them down. The 80/20 rule tells you that 80 per cent of your calls will come from 20 per cent of your callers. Find some other ways to get messages to that 20 per cent.

Developing zone four: Commitment

The three time zones we have discussed form links in a chain. There will be no chain, however, if you are still uncommitted and procrastinating about your goals. Or if you have prepared a brilliant plan but don't have the energy to complete the tasks. The fourth time zone is the zone of commitment, in which you manage any tendencies you might have towards procrastination.

Reasons why I procrastinate . . .
1
2
3
4
5

Identify why you are procrastinating

There are a host of reasons why people procrastinate. It is a bad habit and, like any habit, you need to decide that you want to change and then practise the change until it becomes a new good habit. It may help you start if you can identify the reason(s) why you procrastinate. Use a procrastination notebook. Each time you sense you are procrastinating, jot down your reasons by getting yourself to respond to the questions what, where, when, why and how. Keep track of all the games and excuses you use, categorise them and look for patterns.

Pay attention to what you are thinking when you put things off. What are the excuses you make to yourself? These barriers to action are self-imposed. Are they logical, emotional or ethical? It is most common to feel negative about getting started if you are feeling overwhelmed because a single task seems unmanageable, or if you feel overburdened with an enormous list of tasks. Your subconscious may be giving you the 'logical' message that the job can't be done. One way around this is to split the job into a series of smaller, manageable tasks which, logically, can be done. Perfectionism and boredom are also factors, as are our fears—of risk, of loss of autonomy, of loss of control, of success because the 'prize' may be more hard work. These can be very real emotional barriers to action if we don't acknowledge them to ourselves.

Self-esteem plays a big part in procrastination. If you are plagued by doubts about your self-esteem, you might like to have another look at the section on 'Motivation and self image' in Chapter 3.

If you fear failure because you believe you lack skill, experience or knowledge, then the inclination to procrastinate will be very strong. One of the best ways to procrastinate without appearing to procrastinate is to play a game with yourself called 'when'. To play, you pretend that you are not procrastinating but justify your delay by saying that you will do something 'when' the time is right, or 'when' you are not so busy, or 'when' you are inspired, or 'when' you have the right computer programme, more information, things aren't so hectic—the list is as endless as the procrastination.

Break the mental blocks

Procrastination is a mental block which needs to be broken. One way to do this is to identify the real reason for the procrastination, your personal logical, emotional or ethical barrier to action. Once this has surfaced from the subconscious to the conscious, strategies can be brought into play to deal with it.

Defeat procrastination through visualisation

The next time you are procrastinating over something that needs to be done, take fifteen minutes to unblock and deal with it *now*.

> **Activity: Using visualisation to overcome procrastination**
>
> Find a quiet place where you won't be interrupted. Sit in a comfortable chair with feet flat on the floor. Close your eyes and relax. Visualise the number five. As you see the number, gradually let it fade away. Then see the number five again. Let it fade and bring it back again a third time. Then see the number four and repeat the process with the numbers four, three, two and one.
>
> After you have visualised the number one, see yourself standing in front of that one. Then feel the one being absorbed into your body, moving through your body and slowly disappearing. If you are not relaxed at this point, you can repeat this exercise.
>
> In this relaxed state, visualise a clock and see the time on the clock set for two minutes before you will be starting your task. You can imagine any type of clock you wish: alarm, digital, cuckoo. When you can see this clock strongly, visualise yourself getting ready to do the task over which you have been procrastinating. Visualise organising

papers, moving to another place, whatever you would be doing to get ready for your task.

Now visualise your clock again. The time has moved and it is now time to start your task. Mentally see the clock on the new time.

Now create a visual image of yourself doing the task. Imagine what you will be wearing, your surroundings, any people who will be involved. Imagine yourself becoming totally absorbed in this activity. Notice any associated sounds and feelings. Make this image as strong as possible. Observe the positive sensation of completing this task.

As you focus on your activity, make a strong, positive affirming statement to yourself: 'I am successfully completing this task.' As you repeat this affirmation, see yourself successfully completing the task. Feel the positive sensations that come from success. Smile gently.

Now visualise your clock once again. See that the time has progressed to the time when you will have finished your task, perhaps an hour, perhaps a day. You can repeat this exercise whenever you feel procrastination overtaking you.

To help you even further, try one or all of these five anti-procrastination tricks to get you centrebrained:

1. Consider the 'worst first' rather than 'worst last' approach—eat your broccoli first and then enjoy your chicken and potatoes rather than the other way around.
2. Take 'baby steps' by breaking a job into small bits and pieces to make it more manageable: make a list on paper of each step; try making six phone calls instead of twelve or writing a first, very rough draft rather than trying to finish the entire document. Remember that you don't have to start at the beginning, you just have to start.
3. Use visible reminders to jog your right hemisphere into action. Hang up stick-on notes, signs or pictures in prominent places.
4. Agree with yourself to work on something for only four minutes. This often gets you started and if you stop after four minutes, at least you have completed that much of your task.
5. Go public. Tell a trusted friend or colleague when you should be starting a task and ask them to remind you. Ask them to be persistent.

There is such a thing as purposeful procrastination. This is when you really do need more information, when it may be valuable to wait and see, or when you need a change of pace or a little break. Under those circumstances, it may be valuable to procrastinate—but not for too long. Accept this as a deliberate delay, rather than just more procrastination, and allow yourself to feel OK about it.

Purposeful procrastination

Developing zone five: Energy

The final factor that keeps the chain together is zone five, the energy zone. Energy creates more energy. Research shows that we get energy from excitement, positive stress, doing new things, being creative, daydreaming, being passionate, taking a risk, relaxing, having a challenge, being optimistic, exercising, being committed to goals, having a healthy work environment and balancing work and 'play'. We also become more positive and productive when we get our body rhythms, body cycles and biological clocks in balance.

Prime time is when you feel most alert and capable of creative thought and high productivity. Most of us are either fowls (morning people) or owls (night people). Fortunately, flexitime gives us some opportunity to use our prime time more effectively. This is when you should be scheduling high-priority, high-payoff tasks.

- Find your prime time
- Internal and external prime time
- Cognitive tasks for the morning
- Complete high-energy tasks in high-energy periods
- Take energy breaks

If you don't already know your prime time, jog in place for five minutes early in the morning, in the middle of the morning, at mid-afternoon and at late afternoon. Do this on a non-working day. Whichever session leaves you feeling the most invigorated is your prime time.

Some of us have an *internal* prime time when we are at our best working alone and in deep concentration, and an *external* prime time when we are best working with people.

Short-term memory is best in the morning, long-term in the afternoon.

The mornings are best for cognitive tasks, mid-afternoon for the 'mindless' tasks. Late afternoon and early evening are when we get the most out of a physical workout.

You can gain more energy by getting in touch with your body clock and learning to organise high-energy tasks in high-energy periods and vice versa. Building variety into your day is vital to stimulating the right brain and rest is vital for the left, which tends to get overworked in our left-brain organisations.

Take regular short mini (two to five minutes) energy breaks throughout the day and alternate physical activities with desk work. Check your office surroundings, as the environment you work in can sap or strengthen your energy levels.

Get up fifteen minutes earlier each day to avoid the early morning rush and arrive at work before the chaos begins, have a supportive network of friends and give someone positive feedback every day—about anything.

Keep working within the five time zones to accelerate your time management. It is the journey, not the arrival, that ultimately matters.

Recapping the key points

- Monochronic time can be objectively measured; polychronic time is subjective.
- By adopting a centrebrained approach we can balance external time management pressures with our own rhythm and inner needs.
- The five links in the centrebrained approach are visions, plans, personal organisation systems, commitment and energy. The links combine left- and right-brained thinking.
- Procrastination can be overcome by identifying why one is procrastinating, breaking the mental blocks and visualising the successful completion of a task while in a relaxed state.
- Sometimes procrastination can be useful.
- When you identify your prime time(s) (the time(s) of day when you are most energetic and alert), you can schedule key activities for these times.

Team building using accelerative learning

Robyn Keal

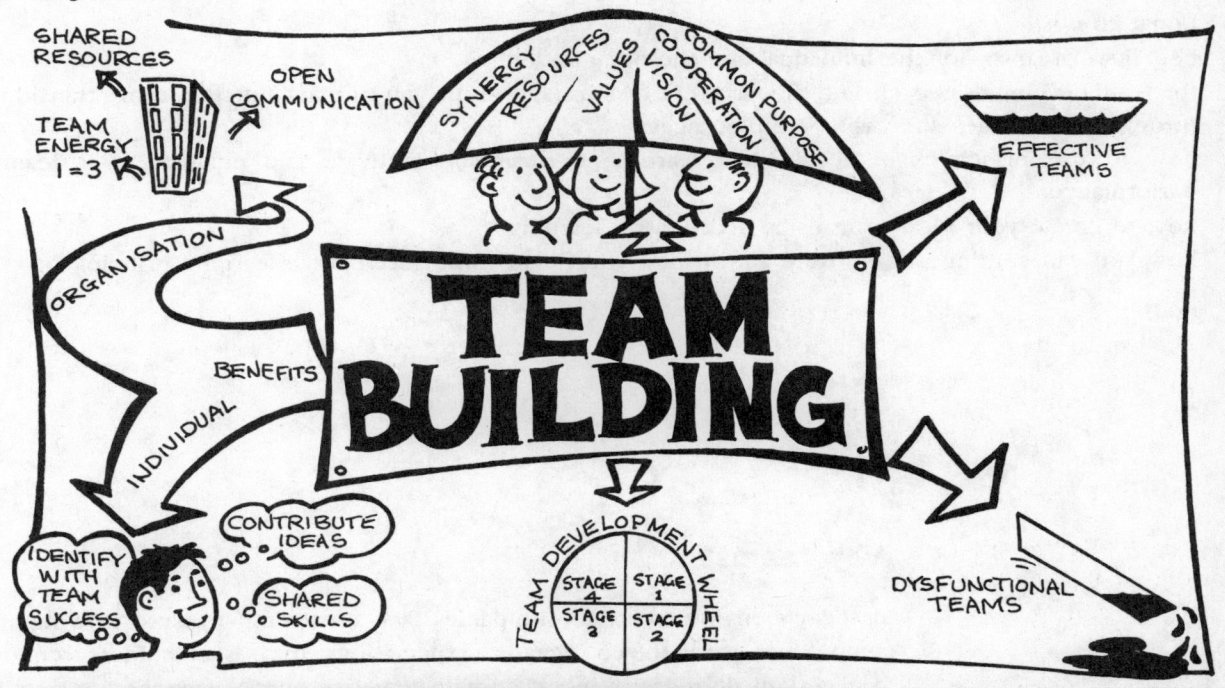

In this chapter

- Why teams?
- What is a team?
- Effective teams
- Dysfunctional groups
- Benefits of building a team
- Development of teams
  - Forming
  - Storming
  - Norming
  - Performing
- Creating your ideal team
- Tools to maintain, motivate and enhance your team's performance

'A new idea is delicate. It can be killed by a sneer or a yawn; it can be stabbed to death by a quip and worried to death by a frown on the right man's brow.'
Charles Brower

Overview

This chapter explains:

- the distinction between a team and a group;
- how to use the mental excursion technique to recognise the features of effective teams and dysfunctional groups;
- benefits of teams—for the individual and the organisation;
- the team development cycle and the features of each stage—how you can facilitate the team's transition through these stages and overcome blockages;
- how to use principles of accelerative learning to maintain, motivate and enhance your team's performance;
- how to create your ideal team using accelerative learning;
- how you can continue to motivate and inspire your team using accelerative learning principles.

Why teams?

In today's environment, all companies face escalating pressure in a highly competitive marketplace. Greater expectations from stakeholders require managers to do more in less time with fewer resources. Everybody wants it done yesterday (or sooner).

Work teams

Consequently, organisations are relying more and more on the output of work teams to produce the desired results. No doubt you've heard all this before. 'You've got to get them working together as a team.' 'Team work—it's the only way to go.' You have probably spent hours in different workshops going through the drill of teamwork and yet you are still unclear.

This chapter will show you the differences between an effective team and a dysfunctional group. You will learn the benefits of building teams, recognise the natural stages in team development and be led through the steps to creating and motivating your ideal team using the principles of accelerative learning.

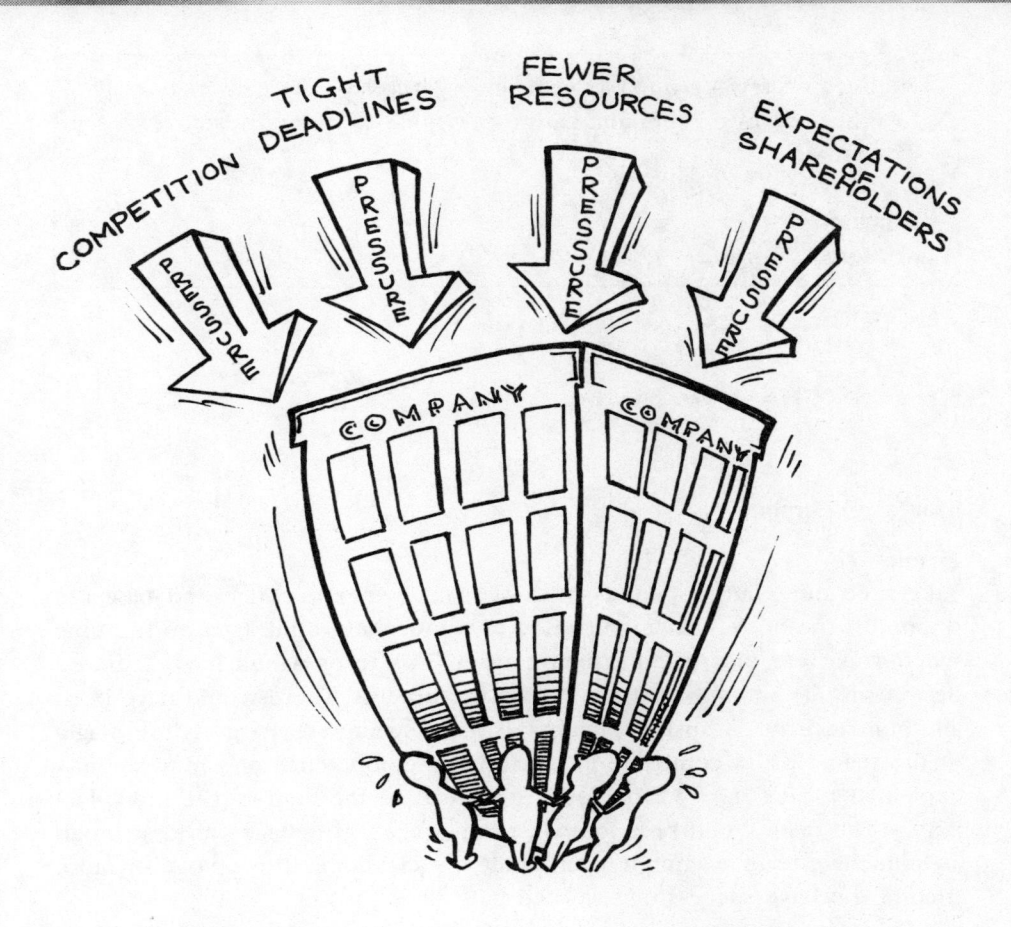

What is a team?

Firstly, it is probably easier to define what a team is not. A team is not just a collection of people doing the same thing—for example, waiting at a bus shelter or in a queue at a bank. That is a group. Members of a team do not have different objectives, agendas or goals.

A team that works cooperatively together towards a common goal is not a chance event—teams don't happen by chance. The skills to work cohesively in a team must be learnt before people can effectively contribute to the team goal. In a nutshell, team building is a process of developing a group of people capable of achieving results more outstanding than would be achieved by one person operating alone.

What is a team?

> Simply, a team is a group of two or more people working cooperatively together, sharing a common purpose, vision, values and resources.
> **T** together
> **E** everyone
> **A** achieves
> **M** more

Step 1: Effective teams

Mental excursion

(5 minutes)
Take time out. Grab a pen, a sheet of blank paper, a coffee and take the phone off the hook. Allow your mind to wander, and think back to the time when you were part of an effective team. This team would have achieved desired results and also had fun during the process. There would have been an abundance of enthusiasm, team spirit and synergy. (Synergy is the magic in the team: it is a combination of strength, competence and motivation— explained as $1 + 1 = 3$. The total is more than the sum of the individual parts.) The team could be a football team, a team at college working on an assignment, a team at church, your family, a social committee or two or more friends you have successfully worked with on a project.

What sets this particular team apart? Think about the team's successes and their failures. How did they communicate? What kept them on track? What motivated them? How did they achieve such positive results?

In the space below record six attributes of that team.

Mental excursion

Synergy is the magic in the team

Attributes that made this team successful
1
2
3
4
5
6

Below is a list of attributes you will find in an effective team.

Effective teams:

- share a common goal/vision;
- achieve results—often the 'impossible';
- openly express thoughts and feelings;
- encourage different points of view;
- provide opportunities for personal growth;
- give honest feedback to each other;
- encourage and appreciate differences;
- give ongoing support to other team members;
- regularly review team processes and structures;
- measure and reward achievements;
- show a high level of trust, support and commitment;
- have fun;
- provide a positive environment where people are motivated and enthusiastic;
- enjoy a sense of belonging;
- recognise and resolve conflict.

Attributes you will find in an effective team

Compare this with your list. Are there any differences? Can you add more to your list?

Note: These attributes are not listed in order of importance. They are all equally important: take one out and the team is no longer as effective.

Step 2: Dysfunctional groups

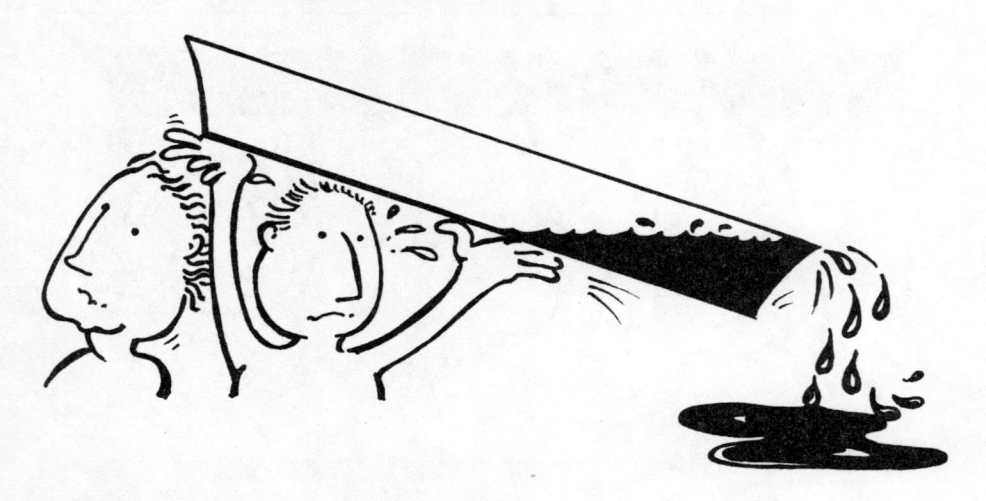

Mental excursion

Mental excursion

(5 minutes)

Now recall another experience when you joined a group which was dysfunctional. You probably felt frustrated and disappointed, as this group would not have had its act together—perhaps it had no purpose and no goal, but lots of hidden agendas. Conflict would have been evident, but whereas in effective teams conflict is healthy and constructive, in this instance conflict would have been destructive and probably resulted in a feeling of hopelessness and eventual disbanding of the group.

What contributed to this situation, in your opinion? Was it due to negativity or perhaps mixed direct and indirect suggestion? For example, a team member might have continued to insist that everything was fine (direct verbal message) yet her non-verbal messages—for example, angry tone of voice, constant criticism of others' ideas, slamming of doors and absenteeism (indirect message)—were clearly spelling out another message altogether.

In the space following record six things that irritated you about that group.

Attributes that irritated me in a team
1
2
3
4
5

Dysfunctional groups:
- argue amongst themselves;
- have no common purpose or clear goals;
- fail to communicate honestly;
- do not respect the roles of other team members;
- blame and label others.

You have now completed a mental excursion clarifying what you admire in an effective team and what you disliked about the dysfunctional group. You will now have a clear picture in your mind's eye of the qualities you want to engender in your team. In other words, you know what you want.

Benefits of building a team

The need to belong is a powerful motivating force, and a main reason we join clubs, get married, go to work and play team sports. As humans, we are motivated to want to form into groups and teams to satisfy this need for social acceptance.

Using teams is beneficial for the organisation, as resources can be shared, communication channels opened up and the resulting team synergy makes things happen.

Other benefits of building teams are the opportunities for individuals to identify with team success, draw on the support, energy and skills of other members and be able to contribute their ideas, expertise and knowledge. As the old adage goes, two (or more) heads are better than one. These collective strengths engender higher quality decisions and often the 'impossible' can be made 'possible'.

Benefits of building teams

An effective team can be likened to an orchestra: all members have a vital role to play in order to create the musical masterpiece. If one member is absent, plays off key or follows a different musical score, discord and disharmony inevitably result. Likewise for a team: all members need to make a universal contribution and strive for harmony in order to create the desired outcome.

Development of teams

It is now common knowledge that teams naturally progress through a team-development cycle. In your role as team leader, it is vital that you identify which stage your team is at, so you are more able to assist in this transition.

Team-development cycle

> Commonly recognised stages are:
> **Stage 1: Forming**
> Honeymoon period—'we are all nice' stage.
> **Stage 2: Storming**
> Stop arguing! My way is the only way.
> **Stage 3: Norming**
> Let's get it right.
> **Stage 4: Performing**
> We are the champions.

Forming

Forming

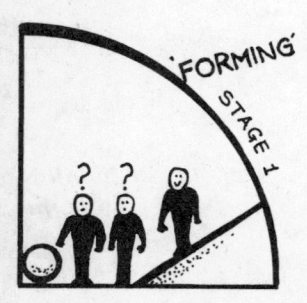

Features of this stage include:
- Individuals are polite and mind their manners.
- They keep opinions to themselves and disclose little.
- There is little trust and some apprehension.

How you can help

1 Provide opportunities for people to get to know one another in a non-threatening, fun environment.
2 Provide opportunities to identify individual strengths and weaknesses.

3 Provide training in team and personal development.
4 Set the guidelines and make your expectations clear.
5 Give regular feedback.

Storming

Features of this stage include:
- Interpersonal conflicts occur—criticism, blaming others, some defensiveness.
- There is a lack of clarity about team roles and responsibilities.

Storming

How you can help

1 Provide training in conflict resolution.
2 Point out that conflict is inevitable and must be worked through. This is vital, otherwise members will mask their thoughts and feelings, and the non-verbal messages (indirect suggestion) will conflict with verbal messages (direct suggestion). Use training to improve their assertive communication skills to prevent this.
3 Be a role model and demonstrate active listening skills. (We learn from observation of others—especially from leaders we respect.)
4 Explain the different roles of the team members.
5 Define roles and responsibilities.
6 Give regular feedback.

This stage is significant, as some groups get stuck here, achieve little and eventually break up. Your role is to guide them through so they can progress to the next stage.

Norming

Features of this stage include:
- Rules and guidelines are decided.
- The team decides which behaviours are acceptable and which are not.
- Members agree to disagree.
- Confidence is engendered.

Norming

- A sense of trust, cohesiveness and harmony develops.
- Team members have a sense of belonging.

How you can help

1. Initially lead the team then take a back seat as team members take charge of their own team processes.
2. Provide resources as needed.
3. Make sure all jobs are well allocated (and one person doesn't 'cop the lot').
4. Give regular feedback.

Performing

Performing

Features of this stage include:
- Goals are being achieved and results measured.
- There is a high level of loyalty and mutual respect.
- Creativity, enthusiasm and resourcefulness are evident.
- Members are ready to compete with other teams and keen to show how the job can be done.
- There is team spirit and synergy.

How you can help

1. Ensure that team members learn all the team tasks (so, if someone leaves or is absent, the team still functions). Apart from this, multi-skilling is beneficial to the organisation and builds confidence in the individual.
2. Provide information as required.
3. Empower the team to follow up on their decisions. (Stay in the background.)
4. Make sure the team acknowledges and celebrates its achievements. Reward its success. (Timely positive reinforcement is vital in accelerative learning; otherwise members lose motivation and performance declines.)

Be aware that this process is dynamic. Situations change, team members will come and go, new leaders emerge and so the team cycle is ongoing. Although the team may be at stage four, the performing stage, the loss of one member and the inclusion of a newcomer may swing it back to the forming stage again.

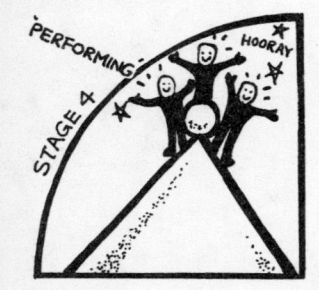

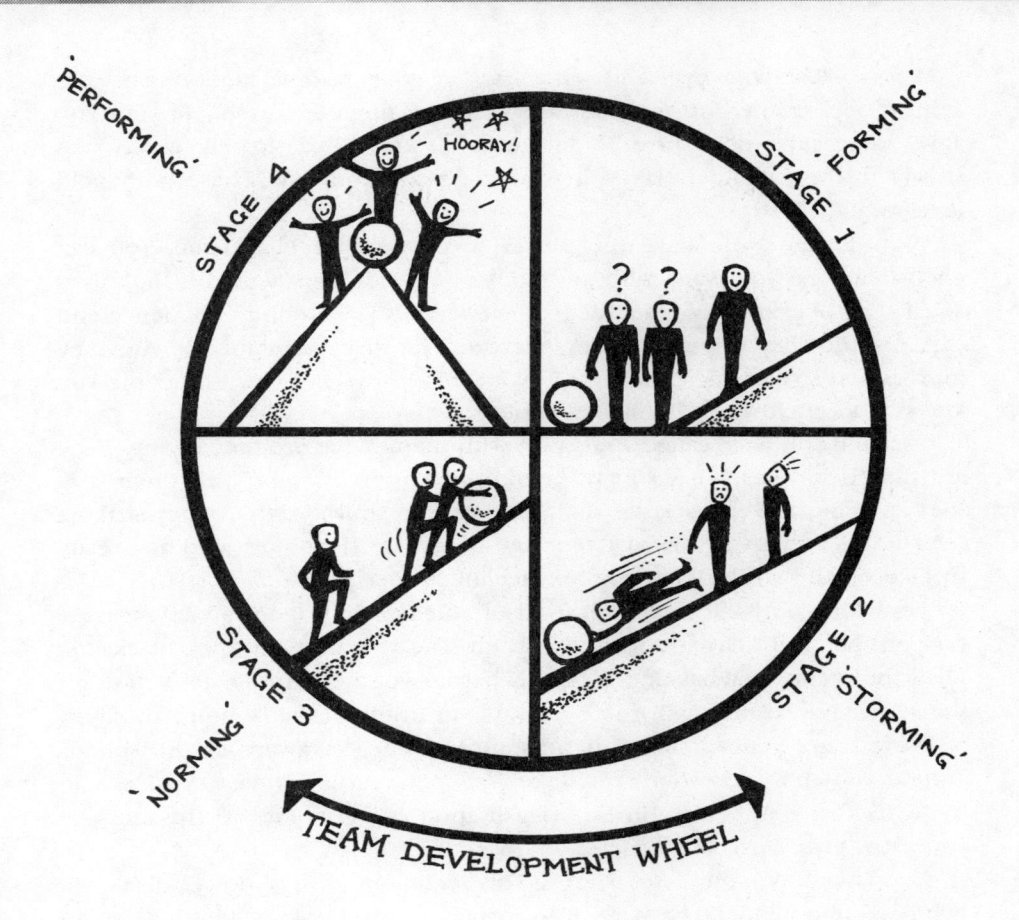

Team building using accelerative learning

TEAM DEVELOPMENT WHEEL

STAGE 1 'FORMING'
STAGE 2 'STORMING'
STAGE 3 'NORMING'
STAGE 4 'PERFORMING'

Step 3: Creating your ideal team

Guided imagery

(10 minutes)
This time you will be working on a subconscious level, practising an accelerative learning tool, guided imagery.

Close the door, take the phone off the hook and make sure you won't be interrupted for ten minutes or so. Have some relaxing instrumental music in the background.

Guided imagery

Relax. Close your eyes and settle back in your chair. Ensure your back is straight, feet planted on the floor and hands resting comfortably in your lap. Take some slow, deep breaths. Imagine you are a leaf floating gently and slowly to the ground. Relax your shoulders and your jaw. These both hold tension.

Now imagine you have the power to create your ideal team. You can choose anyone you want with any skills you need. What would it look like? What type of people do you need? What sort of background experience and expertise do they bring? Are they energetic, creative, spontaneous? Are they movers and shakers or followers? In your mind's eye, conjure up people you know who could easily fulfil these roles.

Imagine you have called a meeting with them. What are they saying? How are they behaving? What sort of energy have they brought with them? Are they laughing and enthusiastic and agreeing with your ideas? Are they shaking their heads and giving alternative suggestions? Are they motivated and ready to take on the world? How are you feeling yourself?

Now look down at a book in front of you. On the page is a vital message for you that will help you form this team. The writing is in thick black ink. Read the message. What does it say? What do you need to do? (If you don't see a message, relax, it will come to you later in the next few hours or days.)

Now bring yourself back to the present time, be aware of the sounds around you and open your eyes. Take your pen and jot down any ideas and thoughts that cropped up in this visualisation exercise. Record the message you were given.

You have now completed step 3. This technique is very powerful, as you will have transcended the state of logical, analytical thinking (the beta state) to the alpha state of creativity, imagination and positivity. Although the beta state is crucial for the thinking, planning and doing tasks involved in day-to-day living, the 'I can'ts', 'I shoulds' and negative blocks also belong to this state of awareness.

To move mountains and create ideal circumstances (and achieve seemingly 'impossible' tasks) you need to call on your inner being in the alpha state (some call it your higher self—your intuition) to transcend the blocks and make things happen.

You are now ready to select your team. As you do so, rely on your intuition (hunches and gut feelings) to guide your selection. Put your rational thoughts on hold for the time being; your intuition is invaluable for choosing the best team players.

Although your logical brain may be shrieking at all this 'fuzzy stuff', you are now drawing on the 90 per cent of the unused potential of your brain. Like some other aspects of the universe, intuition cannot be measured or explained. It is just there and it works. However, like human muscle, the more you use it, the more efficient it becomes.

Tools to maintain, motivate and enhance your team's performance

Once you have the team up and running, be aware of the human tendency to complacency. Many managers and team leaders fall into this trap. They believe that once the team has been selected and has moved through its stages of development, it can now exist alone. Like any other resource, the team machinery must be maintained in order to keep it in peak condition, giving prime performance and outstanding results. The following tools draw on both common sense and accelerative learning principles to enable you to do just this. Choose the ones that appeal to you and use them.

Tools to maintain your team's performance

Tools to maintain, motivate and enhance your team's performance

- Be a role model—'do unto others as you would have them do unto you'.
- Establish a climate of loyalty and trust—don't promise what you can't deliver.
- Listen openly without judgment.
- Ensure your verbal messages are consistent and support your non-verbals. Remember that more than 85 per cent of your message comes across in the non-verbal signals (e.g. actions, posture, tone of voice, facial expressions).
- Tell the team what you want, set the boundaries and clearly define your expectations (people need to know what their limits are).
- Tell them the bad news early. This gives people a sense of control of their destiny. Knowledge is power—information allows them to make choices. Tell them first before they hear a distorted version on the grapevine.
- If you don't know the details, tell them you don't know. This demonstrates honesty and integrity. In return, *they* are then more likely to be honest with *you*.

- Let team members make mistakes—ensure they learn from them. (Don't *rescue* them from the consequences—this is a natural part of learning.)
- Ensure that your positive feedback outweighs your negative feedback. People receive enough negative feedback from other sources. Don't be like others who only call someone into the office when things have gone wrong. People need constant positive encouragement. Yours may be all they get.
- Keep feedback specific—talk in terms of what they did. 'I appreciate your staying back late to finish the project' is more effective than 'You did a great job'. This person will continue staying back if he knows that you appreciate it. She/he can't repeat 'a great job'.
- Remember that different people have different perceptual styles. Use them when giving feedback.

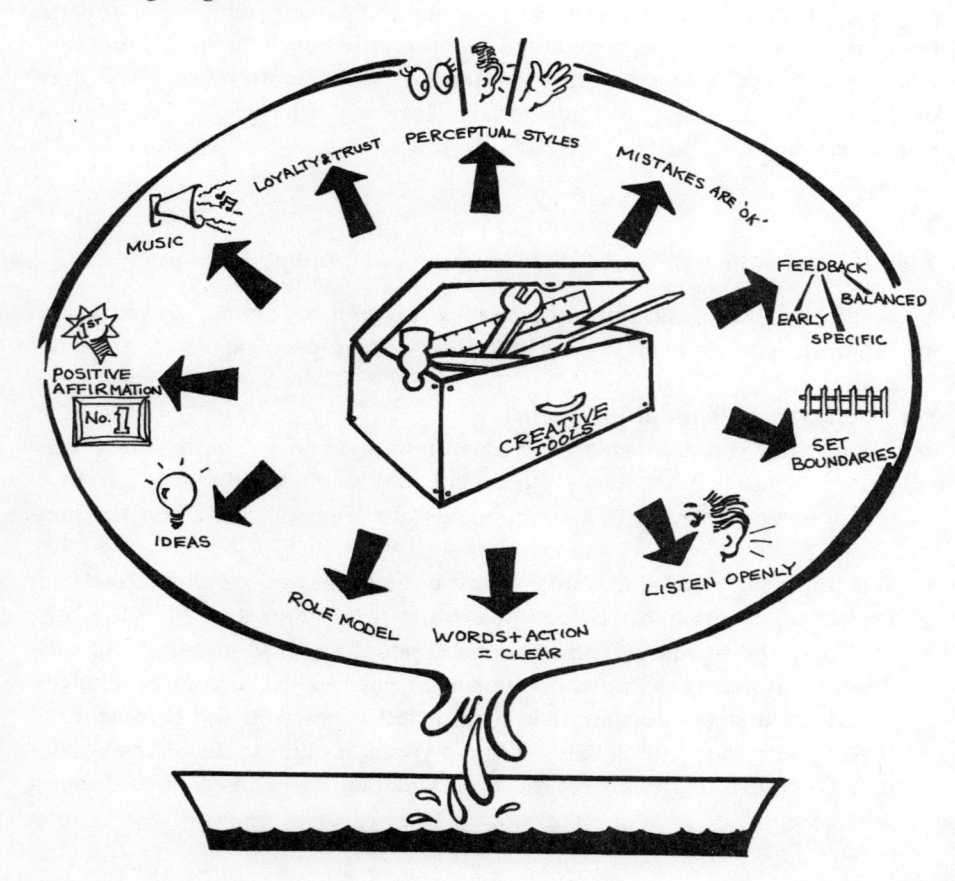

Visual tools

- Write a note on a post-it sticker and put it on their desk. Buy fresh flowers for the office.
- Send a letter or memo thanking them for their help.
- Give them a card, trophy or prize (sounds crazy but people will keep these on their desks for months).

Auditory tools

- Say thanks in person (choose words carefully).
- Express your appreciation in a team meeting.
- Use the company PA system (if appropriate).

Kinesthetic tools

- Shake their hand and say thanks.
- Take them out to lunch. Bring in a cake for morning tea.
- Give them a voucher for a massage.

(If you aren't sure of their preference, use all three channels.)

- Welcome creativity. Bring in an outsider when the team gets stuck. Use other creative tools in this book to stimulate ideas and resourcefulness.
- Ensure their work environment is pleasant, with minimal noise and distractions. If you demonstrate your support by enhancing their work environment, they will get the indirect message that you appreciate them, and regard what they are doing as important. You will see results.
- Encourage teams to provide music, played to stimulate creativity and concentration. Or use music to energise and enthuse. Experiment with different classical pieces. Try feeling unmotivated when Tchaikovsky's 1812 Overture is pulsating through the building! Or play Tina Turner's 'Simply the Best' before team meetings. It worked for football teams, why not for your team?

VISUAL → 'A NOTE' OR 'SOME FLOWERS'

AUDITORY → 'OVER THE SPEAKER' (NICE JOB EVERYONE)

KINESTHETIC → 'A VOUCHER' OR 'A HANDSHAKE'

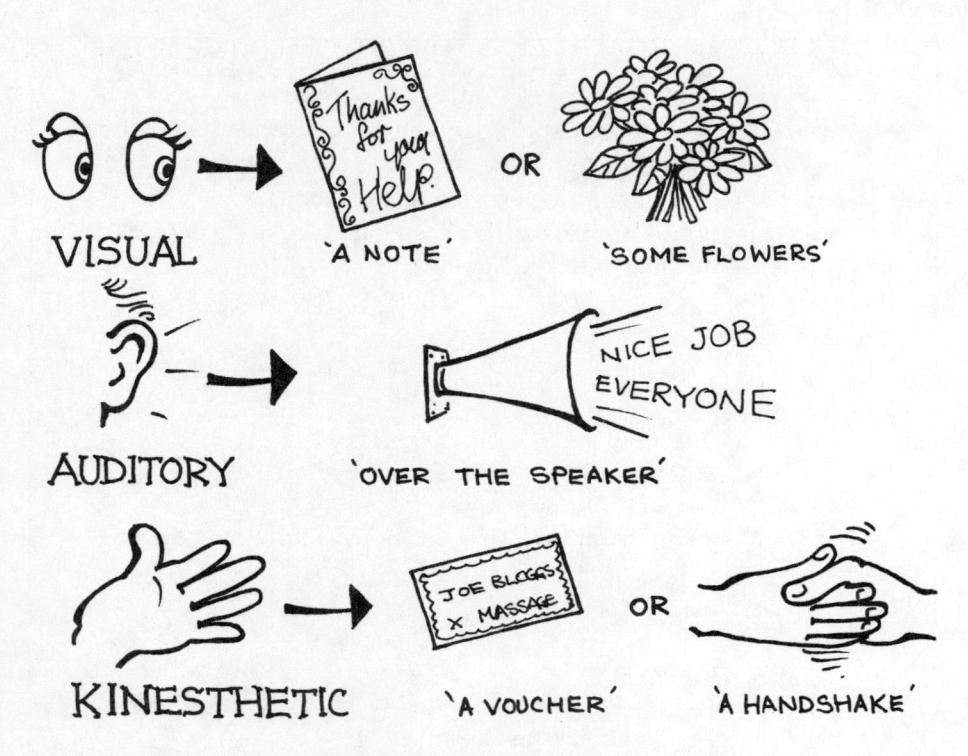

- Surround the environment with success. Post newspaper articles, posters, photos of other successful teams: success breeds success.
- Post favourite affirmations on the wall. Your brain will absorb these messages without your awareness.
- Provide a light atmosphere: people are more effective and productive when relaxed and having fun (another accelerative learning principle).
- Remember the words of Somerset Maugham: 'It's a funny thing in life. If you expect the best you very often get it.'
- Give your team the opportunity to use their potential. Then stand back—the rewards will be there.

Recapping the key points

- The skills to work cohesively must be learnt before people can effectively contribute to a team goal.

- A team is a group of two or more people working cooperatively together, sharing a common purpose, vision, values and resources.
- Synergy in a team is a combination of strength, competence and motivation.
- Effective teams are characterised by many positive attributes.
- Effective teams benefit the whole organisation.
- Team development is a cycle with four identifiable stages. Team leaders have a responsibility to identify the stages which their teams have reached and to provide appropriate resources and encouragement to the team members at that stage.
- Conflict is inevitable. It should be treated as a sign of growth and worked through.
- By practising the 'mental excursion' technique you can draw on the 90 per cent unused potential of your brain to develop your team.
- Like any other resource, the team machinery must be maintained in order to keep the team performing at a high level. This involves sensitive use of feedback and encouragement.
- Ensure that your verbal and non-verbal messages are consistent.
- Match your feedback and encouragement to the individual perceptual styles of team members.

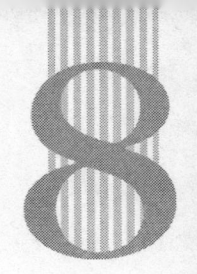

The accelerative learning way to health and stress management

Moni Lai Storz

In this chapter

- Stress management and you
- What is stress?
- The relaxation response using accelerative learning
- Is the relaxation response enough?
  - Physical
  - Mental
  - Emotional
  - Spiritual
- This is how you do it

Overview

This chapter explains:

- how to manage your mind to reduce stress;
- how to create a balance in your physical, mental, emotional and spiritual life.

Stress management and you

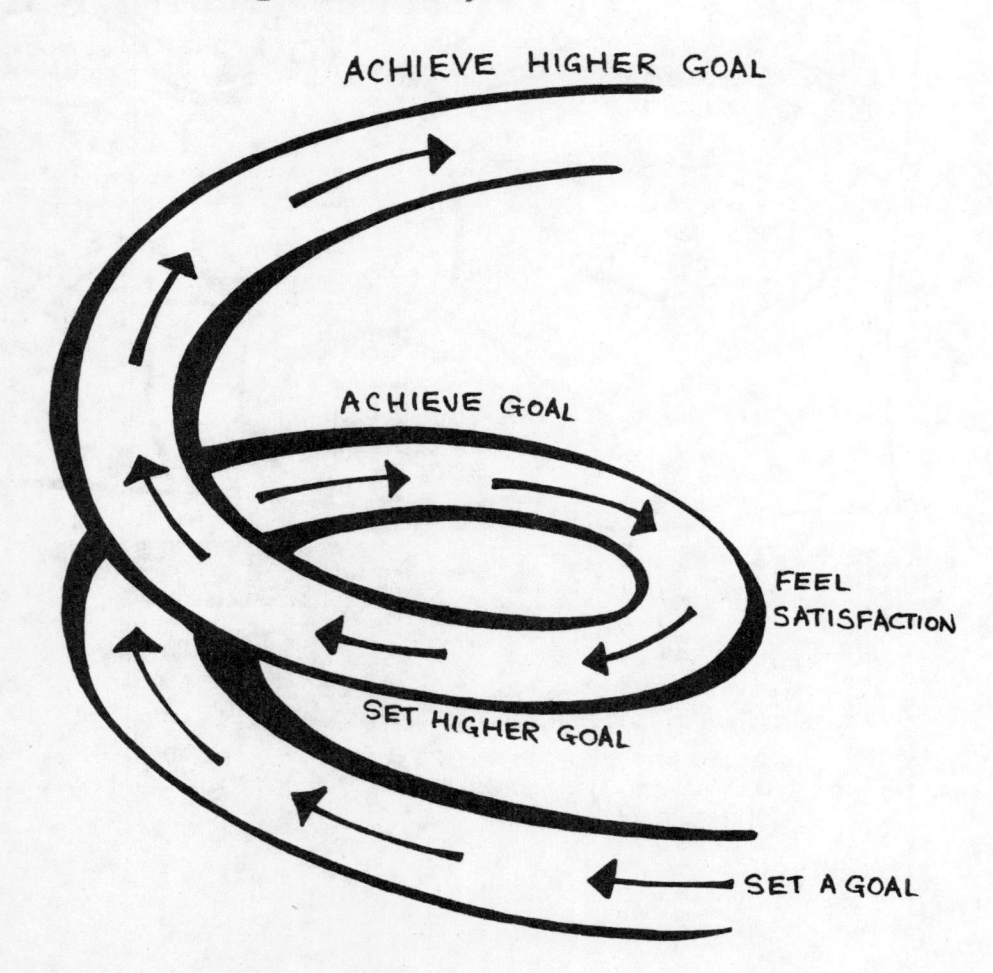

ACHIEVE HIGHER GOAL

ACHIEVE GOAL

FEEL SATISFACTION

SET HIGHER GOAL

SET A GOAL

Health and stress management is about life management. When you manage your health and stress effectively, then you are managing your life successfully. By success I don't mean only financial success, but an all-round success. You have a sense of well-being; you are motivated to do things and to achieve goals; you are energised both in body and mind; you treat those around you with greater goodwill; and you care about yourself. When all these things are present, you feel good and well. This enables you to work for the achievement of your goals. When these are achieved, you feel even better and can go on to bigger and higher goals. You have begun to spin upwards in the spiral of success.

Behind every successful person is an effective health and stress management programme. When we view learning as a holistic process involving the interaction of mental, emotional and physiological factors, it is not too much of a surprise to learn that one of the documented side-effects of accelerative learning is that learners experience less stress in learning. Because of the consistent use of relaxation as a preliminary to the learning process, they may also experience relief from some of their aches, pains and minor ailments.

Learning as a holistic process

An effective health and stress management programme based on accelerative learning principles gives you control over your life—you are in charge. So how is this done? First we need to understand some simple facts about stress.

What is stress?

People define stress differently, and there are variations to the concept. Stress, in physiological terms, refers to a set of biochemical conditions in your body. These conditions are the reactions of your body and its attempts to adjust to stimuli that you perceive as threatening. In short, stress is your body's response to situations that you interpret as pressuring you or causing you tension. For example, if you find your boss irritating, then every time you meet, your body may go into a stress response as you perceive him or her as causing you tension or pressure. So for a stress response to occur, you must first perceive the situation, and in this case the person in the situation —your boss, who may be a neutral object to other staff members—as something or someone who is giving you pressure. This is a subjective experience. You are the one who is responsible for transforming a neutral

What is stress?

stimulus into a stressor. If you can change a stimulus into a stressor, however, then you can also reverse the process. This gives you the possibility of control over your own life.

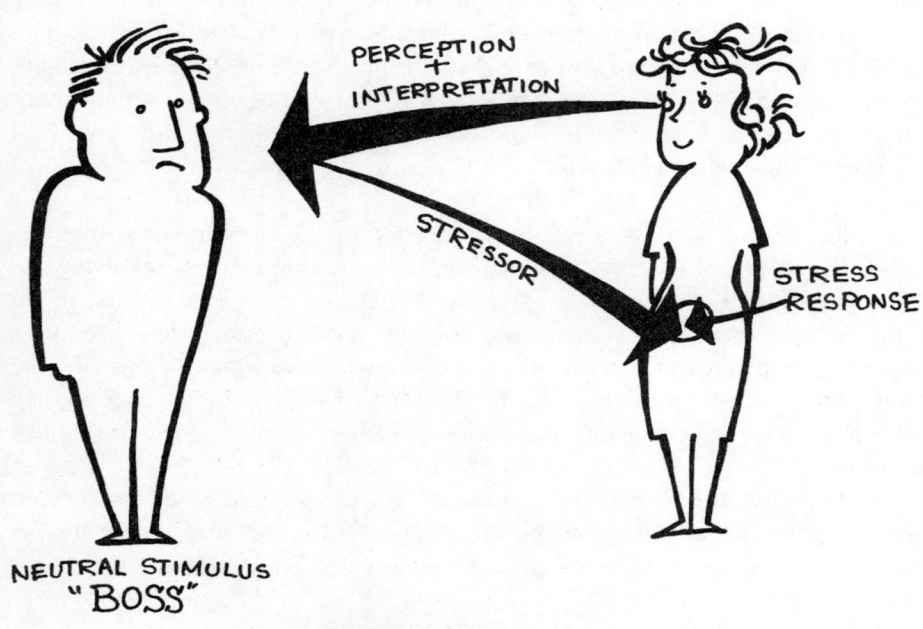

STRESS RESPONSE

Because it is what you perceive as the stressors in your life that cause the biochemical reaction in your body, you can manage your stress by managing your thoughts and your mind. If you can neutralise your thoughts about your boss, for example, then the stress response is minimised. If you can say to yourself 'I can float past this situation' and can convince yourself of this, then the stress reaction will disappear.

Self-talking may not work immediately, however, if the situation is particularly annoying and threatening over a long period. You may feel forced into a 'no fight and no flight' situation. You can neither fight nor flee from the situation. You can neither leave your job nor tell your boss to go jump in the lake. This is the type of situation that increases the stress response. Over a long period, signs and symptoms of stress may appear and your health may suffer. Your life begins to be a journey of more pain than gain.

Manage your stress by managing your thoughts and your mind

Self-talking

The fight or flight syndrome was a natural survival mechanism for our primitive ancestors. When they saw a tiger, they either fought or fled. This enabled their bodies to go back into equilibrium again when the stressor was removed. Modern-day living means we often cannot avoid traffic jams, unreasonable deadlines or changes in the political and economic environment. So how do we counteract the stress response? Relaxation provides a large part of the answer.

Fight or flight syndrome

The relaxation response using accelerative learning

The relaxation response is an immediate and efficient technique to combat the stress in your body. Done daily, it acts as an 'inoculation' against stress. By neutralising the biochemical reaction sparked off by stressful situations, relaxation helps to combat stress that cannot be self-talked away. The relaxation response is rhythmic breathing that slows down your body.

Relaxation response

You can practise this first at home, lying flat on the floor and systematically telling yourself to relax each part of your body. With your eyes shut, breathe to a count of two or four. Your breathing should be natural and done through your nose, with your mouth closed. Do this for ten to twenty minutes. A variation on this is alternate nostril breathing. Hold your nose gently between your thumb and forefinger. Release one nostril and breathe through it to the count of two. Hold both nostrils to the count of two. Release the other nostril and breathe out to the count of two. Count to two without breathing. Repeat the process, starting with the other nostril. Continue for a few minutes. With practice, you can do this without holding your nose! Because the right nostril connects with the left side of the brain and the left nostril with the right side of the brain, breathing in this way helps to create the 'whole-brain' state where each side 'talks' to the other and you are in a more centred, creative mind frame.

At the office, you can develop the habit of regularly spending a few minutes focusing on your breath throughout the day, paying particular attention to creating this 'whole-brain' state before potentially stressful events. As you focus on your breath, visualise yourself remaining calm and centred.

Relax with music

> **Relax with music**
>
> Done with music, the relaxation response is even more beautiful and effective. Not all music is conducive to creating the relaxation response. The rhythm and pace must be right. Have you ever tapped your toes or fingers to the beat of music? The rhythm of music can move us both literally and involuntarily. Listening to music can result in our heartbeats slowing down or speeding up. The average heartbeat is around 70 beats per minute. When we listen to music that is slower—say, 60 beats per minute (largo beat)—then our heart involuntarily slows down.
>
> Music helps in creating the relaxation response in that you can tune out your thoughts and clear your mind as you tune in. Done together with rhythmic breathing, you can go into deep relaxation within ten minutes. At the office, you can practise a modified form of this! The regular practice of rhythmic breathing accompanied by slower paced music which stimulates the right hemisphere of the brain (no vocals, please, as words stimulate the left hemisphere) can help you to sustain the state of relaxed alertness needed for effective decision-making.

Is the relaxation response enough?

The answer is yes and no. Yes, it is better than nothing. But, for a totally effective and successful long-term stress and health management programme, we need to take into account more than just the interaction of the mind and body. We need to balance our life as a whole to include an appropriate level of physical, mental, emotional and spiritual involvement.

Such a holistic approach to effective health and stress management involves managing your life to create a balance that produces harmony in your internal and external environment. Thus it helps you to grow into a well-rounded human being. Four areas should be focused on for holistic flowering into a more balanced and effective human being:

1   physical;
2   mental;
3   emotional;
4   spiritual.

Physical

The physical dimension focuses on your body. Your body can be either a miracle or a dead weight. That is up to you. Use it well, and it becomes a miracle, an ally. Use it badly, and the outcome will be ill health, disease and burnout. Many of us look after our cars and our houses better than we look after our own bodies. Do you give your body a regular service in the form of a workout or a massage?

The body is a miracle, because the more energy it uses, the more energy you have. Energy creates energy. Exercise and use each part of your body and you will find that your body will work for you at your command. You will stay younger.

The body is a miracle

The physical state of your body has to do with exercise. Aerobic exercise is best to keep your heart fit. Aerobic exercise is exercise that increases your pulse rate and heartbeat. Performed daily for ten to tweny minutes, aerobic exercise will keep you fit. Swimming, dancing, cycling, tennis and squash are all examples of aerobic exercise. Golfing and strolling are better than nothing, but they are recreational activities rather than aerobic exercise.

Aerobic exercise

An exercise that can be done with gentle movements is one I call Loving Yourself. To do this exercise, stand in a comfortable posture facing a lovely view wherever possible. Let your arms hang loosely by your sides, keeping your back straight without any strain.

Eyes

Begin with your eyes. Keeping your head still, move your eyes to the right as far they can go, then bring them back to the centre. Next, move your eyes to the left as far as they can go, then back to the centre. This is one cycle of the eyes movement; repeat four times.

Neck

Breathing in, turn your neck slowly to the right. Breathing out, move your neck back to the centre. Breathing in, turn your neck slowly to the left, then back to the centre as you breathe out. Repeat the cycle four times.

Arms

Breathing in, raise both arms above your head and stretch. Breathing out, drop both arms and loosen your entire body.

Waist

Put your hands on your waist. Breathing in, twist the upper part of your body to the right and hold for ten seconds. Breathing out, return to the centre. Breathing in, turn to the left and hold for ten seconds. Breathing out, return to the centre position. Do this cycle four times.

Thighs

Keeping your back straight and breathing in, lower yourself down to an imaginary chair. Holding your breath, sit on this imaginary chair for ten seconds. Breathing out, stand up slowly. Repeat this cycle four times.

Knees

Bend forward slightly and place your hands on your knees, feeling the knobs in your palms. Press the knobs and rub them in rotating motion to a count of ten. Straighten back to normal standing posture. Repeat this cycle four times.

Ankles

Breathing normally, lift your right foot slightly from the floor. Rotate your foot first clockwise ten times, then anti-clockwise ten times. Repeat this for the left foot. Do the whole cycle four times.

To finish this exercise, stand comfortably, close your eyes and breathe normally. Take your gaze inward. Using your mind's eye, visualise your body from head to toe, then travel from your toe back to your head. This is a mental check to see that every muscle is relaxed. Now still with your eyes closed, breathe in deeply, lift both arms above your head and stretch like a cat. Then bring your arms down and wrap them tightly around yourself, giving yourself a big hug. Tightening your clasp, rock gently from side to side and say: I love my body and I love myself. Go deep into the meaning of those words and really believe in what you are saying.

Mental

Mental exercises are for your mind, including both the conscious and the unconscious aspects as explained in Chapter 2. One way to exercise your mind is to learn something new. Our contemporary working lifestyle, with its constant emphasis on retraining and reskilling, is in principle good for the brain. However, you may find that the knowledge and skills you have to acquire at work are not the things that are of most interest to you, so it is important to have recreational mental activities which you enjoy. Some people enjoy learning a new language; others get a thrill from collecting new quotations; still others are stimulated by learning a new dance step. When you enjoy something, you keep wanting to do it because it is pleasurable. Anything that is pleasurable can become addictive—but not all addictions need be negative! What could be more wonderful than having a positive addiction that enhances your mental health?

A positive addiction that enhances your mental health

Although your conscious mind rests, your unconscious mind never does. Because of this, you need to find techniques to give it an occasional rest. If your whole mind does not rest, after a while—like a body that does not have enough rest—it burns out. Mental burnout is mind exhaustion, resulting in a lack of new ideas, a decrease in creativity and innovation.

For warding off mental burnout, creative visualisation is a wonderful exercise since it uses your imagination. Your unconscious cannot distinguish between what is real and what is imagined. Hence creative visualisation is a powerful tool to access your unconscious mind.

Find a quiet place with no interruptions. Make sure that you are away from telephones as their sudden ringing can be shattering when you are in a deep, relaxed state. Sit comfortably. Lightly close your eyes. Use your mind to focus on your breath. Breathing normally, follow the rhythm of your breath, in and out, in and out. To focus your mind, count to four as you breathe in; similarly count to four as you breathe out. Gradually your body will relax through the regulation of your breath. Now let your mind wander. After a while focus on a scene that you like—this can be a sea, a mountain or a forest, whatever suits you and gives you pleasure. So if you choose to visualise a walk by the sea, be very focused on the sensual elements: what can you see in your mind's eye as you walk on the beach? Focus on the colours: the blue of the sky, the white waves, the green of the sea and so on. What can you smell? What can you feel? Perhaps the breeze on your face. What can you hear? The lap lap of the waves, the call of sea gulls. It is important to use all your senses for creative visualisation.

Emotional

Feelings are stronger than thinking with the intellect

Feelings are stronger than thinking with the intellect. For example, you think and know (your intellect) that smoking is bad for you, but you don't *feel* like giving it up. So you don't. You know eating junk food is bad, but you still eat it. Why? Because it gives you pleasure. There is no doubt feelings are often much stronger than mere intellectual rational/logical reasoning. When we feel hunger gnawing away, our rational desire to diet flies out of the window.

The emotional dimension is crucial to our well-being

The emotional dimension is crucial to our well-being. When we feel handsome and beautiful, we *are* handsome and beautiful. When our self-esteem is high, we feel confident. When we feel confident, we feel good about ourselves. When that happens, we feel beautiful. When that happens, you can be sure that others perceive you as beautiful, for you smile and laugh more easily. Often you walk faster, your voice is vibrant, your words enthusiastic and the energy you exude is captivating and inspiring.

When others feel positively towards you, when your work colleagues radiate warmth towards you, a current of synergy or superenergy is created. This means that 1 + 1 equals more than 2.

A very effective exercise to engage your emotions is to read some poetry. Keep a journal and scribble your thoughts in the form of a verse. This is a poem. For example, the same ideas as contained in the previous three sentences can read like a poem:

Engage your emotions
Read a poem
Write a verse
Of beauty
Of joy
Of memories
Keep journal
For your journey

Some of you may prefer reading some quotes of wisdom that make you pause and reflect. Another exercise which is easy to do is to sit in front of a view (this can be a tree or a flower in bloom) and quietly focus your mind on the object. See its colours, imagine you are the flower and feel what it is feeling. If you are an auditory person, put on a piece of a music and really focus on it by sitting quietly and listening. This is good for calming the mind and engaging your feelings.

Spiritual

The spiritual dimension relates to faith. The faith that we are more than our physical bodies is our spiritual food. It is the experiencing of a largeness and awesomeness beyond ourselves and the material world. It is having the sense that the universe is more than simply what we can see, hear, smell, touch and taste.

This belief is not necessarily derived from organised religion. It can also come from a belief in yourself. Whatever it is, the faith factor brings about a sense of peace within you. It is the experience of a togetherness with the universe. This oneness, this non-separateness, this sense of unity and continuity, is essential for health.

The faith factor brings about a sense of peace within you

The spiritual dimension of our lives also needs some exercising. Often the hectic pace of our lives does not enable us to experience the spirituality around us. If you have a religion, the best exercise is praying, talking to your own gods or goddesses. Alternatively, taking time off from the material world, finding a few minutes to do a spiritual ritual that is appropriate for your beliefs, is crucial for your peace of mind. A spiritual exercise following a creative visualisation exercise can be very calming. For example, at the end of your visualisation take a few moments to focus on world peace and the love of humanity. This simple exercise is spiritual insofar as you identify yourself with the cosmos and acknowledge the human ties that bind us as a race of people on this earth.

The physical, mental, emotional and spiritual dimensions are the four faces of holistic health. When all four are balanced, your life is successful and moves forward.

This is how you do it

In a period of allotted time—for example, thirty minutes daily for five days of the working week—your programme should include:

- *Physical:* ten minutes of aerobic exercise (e.g. run or swim followed by deep relaxation and breathing exercises);
- *Mental:* ten minutes of learning something new (e.g. learn ten words of Chinese, read or think about a problem. Use creative visualisation to review a problem or rehearse a sales presentation);
- *Emotional:* take five minutes to write a note of love to someone you care about or send some positive energy through your thoughts via creative visualisation;
- *Spiritual:* appreciation of nature and the aesthetic—take five minutes to stand in your garden, or study the sky and watch the clouds, say a prayer or meditate on your higher self.

Commit a quantity of time to your stress management programme, even if it is only half an hour a day for five days of the week. It can be done if you want to do it. Remember, stress management means attitude management.

Use the remaining two days of the week to recreate, rest and play so that life continues to be a journey of joy and when the pain comes (and you can be sure it will because it is part of your life) your daily stress management programme will stand you in good stead.

Fill in the following chart for your own effective stress management programme.

	Allocated time per day	Activity
Physical (aerobic exercise)		
Mental exercise		
Emotional exercise		
Spiritual exercise		

Recapping the key points

- When you manage your health and stress effectively, you manage your life effectively.
- Learning is a holistic process involving both the mind and the body, the interaction of mental, emotional and physiological factors. An accelerative learning health and stress management programme which takes account of this gives you more control of your life.
- The relaxation response—rhythmic breathing that slows down your body—is an immediate and efficient technique to combat stress. It should be done daily.
- Slow-paced music can enhance the relaxation response.
- A holistic approach to effective health and stress management aims to achieve a balance in the physical, mental, emotional and spiritual areas of life.
- Aerobic exercise increases your pulse rate and heartbeat and keeps your heart fit.
- It is important to have recreational mental activities which you enjoy.
- Use creative visualisation to prevent mental burnout.
- To derive maximum benefit allocate thirty minutes daily for five days of the working week to a programme which includes physical, mental, emotional and spiritual elements.

Memory for managers
Keith Stead

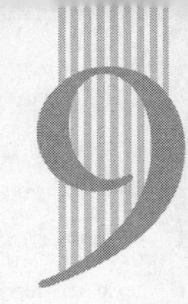

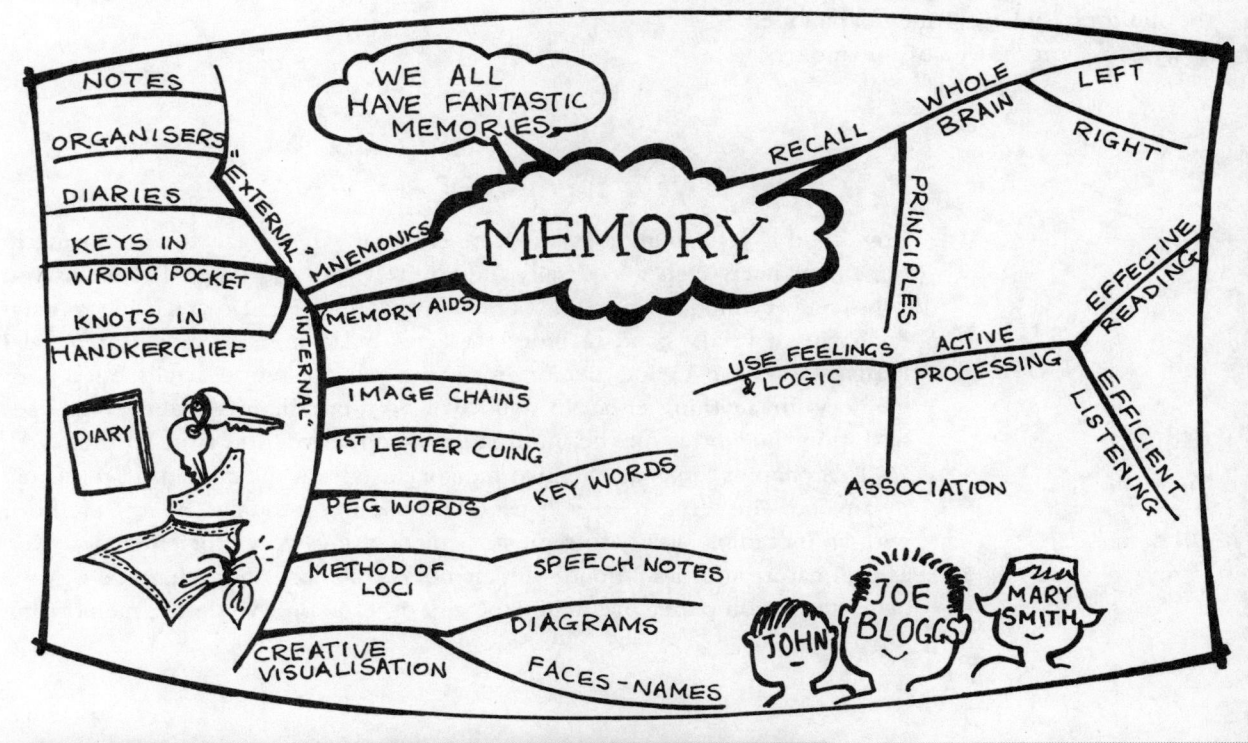

In this chapter

- How good is your memory?
- A neurophysiological memory model
- Focus on recall
- Principles of effective recall
- Aids to memory (mnemonics)
  - Image chains
  - First letter cuing
  - Peg words
  - Creative visualisation
- This is how you do it
- Action plan

'I've a grand memory for forgetting.'
Robert Louis Stevenson

Overview

This chapter explains:

- how to increase your ability to recall information through the use of whole-brain processing;
- the neurophysiological memory model;
- how to use the power of mnemonics.

How good is your memory?

How good is your memory? No doubt everyday you are faced with having to remember many facts and details and you rely on brute mental effort or you consign everything to a notebook or electronic organiser. Do you pride yourself on having a pretty good memory for faces but a poor memory for names? Perhaps you have a good memory for sports facts or music details, but a poor memory for anything else? No doubt you've found many of your employees have poor memories for the information or directives you issue to them.

Effective memory

This chapter looks at effective memory as a skill which can be relearned by anyone. The term 'relearn' is used because we, as human beings, are born with an incredible ability to remember many things very efficiently; however, as we mature into adulthood, our memory skills lose their sharpness as we begin to rely on paper, magnetic tape and other people to do the memorising for us.

A neurophysiological memory model

Memory is linked to the way the neurons in our brain become modified as a consequence of learning. It appears that the terminal buds change shape and specific neurotransmitters are released in response to particular stimuli. We have something in excess of 10 billion neurons in our heads. This allows us to possess phenomenal memories.

> Have you thought how many English words you can make from only twenty-six letters? Most adults have an understanding of about 200 000

> words, each of which are made from combinations of the twenty-six letters. Imagine how many words you could make if you started with 10 billion letters—the mind boggles! In a similar way, the stimulation of different combinations of these 10 billion plus neurons leads to the possibility of thinking that our memories are infinite.

There are no known limits to our memories. Do you think of your memory as being like a box with a fixed amount of space, or as being like an expandable construction set (like Lego) which can be built as large as you like? In fact, the bigger you build it, the more space there is to build even more. Even the slowest of your coworkers actually has a tremendous capacity for continued learning!

> There are people who have total recall. These people are able to recall any event in their lives at any time. (Mozart was able to recall any note in any concert he had ever attended!) The film *Rain Man* (based on actual people), which starred Dustin Hoffman, illustrated this ability. In the film, the character played by Dustin Hoffman displayed a phenomenal ability to recall numbers, such as telephone numbers. Other people have been able to recall details of their childhood when particular stimuli triggered their memories. Marcel Proust recalled a tremendous amount of detail of his childhood when the taste of petite madeleine dissolved in a cup of tea triggered his memory. (This enabled him to write, 'Recollections of Early Childhood'.) You may want to obtain Donald Teffert's book, *Extraordinary People*. This book focuses on people who are mentally retarded to various degrees but who have shown a remarkable ability to recall a variety of different types of information.

The important point to note is that these people had, or have, the same number of (or perhaps fewer) neurons in their brains as the average person. That their ability is considered unusual or 'extraordinary' is a reflection on our perceptions of what is 'normal' ability. To a very large extent, all of us can dramatically improve our ability to *recall* information by using both hemispheres. How can we do this?

All of us can dramatically improve our ability to recall information by using both hemispheres

Focus on recall

Both hemispheres of the brain are involved in learning and memory. Our school system, with its emphasis on logical and factual thinking, is particularly effective in developing the left hemisphere. However, to be able to recall information effectively, we need to utilise aspects of the right hemisphere as well. We need to 'switch on' our intuition, our feelings and particularly our imagination.

We need to 'switch on' our intuition, our feelings and particularly our imagination

Young children have no difficulty in learning rapidly because they have not developed the tendency to rely almost solely on their left-hemisphere logic, analysis and linear mental processing. Holistically, they readily utilise their right-hemisphere functioning. We adults need to again think like young children and to rediscover the power of utilising both parts of our brains. This is particularly useful for enhancing our ability to recall information at will.

As managers, we spend a lot of time getting information into our heads. We tend to think that once the information is there, most of the problem is under control and that recall is relatively easy. Actually, this belief has the problem completely reversed! The problem is *not* with *getting information into* our heads but with *getting it back out* again!

Use external devices such as diaries, planners, memos and visual cues

Many people have difficulty with recall simply because they have not developed appropriate *habits*. As a busy person, you will find yourself being distracted by so many decisions, events, people, questions and 'administrivia' that you will not be able to devote the time required to ensure you can recall everything you need by relying solely on internal recall strategies—you will need to use external devices such as diaries, planners, memos and visual cues to trigger the recall process. Succesful managers have developed the *habit* of using these devices—any useful habit enables you to function without having to think hard about the routine matter and this then enables you to free your thinking for more complex concerns.

Principles of effective recall

Active whole-brain processing, *understanding* and the use of *association* are the keys to effective memory and recall.

Active processing refers to the need for us to focus our attention on whatever it is we are trying to understand and later recall. For example, when we want to be able to recall the name of a person to whom we have just been introduced, we need to pay active attention to the other person's name as we are being introduced rather than listening to hear if our own name is being given correctly! It is useful to repeat the other person's name as we shake hands. 'I'm very pleased to meet you, Mr Betelgeuse!'

Active whole-brain processing

Although passive reception where you learn something incidentally does occur, this is not usually as effective as a deliberate, conscious attempt to make sense of the information being presented. 'Making sense' involves effective listening and reading. *Effective listening* requires you to have clear objectives concerning what you want to take away from the presentation and to 'tune into' the essential ideas being presented by actively sifting out the digressions and irrelevancies. *Effective reading* requires you to have clear objectives for a reading session, to deliberately focus your conscious mind at the level required (e.g. at the 'overview' level; the 'main ideas' level; the 'detail' level) and to note the information in a way which will facilitate subsequent recall.

Effective listening

Effective reading

Understanding occurs when links are established between what you already know and the new information. These links are often facilitated by 'connectors' such as 'how?', 'why?', 'where?', 'when?', 'by whom?', 'for example', 'therefore', 'because'. To illustrate, imagine you are studying the process of photosynthesis in biology and you are seeking to understand the meaning of the word 'photosynthesis' itself. When you make the link with the word 'photograph' by recognising the relevance of light in photography and plants' use of sunlight, you have used the connectors 'how?' and 'when?'. A link has been established between your existing knowledge and the new information being presented to you.

Understanding

An *association* is a mental link. The notion of links is crucial. Our memories are created by the way associations are formed between various elements of our experiences. For example, if I ask you to say the first word which comes into your mind when you hear (or see) the word 'dog' you will most likely say, 'cat' because, for most people (at least those for whom English is a first language), it is closely associated with 'dog'. Thus, recall of one word tends to trigger recall of the other word. The deliberate use of this process of association is fundamentally important in increasing your ability to recall information.

An association is a mental link

It follows that, if we are able to use both logic and imagination, we will retain, process and retrieve information much more effectively than if we do not. This requires us to deliberately incorporate imagination, intuition, emotions and holistic elements into our thinking. Certainly, we may use logic and analytical elements too, but we must suspend the tendency to rely entirely on these. That is, we need to return to the ways of thinking we used as young children!

Aids to memory (mnemonics)

Mnemonics

There are memory systems which have been around for a long time—the early Greeks used mnemonics for telling their long stories (such as *The Odyssey* and *The Illiad*) and delivering long, well-constructed speeches. The beauty of using mnemonics lies in their simplicity, their power and their holistic nature—using them compels us to use both hemispheres of our brains in a fun manner!

Image chains

By deliberating associating one image with another (as we do when we dream), we can dramatically increase our ability to recall specific information as and when we require it. We can condense information, such as that provided in sales presentations or found in technical reports, down to essential 'key' words; the keys provide triggers for the recall of other 'associated' material. 'Image chaining' provides an easy, powerful, fun way of recalling these essential, key words.

To illustrate, the following list of eight key words could have been developed as we summarised an environmental impact survey on local rainforests: 'Plant'; cell'; 'nucleus'; 'photosynthesis'; 'respiration'; 'transport system'; 'life cycle'; 'conservation concerns'. We first need to understand what each of these terms means—to a large extent this requires us to use logical, analytical processing. However, to assist us with recall, we 'switch on' our right hemisphere by using our imagination, emotions, creativity and humour.

Imagine a very large *plant* (perhaps a Triffid!) which has been found guilty of some crime and is locked up in a prison *cell*. However, a *nuclear* explosion, which was *photographed* by someone who then required breathing assistance from a *respirator*, *transported* the Triffid on a *bicycle* to a local *conservatory*. Recalling this 'stupid' story enables each key word to be immediately recognised and its associated information to be readily recalled.

First letter cuing

If you've ever learned to read music, you will be familiar with the mnemonic 'Every Good Boy Deserves Fruit' (or 'Empty Gin Bottles Dismay Fred'!) to help you recall the letters of the notes on the treble staff. Other examples are: 'ROY G. BIV' (or 'Richard of York Gained Battles in Vain') for the colours in the spectrum (the rainbow). The names of the five Great Lakes in North America are recalled with the word 'HOMES'—Lake *H*uron; Lake *O*ntario; Lake *M*ichigan; Lake *E*rie; Lake *S*uperior. No doubt you have invented similar sentences. The most effective ones would be those which employed imagination, creativity, humour and the sense of the bizarre.

Sentences which rely solely on logic tend to be difficult to recall later, because it is so easy to slip up on one crucial element and lose the link (association) with other elements. For example, suppose you wished to raise five important issues at a board meeting and you had identified the key words: '*f*inance'; '*r*esources'; '*m*arkets'; '*a*dvertising' and '*p*urchasing'. A simple, but effective first-letter cuing mnemonic would be '*F*or *r*eal *m*oney *a*dvertise *p*roperly'. Recalling this sentence would ensure you recalled each key word, and their associated issues, without difficulty.

Peg words

This is a similar technique which uses specific words or sounds as triggers for the recall of the associated information. One such peg word system is based on the numerical system where each number has an associated object (the 'peg') derived from the sound of the pronounced number.

The first ten 'pegs' are: gun, shoe, tree, door, hive, sticks, heaven, gate, vine, hen. Each term or key word to be subsequently recalled is deliberately associated with each peg in turn. The strength of this particular technique lies in the ability to recall any word out of order. For example, if the fourth word on the list of biological terms above had been linked with 'door' (for example, by imagining a *photo* of an ornate *door*), it would be readily recalled independently of the word immediately preceding it—this is usually not possible when using the image chain technique.

Figure 9.1 New venture appraisal

```
                        ┌──────────────┐
                        │ Initial idea │
                        └──────┬───────┘
                               │
   ┌─────────────┐             │            ┌──────────────┐
   │    Pros     │             │            │     Cons     │
   │             │             │            │              │
   │  benefits   │             │            │    costs     │
   │opportunities├─────────────┼────────────┤   threats    │
   │ strengths   │             │            │  weaknesses  │
   │  rewards    │             │            │   losses     │
   └─────────────┘             │            └──────────────┘
                               │
              ┌────────────────┴─────────────────┐
              │ Organisation characteristics/    │
              │          climate                 │
              │  (Autocratic/consensual          │
              │   democratic/laissez faire)      │
              └────────────────┬─────────────────┘
                               │
                     ┌─────────┴──────────┐
                     │Implementation factors│
                     └─────────┬──────────┘
              ┌────────────────┴────────────────┐
   ┌──────────┴─────────┐             ┌─────────┴──────────┐
   │     Internal       │             │     External       │
   │                    │             │                    │
   │   e.g. finance,    │             │e.g. markets, advertising,│
   │     personnel      │             │   economic climate  │
   └────────────────────┘             └────────────────────┘
```

Creative visualisation

Creative visualisation

You can use the strategy of deliberately involving the imaginative process of the right hemisphere to assist you to recall diagrams and formulae. Individuals who appear to have photographic memories usually do this.

To illustrate, Figure 9.1 shows a diagram of a scheme for evaluating someone's new idea. You have decided you like the diagram and would like to be able to recall it whenever the appropriate situation occurs. To understand and be able to recall such a diagram, you can first spend time logically exploring its structure and the relationships of the various elements of it.

This is where you are inputting information into your head as you seek to understand. This is a critically important phase. However, once you have reached the point where you can say, 'Yes, I understand this diagram', you should next ask yourself, 'How can I best recall this diagram and the information associated with it?'

To do this, suspend your logical, analytical mind and deliberately switch on your imagination, your feelings, your creativity, your sense of the ridiculous and ask, 'What can I see in this diagram?'

Some people might see this as a robot-like character from a kid's cartoon with its head, body, arms and legs! If this is what you see, later—when you come to recall the diagram—you can deliberately visualise the robotic cartoon character and you will have no difficulty in recalling all the detail. Not only is this an effective way of recalling the information, it is also fun! All effective learning is fun!

The same approach can be used with remembering people's names and faces. Here are some examples: You've just been introduced to these four people:

- *Eve Green*. Imagine her to be *Eve* in the Garden of Eden with her partner Adam and she is wearing a *green* figleaf!
- *Robert Freyberg*. Imagine Robert *fry*ing something on an ice*berg*. Perhaps he had *ro*wed a boat to the iceberg.
- *Mike Watts*. Imagine a singer being zapped with many *watts* when his *mic*rophone short-circuits.
- *Mary Blewette*. Imagine the characters in two childhood nursery rhythms *Mary*, Mary quite contrary blowing the little boy *blue*'s horn.

This may appear to be rather difficult and even a little stupid. Perhaps it is, but it works!

Sometimes you may not develop a particularly strong image but the act of trying will ensure you are actively involved and the key to effective memory is to *actively process* the information.

The hardest step for some people is to suspend their logical, analytical left brain and switch on their creative, imaginative, emotional right brain; however, with practice, the skill can be rediscovered. Remember, we all *do* have fantastic memories and here is a great excuse to act as young children again to rediscover the joy of memorising whatever we need to recall!

This is how you do it

The discussion above emphasises *internal* memory aides, but there are many ways to help recall information by using *external* aides. For example:

- personal organisers (electronic or otherwise);
- personal and/or business diaries;
- memos (to yourself and to others);
- calendars, year planners, notice boards;
- knots tied in your handkerchief;
- car keys placed in your inside jacket pocket instead of your bag or trouser pocket;
- your bedtime reading book placed on the floor instead of on the bedside table;
- asking a friend/colleague to remind you of an important detail.

Regardless of the particular technique(s) you use, the essential elements are that you pay attention to what is to be recalled; you link the information with what you already know and previous experiences; you actively practise recalling the material on a regular basis. You will not be able to grow more neurones to improve your memory, but you *can* change your habits! Just developing the habit of recalling regularly will improve your memory.

Action plan

1. Some people have extremely good recall for particular information—such as cricket statistics, popular music titles and artists' names, types of wines and varieties of grapes, motor vehicle types—yet have difficulty remembering where they left their car in the parking lot. This is because they did not actively take note of their car's location. Develop the habit of deliberating noting the geographical features of your car's position—perhaps near the lamp post with the graffiti on it.
2. Why do so many people claim that they have a 'good memory for faces but a poor memory for names'? Some good advice is to develop the belief, 'I have a fantastic memory and I'm proud of my ability to remember names and always use a mnemonic when meeting people' (and always record their names in your diary as soon as possible!).

3. Sometimes we find we have something we're trying to recall on the 'tip of our tongue'. To assist with the complete recall, relax, let the subconscious mind make the connections and gently run through your previously learned mnemonics. Perhaps write something (anything) down. So often an apparently unrelated word or phrase will trigger the required association.
4. Learning a foreign language is always easier when you reside in the country where the language is spoken than learning it in your own country. This is because of the inevitable constant rehearsal. Therefore to learn a second language, if it is not possible to reside in that country, use your powerful, creative imagination to constantly pretend you really are in that country and rehearse, rehearse, rehearse! Remember, it took you four or five years of total immersion in the language to learn your first language reasonably well—considerable practice is always required.
5. When learning to recall diagrams and charts for an impromptu presentation, deliberately use both hemispheres of your brain by combining elements of logical, rational thought (left hemisphere) with creative, emotional, imaginative, child-like (right hemisphere) ideas.
6. Regularly practise using verbal mnemonics (use either 'first letter cuing' or an 'image chain') to recall at least eight points from speeches or from journals (or newspaper) articles as you read them.

Recapping the key points

- We all have a phenomenal memory capacity.
- The problem is not getting information into our heads, but knowing how to recall it.
- Like any skill, recall strategies can be learned.
- Pay active attention to the incoming information (listen, read, observe effectively).
- Understand the information by creating links with existing ideas (use association).
- Deliberately use feelings, imagination and creativity, as well as logic (use your whole brain).
- Use mnemonics and/or external aides.
- Practise recalling the information regularly.

Memory and graphs
Geoff McDonald

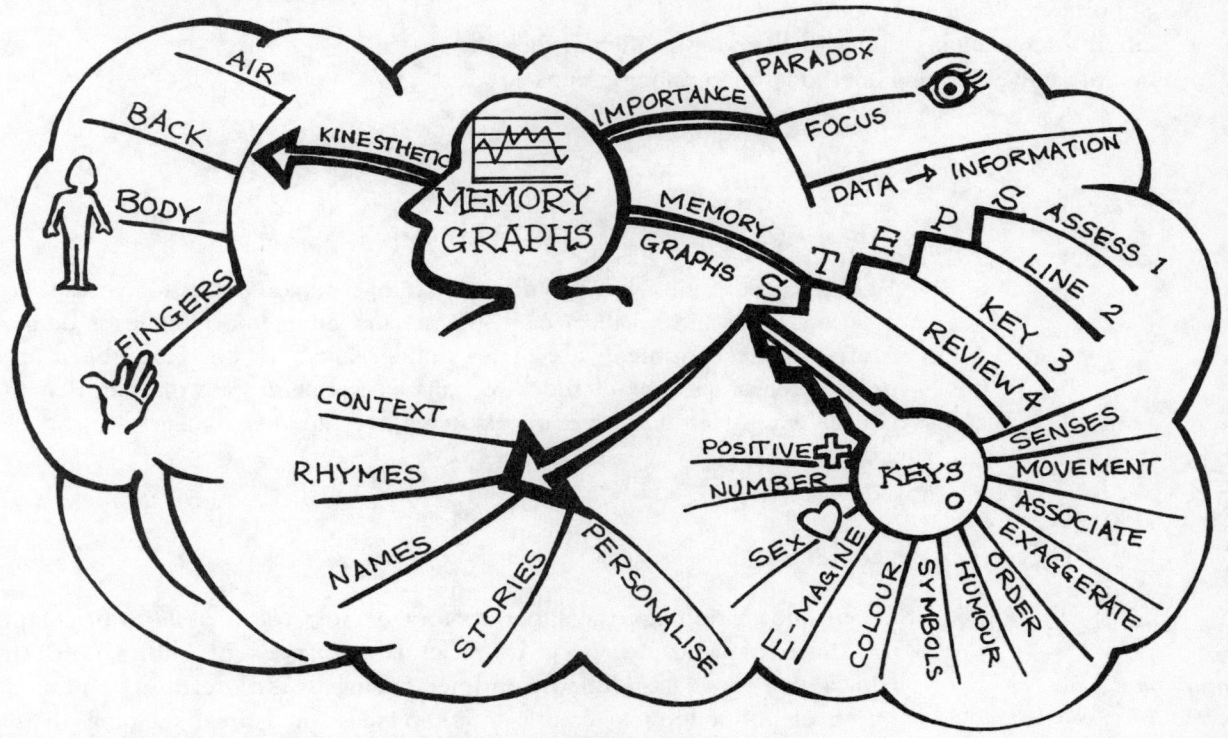

10

In this chapter

- The importance of memory and graphs
  - Shift of focus
  - Data and information
- Memory graphs
- Memory keys
- Connections
- Using kinesthetic graphs in a presentation
- Kinesthetic methods
- Creating finger graphs
- Conclusion

'There can be no learning without memory.'
Colin Rose

139

Overview

This chapter explains:

- the importance of memory and graphs;
- a method for recalling column or line graphs: memory graphs;
- a range of 'active learning' methods for recalling graphs.

The importance of memory and graphs

Traditional education has promoted a strange paradox. The focus has been on the storing and recall of facts, figures and other information (as demonstrated in the continuing use of tests and exams). Yet there has been little or no attempt to offer methods to enhance recall, despite the fact that the Greeks extensively used memory systems over 2000 years ago.

Shift of focus

Educational focus has shifted from memorising to the organising and structuring of information

In our information age, the superior storage and retrieval abilities of computers have reduced the need to recall large masses of information. The educational focus has shifted from memorising to the organising and structuring of information to create new knowledge and understanding. In this area, the human brain is significantly superior to today's computers. Within this process, the importance of memory is vital. It is within this context of structuring information that graphs should be viewed.

Data and information

Usefulness is a key difference between data and information. A mass of numbers represented in a table (data) may mean very little unless they are studied to find a meaningful pattern (information). If these numbers are plotted on a graph, a pattern or trend will emerge more readily and give greater meaning. Effectively, data will be transformed into information.

Memory graphs

The purpose of using graphs is to show information visually. Memory graphs are an aid to recalling the trend of a graph.

The process of creating memory graphs relies on using an image, object or situation to create a metaphorical association with the graph. The emphasis is less on the accuracy of the individual number and more on the overall pattern or trend. Focusing on the trend generally increases the ease of comparison, the speed with which the information can be understood and the potential for recall. If accuracy is important, this can sometimes be overcome when the graph is simple or where the figures can be added to accompany the graphic representation.

Look at Figures 10.1–10.4. If you are particularly skilled at memory techniques, you may be able to recall Figure 10.1 as the numbers themselves. But how accurate do you need to be? Recalling the overall trend is usually sufficient. The focus of memory graphs is on the trend of the graph and not on the particular quantities. Some range of quantity—be it thousands or millions—should be accessible from your general knowledge of the subject.

Creating a memory graph

To create a memory graph there are four simple steps:

1 Assess the graph

Is the graph accurate? Before committing it to memory, assess the graph for the accuracy of its representation. In the same way that emotive word choice can distort a viewpoint, an inappropriate choice of scale on either or both axes of the graph can create distortions.

> Distortions to look for include the following:
> - Does the information appear to be realistic? Is the comparison between a large and small object fair?
> - Is the graph an irregular shape? Is it tall and thin or short and wide? Does this exaggerate the graph's trend?

Figure 10.1
A generic example

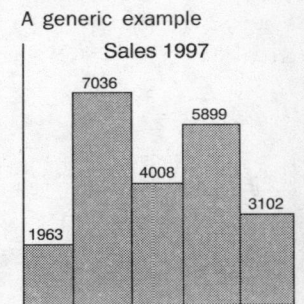

Figure 10.2
Converting to a memory line

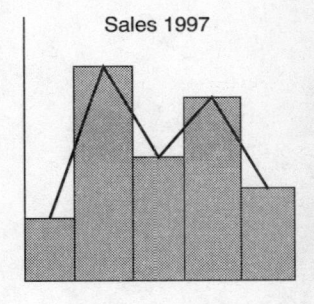

Creating a memory graph

Figure 10.3
A straight line memory graph

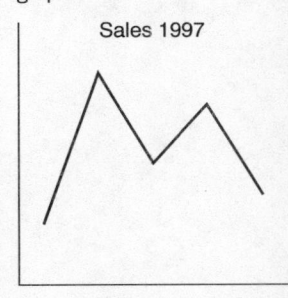

Figure 10.4
A curved line memory graph

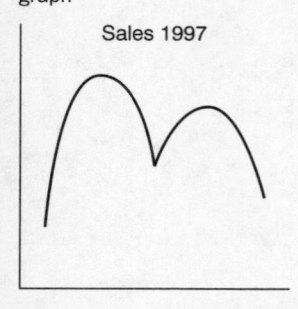

Sales 1997

> - Are the scales consistent? Beware of exponential scales or axes that do not begin at zero. Both radically alter the rate of change.
> - Is a bar graph portrayed as a volume? For example, Wurman asked whether oranges are drawn as circles or spheres. Are we comparing the height or width?

You should be dubious of graphs like Figure 10.1. Although there are numbers on the graph, neither axis is labelled, there is no indication of what the sales are measured in (Australian dollars? Japanese yen?) and there is no indication that the graph is to scale.

2 Convert to a line

Typically the best way to create a memory graph is to translate the trend to a single line, as in Figures 10.2 and 10.3. A single line works best, because it allows the shape to be imagined as if it is drawn in many different ways (for example, a plan view, a silhouette or in perspective). The memory graph can then be drawn as a straight or curved line, as in Figures 10.3 and 10.4. This option provides further opportunities to create a suitable memory key.

3 Create a memory key

Make a suitable memory key by linking the shape of the line to an image of an object or place that you are familiar with.

4 Review

Test yourself and review the memory key within ten minutes of creating it. This is an important step in transferring the information from your short-term to long-term memory. This process should only take ten to twenty seconds. Simply recall the memory key you have made and link it to the original graph. Further similar reviews one day, one week, one month and six months later will increase your recall ability by around 70 per cent over those who do not review.

Here's a simple rhyme to remember the four steps by:

*Make sure it is fine,
before you make it a line,
make the key special to you
and reinforce with a review.*

Memory keys

Memory keys can be used to 'lock' the memory into the mind and to 'unlock' the memory when recall is required. This is accomplished through imagination and association. Use your imagination to associate or link the item to be remembered with something you already know.

To highlight the association and enhance recall, make as many vivid connections as you can. This process not only enhances recall but also your creativity. Tony Buzan suggests the following as powerful keys:

1 *Senses*. Incorporate your full range of senses into the image. This is a very powerful technique and is used by many of the great mnemonists (people with super-memories). Since graphs are a visual method, you may begin your description with: 'The graph looks like . . .', then elaborate with what that image sounds like, tastes like, feels like, moves like and smells like.
    Example: Imagine you have a stick of celery in your hand. Break the celery into the shape of the graph. Listen to the sound as the celery snaps within your fingers. Feel the texture of the crisp stick of celery in your hands. Then taste the graph as you eat the celery.
2 *Movement*. Turn your image into a 3D movie.
    Example: Picture the graph trend as a child's line-drawing of a bird. See the bird flapping its wings as it flies. Watch it fly towards you, growing bigger as it comes closer.
3 *Association*. Link the image to an object, place or event that will help you recall it. If you are in a particular room where you are likely to need to recall this information—perhaps your office or the exam room—link the image with the items that are around you, such as your desk, a telephone or a picture on the wall.
    Example: The graph line reminds me of the big crack in the wall of my office. Each time I see the crack, it will remind me of the shape of the graph.

Memory keys can be used to 'lock' the memory into the mind

4 *Sexuality*. Turn it into a sexual fantasy and you will definitely remember it. (But don't worry, no one else need know which associations you use!)
   Example: The graph forms a pair of smooth-flowing curves that remind you of a pair of breasts.
5 *Humour*. The more absurd and surreal the image you create, the easier and more fun it is to recall.
   Example: The graph reminds you of the big, hairy eyebrows of the presenter—two big, fuzzy, sleeping caterpillars perched on his forehead.
6 *Imagination*. By making your images more interesting, bizarre and varied, you enhance your recall and stimulate your creativity, which can be put to use in other ways.
   Example: It is not so much a line, but a crack on the projection screen from an earthquake. You can see it shaking . . . you can feel the whole room shaking . . .
7 *Number*. Numbers create order and sequence and counting is a great method of encoding information for greater recall.
   Example: Count the peaks (2) and the troughs (1).
8 *Symbols*. Use symbols as a means to link abstract ideas.
   Example: It looks like the letter 'm' (or the number '3' on its side).
9 *Colour*. Use colours wherever possible, not only to brighten up your day, but to provide an extra key for locking away your memories.
   Example: Imagine the line on the graph is shining like a jewel. At the low points the line is a dark, dull grey, but at the high points the line is a brilliant, shining silver.
10 *Order/sequence*. Encode the information through numbers, size, shape, colour, direction or any grouping you like. This provides structure to random information.
   Example: Remember the sequence of your journey by imagining you are on a roller coaster—going slowly up the first very steep climb, quickly down the shallow slope . . .
11 *Positive association*. Often we don't like to recall negative images, so seek out pleasurable scenes to assist your recall.
   Example: The memory of the snow-capped mountains you visited on your honeymoon is more pleasant than the memory of the ski slopes on which you broke your leg.
12 *Exaggeration*. Marketing people know that the biggest, the best, the smallest or the widest is the way to create a lasting impression. It will work for your images too!
   Example: The line on the graph is the thinnest line you have ever seen.

It is so thin, it looks like a hair on the projector screen that isn't meant to be there.

> **Exercise**
>
> Consider Figures 10.3 and 10.4. Relate them to the examples above. Can you break your celery into this shape? Can you imagine the bird flying towards you? How many peaks and troughs are there? What does it feel like to ride the roller coaster of the graph? Can you breathe the fresh air of the mountains? Is it the thinnest line you have ever seen? What other associations can you make from this simple example?

Connections

It is no use remembering the graph as the letter 'm' if you cannot recall what this refers to—does the sales graph look like an 'm' or is it the productivity graph? Make the connection between your image of the graph trend and the information that is being portrayed as vivid and powerful as you can. Here are several ways to heighten this connection.

Make the connection

Context

Research has shown that if you were drunk at the time of a particular event, the potential for recall of that event is enhanced when you become drunk again. This is not to suggest that we all begin drinking, but it does highlight the importance of the context of the learning situation. The place of learning becomes a powerful anchor for recalling the lesson.

The place of learning becomes a powerful anchor for recalling the lesson

Consequently, it makes good sense when you first move into a classroom or office to heighten your awareness of your surroundings. What colour are the walls? Does the room have a particular odour? Recall your movements ('I walked through the door, and around the filing cabinet . . .')

When recalling information from a talk, meeting or conference, mentally revisit the room in which the event occurred and you will have taken a big step towards better recall of those events. The relevance of any graph can then be linked to the room and why you were there.

> **Rhymes**
>
> Advertisers know that rhythm and rhyme are great ways to remember the products they are marketing. Make up your own jingle to ensure your recall.
> *Example:* You have used the memory key of a roller coaster ride to follow the trend of the graph. The rhyme could then become:
>
> > *The sales in '97*
> > *make us think we're in heaven*
> > *enjoy the thrills*
> > *of riding up and over the hills.*
>
> Simple but effective! (Can you remember the rhyme of the four steps to creating memory graphs?)

Names

Personalise your understanding of the information through 'naming' the graph pattern.
Example: Instead of simply '1997 sales', rename the graph: 'The 1997 earthquake sales'. (Feel the sales figures shake! See the building in the shape of the numerals '97' crash to the ground to reinforce the overall connection.)

Stories

The Russian mnemonist nicknamed 'S' used stories to recall lengthy mathematical formulae. The ordering of the information provides an opportunity to link seemingly unconnected images. If one item is at first forgotten, the surrounding parts of the story quickly fill in the gaps. This is a great way of linking several graphs into one memory key with each piece reinforcing the others.
Example: If the 1996 sales figures were linked to the image of a bird and the 1997 sales figures were linked to an earthquake, then: 'The giant, black bird came flying toward me. It had strange yellow markings on its feathers—it looked like the number "96". In the bird's beak he carried a small, shiny, silver cash register (where the sales are made). But then everything began to shake. It was an earthquake! A blue building in the shape of "97" collapsed

to the ground. The bird dropped the cash register into a crack opening upon the ground.'

It may be a bizarre story—but what a funny and effective way to link the sales figures of 1996 and 1997!

Personalising

Wherever possible, a personal encoding of the information is more effective than a memory key provided by someone else. Make it special for you and increase the effect.

Note: Memory graphs should be seen as a device for recall. They should be added to reinforce other material. If presented in isolation, a memory graph will mean very little to your audience and remove the opportunity to review the accuracy of the graph.

Using kinesthetic graphs in a presentation

Catering for all preferences

Research has shown that everyone has a dominant sensory system, a preference to learn or communicate through a particular sense (see Chapter 5). The major groups are the visual (seeing), the auditory (hearing), and the kinesthetic (doing).

During a typical presentation, the preferred style of most learners is catered for through a verbal description and visual graphics. However, the kinesthetic learner is often forgotten or ignored. Movements of the body are distinctly recorded by the brain and should be pursued as an opportunity to enhance communication and learning.

Preferred style of most learners

Further advantages

Beyond catering specifically for the 'active learner', incorporating activities into your presentations has several important advantages:

- The incorporation of all three modes of learning provides a more complete and powerful presentation. This includes a complementary range of cues to aid all learners.

- Activities provide a great way of changing the flow of a presentation. Asking the learners to stand and participate in an activity revives any flagging interest and provides an event that can aid recall.
- Kinesthetic exercises provide an opportunity for interaction between learners.
- Having fun is a very positive learning experience that both increases interest and unlocks the door to the subconscious mind to increase recall. Activities show that learning can be fun and effective.

Kinesthetic methods

Air graphs

Draw the graph in fresh air

One of the simplest activities for recalling graphs is to draw the graph in fresh air—first with the eyes open, then several times with the eyes closed. For added effect, say the title of the graph aloud as you write. Turn the lights off and use a torch or flashlight for extra fun.

Back graphs

Draw the graph on the back of the person seated in front

To incorporate the sense of touch and increase interaction with other learners, draw the graph on the back of the person seated in front. Say the title of the graph and write simultaneously.

Walking graphs

Walk the pattern of the graph

Stand and walk the pattern of the graph as if it were painted on the floor. Since crawling is an unusual activity for most adults, it will be even more effective for recall.

Body graphs

Shape your body in the same way

Can you shape your body in the same way as the graph?

Finger graphs

Finger graphs represent the information within a graph with the finger positions poised in relation to the height or length of the statistical data. At least four hand positions are readily available: finger closed at the knuckle (a closed fist); closed at the first joint; closed at the second joint; or the fingers in a straight position.

Finger graphs

Creating finger graphs

Graphic notation

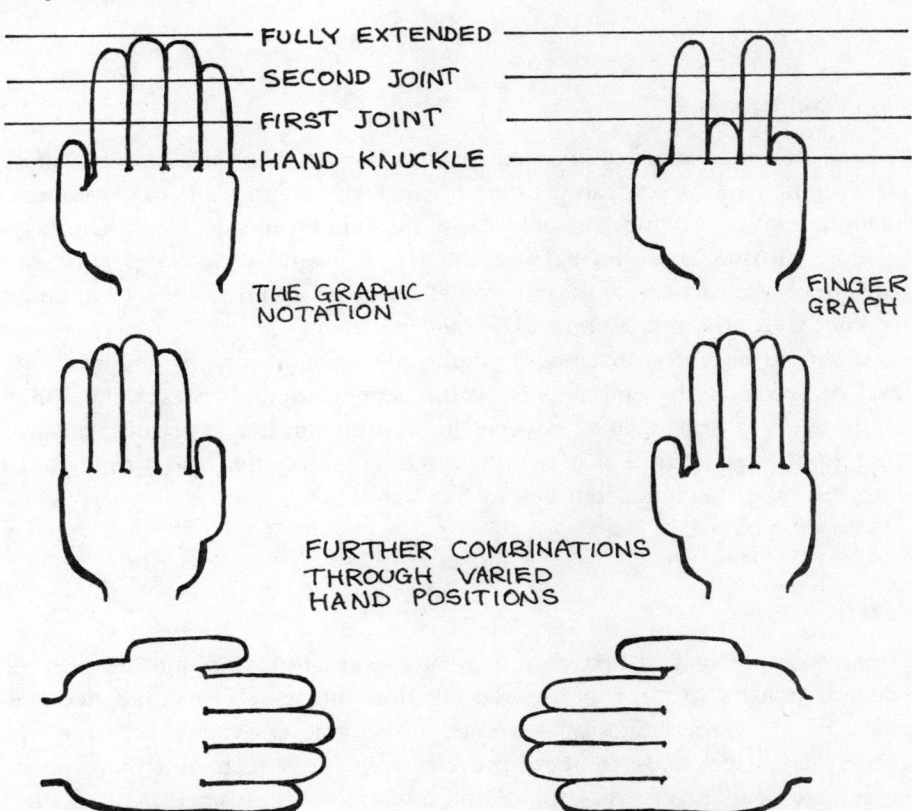

In presenting a graphical account of a finger graph, it is suggested that the four horizontal lines that denote the four extensions of the fingers be shown. This creates a valuable reference point to read the position of the fingers; a similar role to the lines in a musical score.

Approximation

The aim, as with memory graphs, is to create an approximation of the data. We are not trying to mimic the accuracy of the graph itself, but simply to reflect the overall trend, as in Figures 10.3 and 10.4. The generic example graph similar to Figures 10.3 and 10.4 may be created.

Create the pattern with your fingers and say aloud the name and relevance of the information it represents.

More combinations

This approach is obviously limited to how many fingers you have and how many combinations you can create, but since the emphasis is on an approximation, enough variations should easily be found. Consider each hand as a separate measure and you have doubled your memory capacity; shift your hand from the vertical to the horizontal for more combinations. (You could try your toes also, but 1 don't like your chances!)

It should be noted that finger graphs, like memory graphs, record a low level of accuracy: the emphasis is on the general trend. However, the ability of the brain to bridge gaps between the information that is recalled ensures the role of finger graphs as a 'net' for catching information and forming links with the other details stored within our minds.

Practice

These positions may at first be difficult to form and may require the use of your other hand to form the desired position. But with a little practice it is possible! Remember, it took us twenty, thirty or forty years to develop our current language skills to their present level. This technique may be of immediate benefit to the hearing disabled, who are accustomed to using their fingers for sign language.

Further connections

The enormous abundance of possible images and associations for memory graphs highlights the narrow range of options for finger graphs. After recalling five to ten graphs, the messages about which finger positions relate to which graph (e.g. sales, productivity) may become confused. However, this can be overcome by linking the finger graph to any of the other methods outlined in this article (i.e. memory graphs, air graphs, back graphs, walking graphs or body graphs).

Conclusion

The following rhyme will help you recall the main ideas of this chapter:

>Structure *to inform,*
>*So easy* understanding *is the norm;*
>*Enhancing recall is the* key
>*If you* listen, do *and* see.

Recapping the key points

- Graphs can be seen as a way of structuring information to show it visually.
- Memory graphs are an aid to recalling the trend of a graph rather than the detailed figures.
- A memory graph uses an image, object or situation to create a metaphorical association with the graph.
- The four steps to creating a memory graph are (1) assess the graph; (2) convert to a line; (3) create a memory key; and (4) review.
- To highlight association and enhance recall, make as many vivid, varied and bizarre connections as you can.
- Memory graphs should not be used in isolation but in context to reinforce other material.
- Kinesthetic graphs may help kinesthetic learners to remember the trend more easily.
- Finger graphs provide another readily available means to help remember trends. As you create the pattern with your fingers, say aloud the name of the graph and the relevance of the information it represents.

An earlier version of this chapter entitled 'Finger and Memory Graphs' was published in *ALSA News*, Accelerative Learning Association of Australia, Victorian Branch, August 1982.

Strategic planning: An accelerative learning approach

Jeffrey Lai

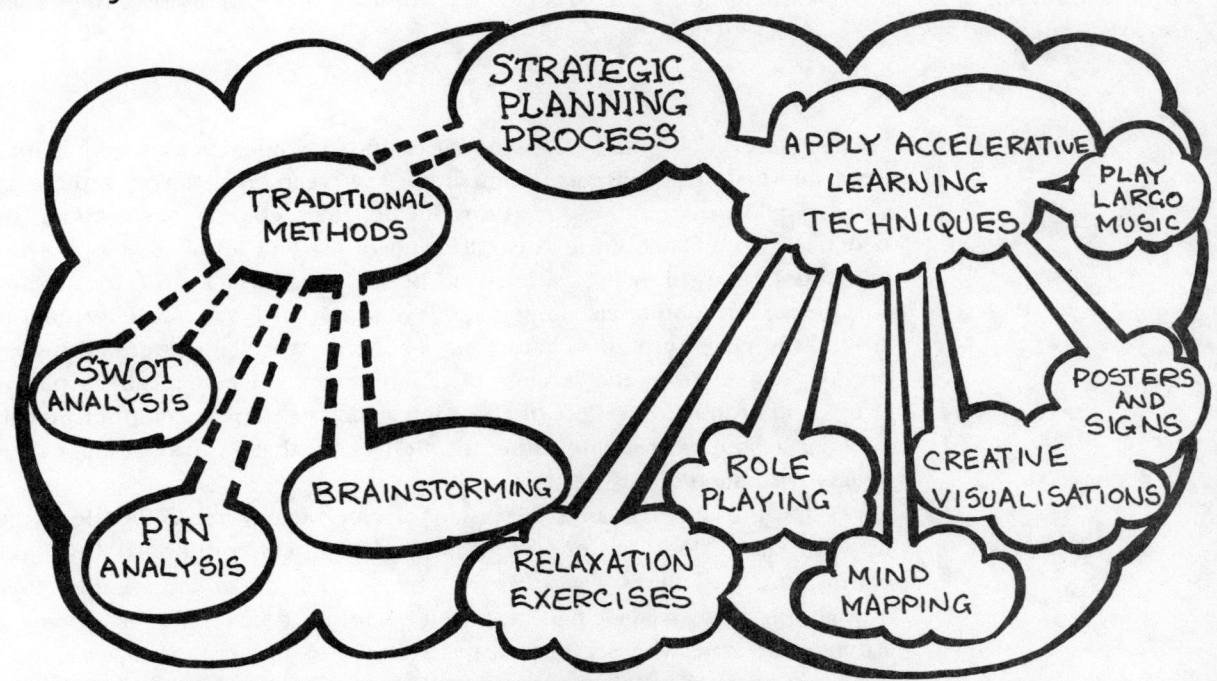

[Mind map diagram showing: Strategic Planning Process connecting to Traditional Methods (SWOT Analysis, PIN Analysis, Brainstorming) and Apply Accelerative Learning Techniques (Play Largo Music, Posters and Signs, Creative Visualisations, Mind Mapping, Role Playing, Relaxation Exercises)]

In this chapter

- Strategic planning—a process
- The planning process
  - Step 1: Understand the environment
  - Step 2: Establish key strategies
  - Step 3: Set objectives
- Traditional methods
  - SWOT
  - PIN
- The accelerative learning approach to strategic planning: Action ideas
- This is how you do it

Overview

This chapter explains:

- why an accelerative learning approach gives you better results from strategic planning
- how to apply an accelerative learning approach to strategic planning to obtain more intuitive and creative results.

Let me describe a planning session I attended while I was working for a large multinational computer company a few years ago. It was a three-day activity held in a picturesque resort located in a country town about 100 kilometres from Melbourne, Australia. The resort had tennis courts, a swimming pool, large sprawling gardens and, best of all, gourmet meals for morning tea, lunch, afternoon tea, dinner and even supper. I can recall wandering around the resort grounds chatting about the most trivial matters during the breaks we had from the intense planning sessions. I can recall us playing tennis and croquet. But most of all I can remember those scrumptious meals. Looking back now, it is interesting for me to note that I can remember these details with such clarity.

As for the actual planning sessions, I can vaguely remember long and tiresome discussions and brainstorming activities which did not spark much enthusiasm. Most times it was like watching a long, drawn-out B-grade movie of a couple of managers 'fighting it out'. At other times it was like being in a trance-like state where everyone just stared into an empty void, waiting for the next break. We did achieve a few things. We came up with 'numbers'—sales forecasts; headcount numbers; customer opinion ratings; budgets. And we designed a huge action plan which was supposed to represent the strategies we had developed. At the end of the three days, we all got into our cars and drove off into the sunset.

Strategic planning—a process

The scenario I have just described is perhaps a bit unfair. Maybe it is a touch too cynical. More likely it is a jaded recollection of a process which was so critical to our business, but produced results which were so average.

Strategic planning, including business planning, has far-reaching implications and consequences for a business, and also for the individuals who contribute to the enterprise. It is an indispensable process which every business, large or small, undertakes in an attempt to achieve success. Strategic planning comes in many forms and produces a variety of results, depending on the specific business requirements at that point in time. It usually involves such matters as:

Strategic planning

- the organisation's strategic vision;
- its mission;
- its objectives;
- its marketing plan;
- competitive analysis

and a whole host of other business issues including the development of an action plan for the implementation of various strategies. The planning process will in general involve key personnel of the business or organisation working together. In addition, the planning process itself is often an educational activity for the people involved and should create a greater awareness of the environment in which they and their business exist. It is in the planning process that I believe accelerative learning can be used.

Accelerative learning can:

- improve the quality of the output;
- increase creative input;
- elicit more intuitive managerial responses.

I will start by outlining the planning process and describing two—predominantly left-brain—methodologies that are commonly used. I will not be talking about the various intricacies of strategic planning. This would include a myriad of theoretical and esoteric matters ranging from market forces analyses to value chain investigations. What will be addressed is how to obtain more creative and intuitive results when we get a group of people together to plan.

Methodologies

The planning process

The planning process is used to develop strategies and allocate resources in order to achieve the organisation's objectives.

Figure 11.1 Strategic planning

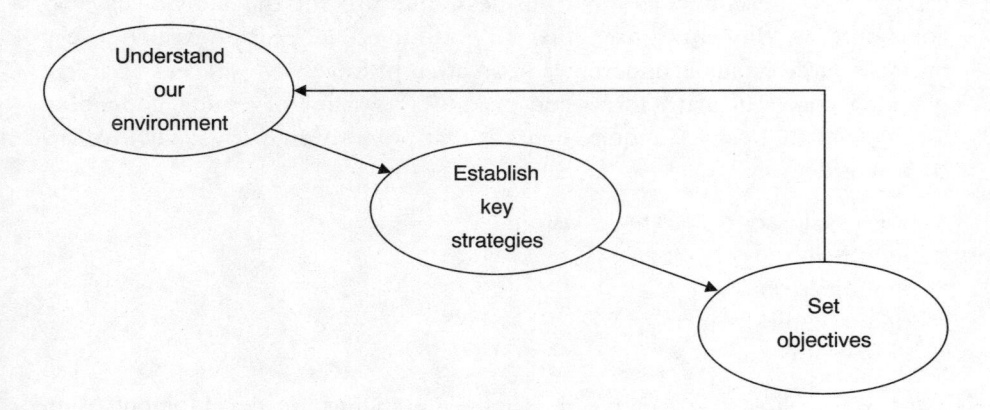

```
        Understand
        our
        environment  ←─────────────┐
             │                     │
             ▼                     │
        Establish                  │
        key                        │
        strategies                 │
             │                     │
             ▼                     │
                            Set
                            objectives ──┘
```

Some examples:

1 What is the best way of marketing your company's products or services given a finite amount of human resources, time and budget?
2 How can we accurately forecast sales for the coming year so that the appropriate human and other important resources can be focused on winning a greater market share of business?
3 How can we use information technology to achieve a competitive edge in the marketplace?

Planning usually includes three major steps, as shown in Figure 11.1.

Step 1: Understand the environment

The environment

Understand the environment in which the organisation or business exists. Typically, this includes the economic, political and social environment—internal as well as external—of the organisation. For example:

- What market forces are out there which could affect the business of the organisation?
- Are there any trends which the business could exploit to its advantage?
- What about the competition? Are they succeeding or failing in certain areas?

- What is the morale of the people in the organisation like? Is the attrition rate high?
- Where can productivity be improved?

The list of questions could go on ad infinitum.

The trick is in identifying these issues and environmental factors. Following this, it is important to give the more important issues priority.

Step 2: Establish key strategies

The strategies are related to the vision and the mission of the business. For example:

- Where is the business going?
- Where do we want it to go?
- Do we want to be the largest supplier of widgets in Australia by the turn of the century?
- Or are we just interested in making a one million dollar profit for ourselves in three years' time, no matter what the cost?

Vision and the mission of the business

Thus the need to understand our environment.

Step 3: Set objectives

Set objectives for the business and organisation. As well as financial and profit-related objectives, business objectives should cover human resources, organisational structures, technical resources, physical resources, productivity and social issues.

Set objectives for the business

For example, your organisation may want to make a net profit of one million dollars over the next twelve months and also to open office branches in every capital city on the eastern seaboard. Or your business may be interested in raising its corporate profile through an advertising campaign and also at the same time reduce its headcount by 20 per cent over the next six months. No matter what your objectives are, they should be set as part of the overall business and organisational strategies.

The above process is cyclical and should be seen to be evolutionary, subject to constant review and adjustment. Sometimes businesses develop a plan and it stays in the filing cabinet. In today's fast-moving environment of

Process is cyclical

Figure 11.2 Example of a SWOT analysis

Strengths	Opportunities
- Best widget technology	- Target Asian market
- Good reputation in the marketplace	- Marketing through Internet
- Excellent support staff	- New wonder widget
-	- ....
Weaknesses	Threats
- Supply leadtime are long	- Major competitor copying our technology
- Low margins	- Domestic market is shrinking
- Sales staff not prospecting much	- More stringent environmental policies
-	- ....

constant change and competitiveness, the planning process must be an integral and constant part of the management of a business. This is not to say that we excessively plan to the extent that we forget about the implementation of the plan or our role in life, but that the 'plan' is a constant reminder of our strategic directions and the achievements we are meant to accomplish in a given time frame. The plan has to be revisited regularly and not be treated as a 'once a year' document.

Traditional methods

SWOT

SWOT analysis

One of the most popular methodologies used as part of the strategic planning process is the SWOT analysis. The purpose of the SWOT analysis is to get participants in a planning session to have a better understanding of the business they are in by having them 'brain dump' the Strengths, Weaknesses, Opportunities and Threats (thus the acronym SWOT) of the situation they are in. This type of planning activity is meant to be short and sharp and is a very good way of creating a high level of awareness of issues amongst the participants—hence its popularity in most organisations today as a starting point for the planning process.

It is typical for a planning session like this to be limited in usefulness. This is especially so when the SWOT analysis is conducted as a traditional business meeting. There may be hidden agendas, power plays and a lack of assertiveness or enthusiasm. It is frequently the case that participants in a typical business planning session have various reasons for not being able to contribute as creatively as they should to the strategic plan.

Another reason why such planning sessions may not yield the desired results is inherent in the 'left-brain' nature of the process. Business meetings are usually—and for good reason—conducted in a logical, linear, step-by-step way which favours left-brain analysis and decision-making. To maximise the benefits of strategic planning, however, we need to adopt a 'whole-brain' approach which involves both the logical and the creative, intuitive aspects of our thinking.

To overcome some of these problems, organisations sometimes inject some 'play' time into a planning session and include various forms of recreational activities over the course of a two- to three-day planning exercise as described above. This recognises the importance of right-brain involvement as these activities inject an element of fun to the exercise. However, they do not maximise the creative and intuitive potential of the participants. One major reason for this is that the right-brain involvement is not related to the purpose of the activity. In the example above, I can clearly remember the gourmet meals, the recreational activities and the trivial conversation between sessions—all activities involving more 'right-brain' activity—but I have no clear recollection of the strategies and action plans, the left-brain emphasis of the planning sessions.

PIN

Apart from SWOT analysis, the PIN process, a brainstorming activity highlighting the positives and the negatives of the year gone by, is another technique used. From a list of positive and negative key issues, the group sets priorities. After discussion, the group decides on its objectives, taking into account those negatives which are considered to be critical. Strategies are then developed to achieve these objectives and finally an action plan is established to implement these strategies.

PIN process

A typical example could be something like this. Imagine that the group identifies a high rate of attrition of staff as a negative for the past year. Its objective might then be to reduce the attrition rate to an acceptable level in the coming year. To develop a strategy to support this objective, the group will have to identify key factors that account for the high attrition rate. Once these are established, these strategies can then be formulated into an action plan to resolve the problem. This sounds simple enough, but a closer examination of the example highlights several potential stumbling blocks in this type of process.

Given its highly analytical nature, the process is predominantly left-brain. Yet such a process calls for a whole-brain solution in that it demands that the group adopt a very creative mode of thinking to come up with an action plan. One may argue that this process is not meant to resolve issues at that point, but rather it is a forum whereby ideas are tossed around and the eventual development of a strategy may be done 'offline'. This may be true, but the strategic guidelines have to be established—hence the importance of creative or intuitive input.

For example, the high attrition rate may be considered to be acceptable as part of an overall strategy to reduce the headcount in the organisation. On the other hand, the people who are leaving the organisation may be the people that are desperately needed to keep the business going. If that is the case, then how do we keep the good people and let the non-performers go? Looking at the situation from yet another angle, maybe the non-performers are not performing because of low-quality management. In this case, we need a different strategy and action plan.

The traditional approaches to planning mentioned so far are tried and tested methods to achieving good results from a planning session. Can we get better results?

Incorporation of whole-brain techniques into the planning process

In the rest of this chapter we will examine an alternative to traditional planning methodologies. The incorporation of whole-brain techniques into the planning process through the use of accelerative learning can only improve on what is usually seen as a very left-brain and sometimes a very stressful activity.

The accelerative learning approach to strategic planning: Action ideas

Whole-brain approach

The incorporation of accelerative learning into the planning process using a whole-brain approach can:

- produce results that are more creative;

- promote intuitive and lateral thinking that produces more options;
- assist members of an organisation to achieve better understanding and appreciation of the business environment and the organisational complexities involved;
- enable participants to grasp the complexities of issues that face their colleagues in other areas of responsibilities more readily and quickly, as they are more receptive to empathic feelings;
- make the process more enjoyable and less stressful.

So how do we incorporate such a technique into the planning process of a business? The aim in incorporating accelerative learning into strategic planning is to create an atmosphere whereby participants are able to realise their full potential in the planning process.

STRATEGIC PLANNING PROCESS + ACCELERATIVE LEARNING TECHNIQUES = MORE CREATIVE AND INTUITIVE RESULTS

Creating the right atmosphere

- *Play largo (slow tempo) music.* One of the basic tenets related to accelerative learning is that people will learn best under conditions of relaxation and joy. If specific relaxation techniques are used throughout a planning session, then we find that participants are in a better state of mind to produce more effective results. For example, I find that having largo music played during the planning sessions helps enormously. Guiding participants through short meditative breathing exercises at various points of the planning session is also important.
- *Put up posters.* A major principle related to accelerative learning is the ability for individuals to absorb suggestions at both a

Largo music played during the planning sessions

Figure 11.3
Accelerative learning process of strategic planning

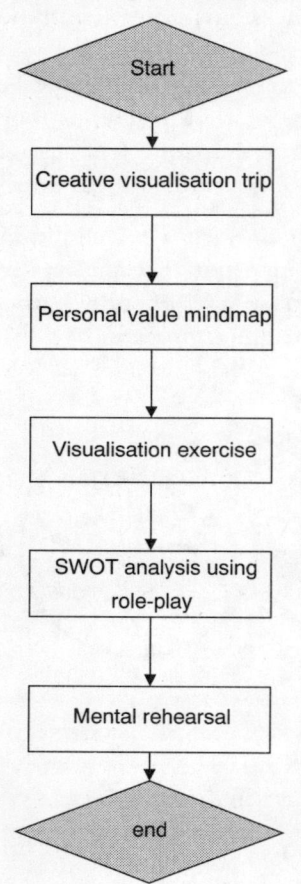

```
        Start
          │
          ▼
┌─────────────────────────┐
│ Creative visualisation trip │
└─────────────────────────┘
          │
          ▼
┌─────────────────────────┐
│  Personal value mindmap │
└─────────────────────────┘
          │
          ▼
┌─────────────────────────┐
│  Visualisation exercise │
└─────────────────────────┘
          │
          ▼
┌─────────────────────────┐
│  SWOT analysis using    │
│       role-play         │
└─────────────────────────┘
          │
          ▼
┌─────────────────────────┐
│    Mental rehearsal     │
└─────────────────────────┘
          │
          ▼
         end
```

conscious and subconscious level. The use of certain suggestive peripherals to give positive and affirming messages to the participants can be very useful in setting the mood of the sessions. Posters with slogans like 'CREATIVITY and INNOVATION' or 'AIM FOR NUMBER 1!!!' strategically placed around the meeting room are examples of such affirmative messages. Another useful technique is to use pictures or advertising posters which convey the success of the enterprise to date. Or such materials from other successful or benchmark organisations could be used for inspirational purposes. Through careful use of direct and indirect verbal suggestions, it is possible for the facilitator of the planning sessions to obtain more positive outcomes from the participants.

CREATE AND INNOVATE TO BE "TOP GUN"

- *Use creative visualisation.* Creative visualisations incorporated as part of the relaxation process can also spur the imagination of the participants when performing scenario analysis. For example, taking participants through a visualised journey of exploring a forbidden city could be used to untap the mental reserves of participants in terms of creating a curious and inquisitive mindset with the participants. Further, through the use of visualisations, it is possible to attain a 'helicopter' view of the problem or issue at hand. It is important to achieve such a view so that more creative solutions may be arrived at.   *Creative visualisation*
- *Encourage role-playing.* Role-playing can also be used very effectively, especially to overcome the reticence of certain participants and also to minimise the negative effects of hidden agendas. So, instead of leaving managers to be themselves when doing SWOT analysis, have them role-play that they are consultants from a make-believe company. This is a very useful way to get participants to open up, yet still protect their self-esteem.   *Role-playing*
- *Use mind mapping.* Alternatively, or as an adjunct to the SWOT analysis, the use of mind mapping can be a very powerful tool. Mind mapping should be initiated using 'Strengths' or 'Opportunities' as starting points.   *Mind mapping*

This is how you do it

Here is an example of an accelerative learning planning session. Figure 11.3 depicts the steps in conducting a SWOT session with a difference. The difference is that participants will be able to learn about their environment faster and more intuitively. They will be able to generate ideas more effectively.

This session would take half a day. The process starts with a creative visualisation trip which guides participants through a journey of discovery. Begin by encouraging the participants to make themselves comfortable, and explain that you will be trying some different techniques which are designed to encourage greater creativity. They may close their eyes if they wish.

Then ask them to imagine themselves to be eagles, flying high up in a blue sky with wisps of cottonball clouds. They soar up and glide down and around, just feeling the wonderful sensation of having the wind beneath their wings. They continue flying around and then look down to the earth beneath, noticing the gentle rolling green meadows below.

Next guide them to observe various details in the landscape far below. A brook is warbling across the green fields. Scattered clumps of trees dot the landscape. Suggest that they observe how the sunlight is reflected in the gentle streams of the brook while they feel the wind lifting them. What a glorious feeling!

The purpose of this guided imagery exercise is to put the participants in a relaxed state of mind where they can recall feelings associated with the wonderful sense of discovery, the sudden flash of insight or the sudden realisation of something profound that is happening to them. This sets the mood for the whole process.

The next step is to break down barriers that are typically present in a group of people, especially if they represent different levels of a hierarchy. It also builds individuals' vision of the role they play in the bigger scheme of things.

'Personal value' map

Invite participants to create a 'personal value' map. Request them to draw 'maps' of some of the things that affect their contribution to the organisation: their assets, liabilities and their own uniqueness. Next, invite them to discuss their maps in small groups. As individuals take turns to speak, ask the group to 'shoot down' any liability or weakness that is spoken about. Following this, invite the group to visualise their liability dissolving into 'thin air'.

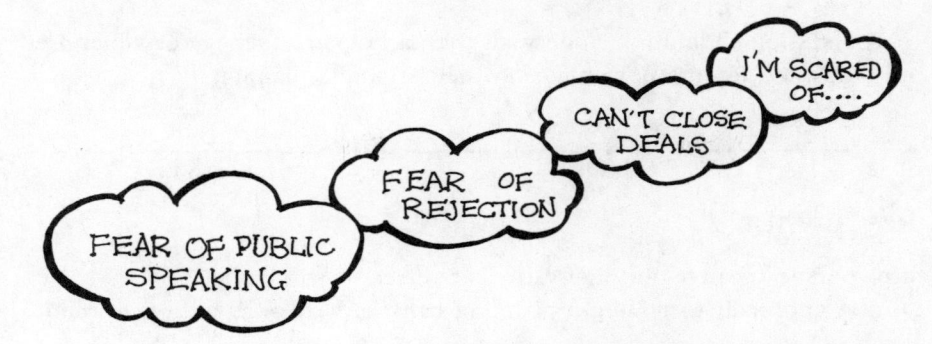

For example, participants could be asked to imagine lugging this 'liability' with both their hands, dragging it across the room and lifting it onto a small white cloud. The cloud with this heavy baggage then effortlessly floats into the air and is blown away by a gentle breeze. The cloud disappears further and further away with the heavy baggage and soon it becomes so small and distant that they cannot see it any more.

This personal value exercise sets a frame of mind that links the participants individually to their business or organisation. This is a powerful step in getting them to use their subconscious minds to start to understand the environment they are in.

The next phase of the session enables the participants to understand the internal and external environment of the organisation. It gives them the opportunity to be aware of the issues they face in the business.

Invite participants to assume roles as external consultants and to conduct a SWOT analysis. The role of external consultant discourages hidden agendas or power plays during the activity. In addition, the occupation of these roles provides a high level of protection for the participants' self-esteem.

During the SWOT analysis, the facilitator should constantly feed in positive suggestions. It is extremely important to protect the self-esteem of the participants at all times. For this reason, it is recommended that the whole SWOT analysis be conducted by a facilitator who is not a member of the team involved in the planning session itself.

The final step in the whole planning session is a relaxation-based exercise used to review the whole planning session and to summarise the results gained from the SWOT analysis.

The facilitator revisits the events of the planning session. In a relaxed state, ask the participants to remember in their mind's eyes the Strengths, Weaknesses, Opportunities and Threats of the business. Guide them through some of the points raised during the SWOT analysis.

The session should conclude with the participants feeling very energised and motivated for the next phase in their strategic planning.

Recapping the key points

- Organisations need to pursue creative and innovative strategies to survive.
- An accelerative learning approach to strategic planning can help an organisation to gain a competitive advantage.
- A holistic approach involving feelings as well as thinking will generate a higher and better quality output of ideas.
- An accelerative learning approach tends to raise self-esteem and reduce anxiety. This, in turn, can facilitate greater commitment from staff and reduce or resolve any conflict within management ranks.
- Treat the planning process also as a team-building exercise and a learning event for all participants.
- Lastly, remember: if your planning process is enjoyable and fruitful, participants will have more ownership in the outcomes from the process.

Managing for the future: Developing a whole-brain organisation

Justus Helen Lewis and Moni Lai Storz

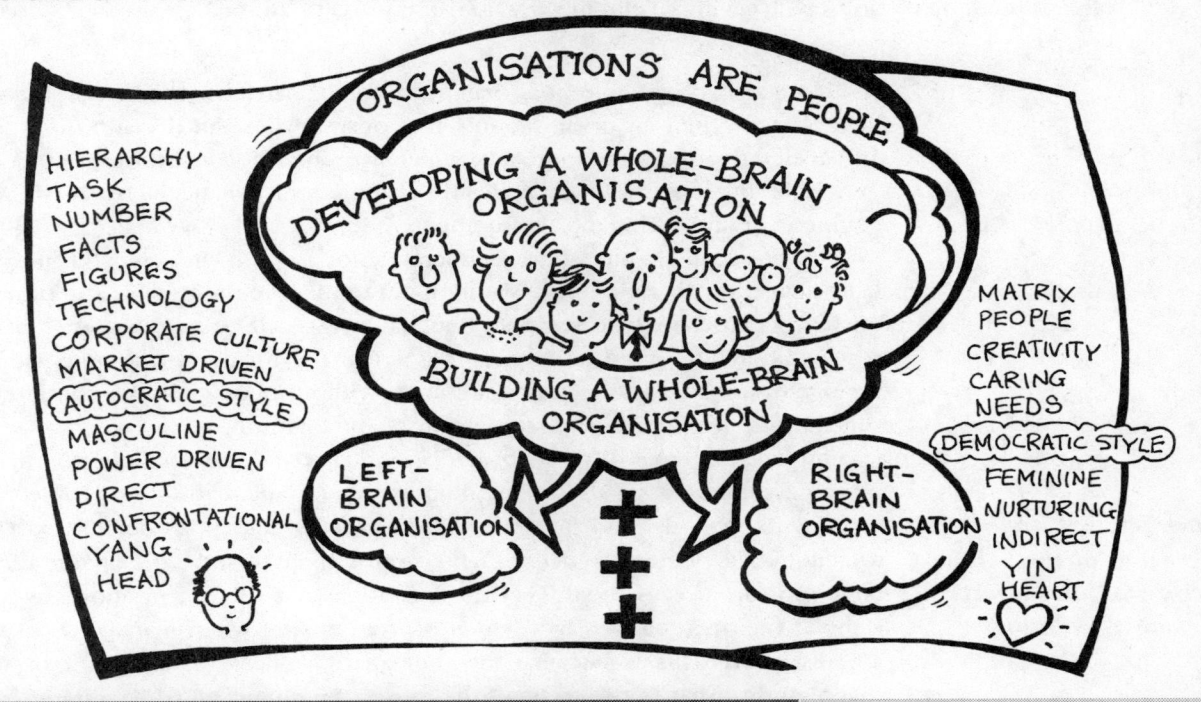

In this chapter

- Implementing the whole-brain organisation
  - Stage 1: Conducting an audit of the organisation
  - Stage 2: Conducting an audit of the people
  - Stage 3: Using the findings of the audits
  - Stage 4: Creating a whole-brain environment

Overview

This chapter attempts to tie up the threads of the previous chapters and bring them into focus on the implementation of accelerative learning in an organisation. It covers:

- typical differences between left-brain and right-brain organisations;
- the stages of implementation involved in developing a whole-brain organisation.

There is no organisation without people

In a sense, this whole book has been about managing the future, for we believe that when an organisation consciously makes the decision to adopt an accelerative learning approach, which we characterise in this chapter as 'whole brain', it starts to generate the synergy which it needs to thrive in a competitive and turbulent environment.

The previous chapters have deliberately focused on the needs of individual managers with a view to assisting them to manage themselves and others. This is because we take seriously the statement that an organisation's main resources are its people. Organisations are made up of people and people are organisations. There is no organisation without people and no continuing survival for people without some form of organisation.

Our writers have dealt with managers' skills and areas of development. They have focused on the theme: know yourself and know the people you work with. Personal and interpersonal knowledge and skills do not exist in a vacuum. They belong to people who can use them to serve the organisation, which in turn serves them. That the individual and the organisation are two sides of the one coin is a fact which is often missed when managerial issues are discussed. This is because the 'human being-ness' is taken out of the organisation—that is, the feelings, the music, the colour, all of which are part of the functioning of the right side of the brain. When feelings are taken out of the picture, organisations become essentially left-brain. This impoverishes both the organisations and the people in them.

When feelings are taken out of the picture, organisations become essentially left-brain

The two sides need to be brought into dialogue

In Table 12.1 we give you a comparison of some of the important organisational differences which we see between left- and right-brain organisations. Both have their strengths. The principal weakness of both is that they are operating with only half their potential—half their 'organisational brain'. The left-brain organisation concentrates on tasks and is particularly attracted to 'doing things right'. In contrast, the right-brain organisation tends to revolve around people's personal needs. It gets sidetracked by the infinite diversity of human differences and may spend too much time speculating on 'doing the right thing'. The two sides need to be

Table 12.1 Comparison of left-brain and right-brain organisations

Left-brain organisations tend to be	Right-brain organisations tend to be
• Hierarchical in their organisation chart	• Flatter or matrix-structured in their organisation chart
• Task-focused—value is placed on completing specific given tasks	• People-focused—value is placed on creating a supportive environment
• Places where people who are good with numbers get high status and recognition	• Places where people who are nurturing and creative get high status and recognition
• Places where the bottom line is facts and figures	• Places where the bottom line is caring for the other person
• 'What's in it for me?'	• 'What can I contribute?'
• Strong on corporate culture	• Strong on meeting individual needs
• Technology-driven	• Sceptical of technology
• Market-driven	• Driven by intrinsic values
• Autocratic in management style	• Sharing roles and responsibilities
• Masculine	• Feminine
• Power-driven	• Nurturing
• Direct in confronting issues	• Indirect in dealing with issues
• Favourable to memos and 'one-to-many' types of communication	• Favourable to person-to-person discussion of important matters
• Keen on buzzwords like productivity and quality	• Keen on buzzwords like human potential and development
• Populated by people who project their stress on to other people	• Populated by people who internalise their stress
• Typically large business corporations	• Typically small family businesses, theatre groups, community centres
• Run by people who enjoy dealing with details and numbers (consequently, they make well-considered business decisions that lead to profit and business survival)	• Run by people who are bored by details (consequently, they work themselves into the ground, but don't do very well financially)
• Usually run by men	• Often run by women

brought into dialogue, just as the two hemispheres of the brain need to interact to achieve focused and creative states of mind. Tasks cannot be completed without people and it is people who ultimately give meaning to tasks. By integrating both left- and right-brain qualities in our organisations, we create the synergy that characterises a whole-brain organisation.

Implementing the whole-brain organisation

Organisational awareness

Implementing the whole-brain organisation is a process of organisational transformation. Before you can begin to implement these changes, you need to know the current status of your organisation. Organisational awareness is the first of four stages of implementation which are:

1. conducting an audit of the organisation;
2. conducting an audit of the people;
3. using the findings of these audits to implement recruitment and training programmes based on accelerative learning paradigms;
4. creating an environment which lowers stress, enhances motivation and encourages problem solving, critical thinking and creativity.

Stage 1 Conducting an audit of the organisation

At this stage you should examine your organisation from a global perspective, taking into account its management policies and procedures. For example, check out:

- the organisation structure;
- the appraisal and reward practices;
- recruitment;
- management and communication styles.

Use Table 12.1 to guide your thinking about the questions to ask in conducting your audit. Look at company documents, such as mission and vision statements, quality policy statements, departmental mission and quality statements, public relations and promotion material and ask yourself what is the main focus of these documents. Are they more concerned with 'doing it right' (i.e. encouraging a purely left-brain approach which is linear and sequential) or do they also provide a creative 'space' where people can collaboratively problem solve what 'the right thing' is (i.e. encourage a right-brain approach)? Do they show more concern with conforming to industry standards (left-brain needs), or with meeting the ever-changing needs of customers? Do your policy and procedure documents reflect a balanced preoccupation (left and right brain) with meeting the needs of employees, customers and the marketplace?

Look at your practices and ask the people involved about their perceptions of how well practice matches the stated policies of the documents. A useful technique is to ask a team to generate a list of 'buzz words' that are commonly in use in their department as well as in the organisation in general. What are the catchphrases that sum up where people are at? Is there a focus on 'getting runs on the board' or is it a case of 'consolidating our competitive advantage'? Notice how many of the motivational and descriptive expressions commonly used in business reflect a kinesthetic orientation to the world. We generate ideas, we let them brew, we put them on the back burner, we walk them past our boss . . . If you think of the physical situations from which these metaphors are drawn, you will notice that they all typically have some emotion or feeling connected with them. Organisations may encourage us to suppress our natural expressions of emotion, but they still creep into our language.

At this stage of the game you are doing an awareness exercise. You should be attending to descriptive accounts rather than jumping to judgments and evaluations. Right-brain and left-brain organisations each have their unique strengths, as Table 12.1 demonstrates.

Another useful technique for encouraging people to contribute to and participate in this organisational awareness activity is to draw a map of your findings and put it up somewhere where people can see it, talk about it and even add to it. Encourage people to contribute the buzzwords from their particular departments and invite them to draw pictures of how they perceive that their departments and people relate to the rest of the organisation.

Stage 2 Conducting an audit of the people

Stage 2 is to conduct an audit of the organisation's people, particularly those in top and key positions. They are usually role models for the rest of the organisation.

You should consider using an instrument like Myers-Briggs (discussed in Chapter 4). This will help you to be more objective in your approach. In achieving a whole-brain organisation, it is crucial to take into consideration

Audit of the organisation's people

the preferred styles of your managers. Remember, it is not a question of good or bad: people have different styles and all styles are acceptable.

This stage of the process may reveal that some managers occupying strategic positions have radically different styles. Remember that team synergy is created when individuals are encouraged to make their unique contributions. You should welcome this as a challenge to improve the organisation by incorporating the strengths from each. Too often differences in operational style are seen as management issues in which one individual is the loser.

By the time you have completed these two stages, you will have amassed quite a pile of information. Some of it will be extremely sensitive and restricted, but other parts of it can be communicated both within and outside the organisation. Studies show that regular feedback is one of the best motivators. So you may wish to stimulate the different parts of your 'organisational brain' by communicating some of this information to your stakeholders, internal and external, using channels such as memos, reports, newsletters and email.

Stage 3 Using the findings of the audits

Stage 3 consists of reviewing your recruitment and training policies and practice in the light of your findings from Stages 1 and 2.

Reviewing your recruitment and training policies and practice

Here you can analyse your data and determine your strengths and weaknesses. Do your findings indicate that you have a balance in your policies and practices that produces the team synergy you need to maintain your competitive edge in the marketplace? If you are not satisfied on this score, what do you need to do to change the situation?

Use an accelerative learning whole-brain approach, keeping your language positive (a 'learning experience' rather than a disaster, a 'challenge' rather than a problem; a 'chance to explore our flexibility' rather than a difficulty). Pay attention to your strengths and how you, with the help of your team, can integrate them to produce a more focused, productive and flexible team (see Chapter 7 on team building).

Recruitment

Recruitment

What kinds of people are you looking for to fill vacancies and occupy new positions? The human tendency is to look for people who match the staff you already have. This has a certain amount of logic. It is likely that similar people will have similar styles and adjust well to the organisation. However, is this enough?

If you are a very right-brain organisation, you may need some strongly left-brain people to keep you on track in day-to-day matters, set realistic goals and monitor your progress regularly. If your organisation is very rigidly left-brain, then perhaps you need to create some positions for more right-brain oriented people to evolve new possibilities and a more elastic approach. With the right mix of talents and collaboration, you can create the synergy that propels your organisation forward and makes it a rewarding place in which to work.

Training

Training is an ongoing function. Many employees, however, do not relish the prospect of attending training courses. They erect logical, intuitive and emotional barriers at the very mention of the word. And many training courses, particularly skill-based ones, are presented in ways which are inimical to retention and application of the material back on the job.

This is why more attention is being given to on-the-job and just-in-time training, along with the development of job aids and online help for software applications. It makes sense to give people the training and assistance that they need when they need it. It also makes financial sense to tie the learning to the application and realise immediate returns from training time.

The development of multimedia packages which allow people to learn on an individual basis at the time when they need the information is also becoming widespread. The combination of words, pictures, sounds and interaction at the keyboard incorporates many of the features which have been seen to be conducive to accelerative learning.

Giving people control of the learning process is another factor, using the multimedia packages which stimulate motivation. It is important, however, that sound instructional design principles be incorporated into such multimedia developments in order to obtain the maximum return in learning and productivity from the considerable outlay that is involved.

Giving people control of the learning process

These developments are on the increase and we can foresee a time when the evolution of multimedia and computer-managed learning, coupled with the ongoing need to provide training to individuals and small groups in diverse locations, will make it more cost effective to conduct a great deal of the more routine types of training using distance education methods enhanced by frequent computer conferencing.

Whether we are using a face-to-face or distance education approach to meeting our training needs, it should be a top priority to train the trainers in the accelerative learning paradigm and to ensure that the accelerative learning elements are systematically and sequentially processed.

Stage 4 Creating a whole-brain environment

This is the easiest and most pleasant stage. For that reason, some people think it is the most important—or even the only—aspect of accelerative learning. It involves the creation of an environment which lowers the stress levels of people at work. Some suggestions given in the earlier chapters include having piped largo music at certain periods of the day, creating a colourful and pleasing office environment, putting up positive affirmations and encouraging people to make constructive suggestions to improve productivity.

Creation of an environment which lowers the stress levels of people at work

> It is common in Muslim countries for people to be given time at work to say their prayers. Why not ten minutes of company time for a 'meditation break' for those who appreciate the value of this activity? Rather than rush from beginning to end of a hectic day, why not encourage people to have a half-hour siesta to refresh their minds?
>
> You might also encourage your employees to look after their physical health by providing a choice of 'healthy' food in the canteen. Many companies are moving in the direction of this healthier lifestyle by providing purified water on tap for their workforce.

A caution is in order here: don't jump to Stage 4 without going through the previous stages. If you attempt to do this, you simply lose your credibility. If people have not grappled with difficult issues such as managing conflict engendered by different personality styles or becoming aware that the consciously expressed vision of the organisation is out of line with the everyday experience of people at work, your gestures towards accelerative learning will be seen as hollow and you may be very surprised at the interpretation put on your actions by those inside and outside your organisation.

The external has to be a manifestation of the internal, or it is unlikely to last. We have met and talked to people in such situations, working in organisations espousing accelerative learning principles, and in some cases we have found that although some of these people found the accelerative learning paradigm interesting, they were not fully convinced. They had not been challenged to think through some of the basic principles discussed by the writers in this book. This showed itself in them enjoying what they perceived to be an easy-going environment, but not fully aligning themselves with the organisation's mission. In other instances, we have found organisations that have adopted the superficialities of an accelerative learning environment: pot plants; attractive decor; positive affirmations on the walls. But the staff had a different story to tell. They perceived that their managers were acting in ways that were totally inconsistent with the first impressions of visitors. Self-esteem and morale were low, as staff perceived the incongruence between the show and the reality.

Always remember that a whole-brain organisation is an integrated place. It incorporates left-brain and right-brain policies and procedures. By allowing its people to use more of their brains, the organisation itself becomes richer, more diverse and more productive.

Recapping the key points

- There is no organisation without people and no continuing survival for people without some form of organisation.
- Organisation can also be characterised as predominantly right- or left-brain. The whole-brain organisation integrates the qualities of both right- and left-brain organisations.
- The process of implementing a whole-brain organisation has four steps which involve auditing the organisation and the people in it, using the findings to implement accelerative learning training and recruitment programmes and creating an environment which lowers stress, enhances motivation and encourages problem solving, critical thinking and creativity.
- To be successful, this four-stage process must allow for maximum participation and input from the people who work in the organisation.
- If the internal interpersonal environment of the organisation does not match the externally percieved environment, then accelerative learning principles are unlikely to take root in that organisation. Accelerative learning implies a harmony between the unconscious and the conscious, the internal and the external.

Managing your work with accelerative learning

Justus Helen Lewis

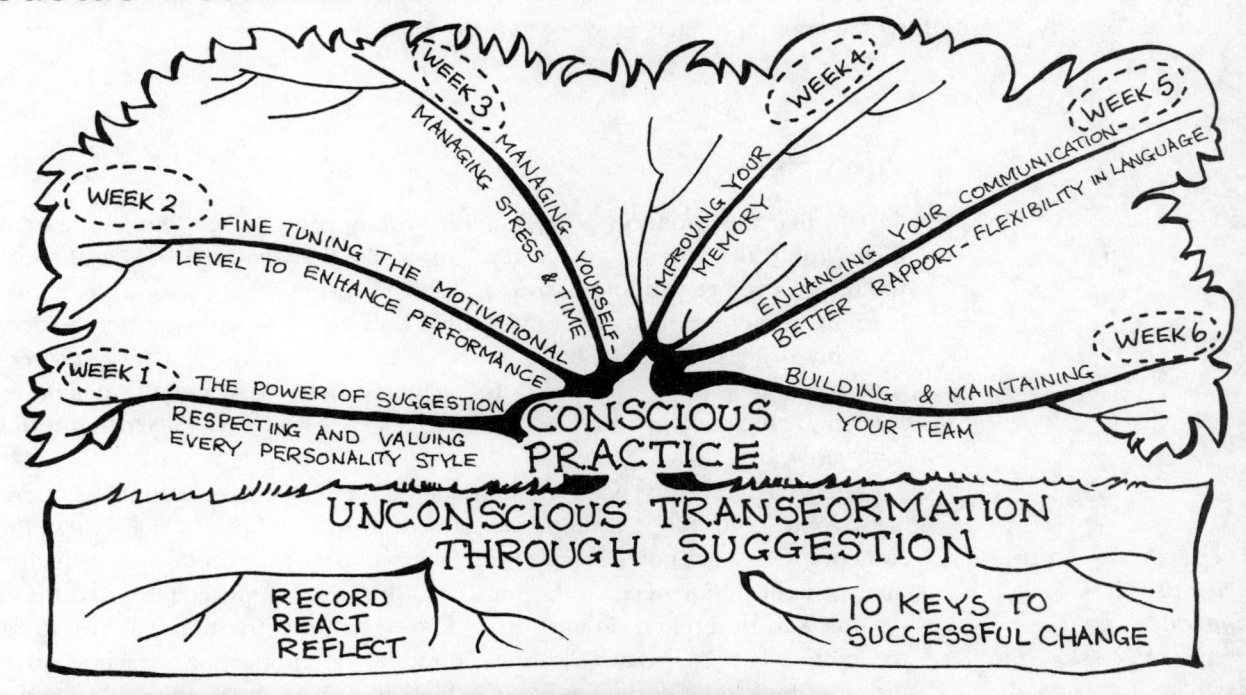

In this chapter

- What next?
- The six-week plan
- A final word: keys to successful change

Overview

This chapter attempts to finalise the book by:
- presenting a specific six-week repeatable plan of action which provides a medium which readers can use to implement relevant accelerative learning practices in their own specific work situation;
- sharing ten 'maxims' which I have found to be vital to implementing my personal interpretation of the accelerative learning whole-brain approach to work and personal life.

What next?

So you like the sound of accelerative learning, you can see how some of it might apply and you feel you would like to take it a step further. Is it possible to change, even revolutionise, your approach to work by applying accelerative learning principles, and just how should you go about it? So much advice, so many suggestions have been given along the way. Yet you may still feel that something more is needed to enable you to implement accelerative learning principles in your working life. This chapter has been written to fill that gap.

There are as many ways of implementing accelerative learning as there are people who adopt it, because each person is unique.

There are as many ways of implementing accelerative learning as there are people who adopt it, because each person is unique. What is best for someone else may not necessarily be what is best for you. Just as a quality management policy needs to be translated into a set of procedures and these too need to be broken down further into specific instructions, so you need to define what you want to achieve through the application of accelerative learning, pick out the key areas in which it will be most effective for you and develop your own day-by-day plan to achieve it.

The following six-week plan commits you to five minutes every day. Is that really enough? Well, probably not, and once you become 'hooked' on the idea of using more of your mind-brain you will certainly spend a lot longer doing so. The important thing to remember is that you are embarking on the delicate task of persuading and enticing yourself—and particularly the feelings part of you—into a more expanded and satisfying expression of what you are capable of. Another way of putting it would be to say that you were engaged in developing a *positive addiction*, a way of behaving that is not only good for your entire system, but also gives you a regular 'high'. Even a five-minute 'mental excursion', if you do it regularly when you are at your best, in a spirit of relaxed yet alert enjoyment, reinforced with brain-syn-

Developing a positive addiction

chronising music or sound, can cumulatively have an enormously beneficial effect on your productivity and creativity. Some people will find this easier than others, and the more you focus your mind on the greater you that you are capable of expressing, the quicker you will switch on more of your brain and experience the benefits. Just remember, everyone—including yourself—can enjoy at least five minutes a day of this pleasure.

The six-week plan

Spend five (or more, but at least five) minutes each day, when you are at your best and most energetic, thinking over the questions given below. They are based on the chapters of this book and you will find they are easier and more fun to do if you quickly review the chapters as you go. At the end of each session, jot down a reminder of your reflections on the chart which follows. Or use a pocket notebook or electronic organiser—whatever gives you the most satisfaction.

Six-week plan

First month

Week 1

Questions relating to Chapter 2, What is accelerative learning?

- *Day 1.* What barriers to learning can you see in yourself and those around you at work? How could you apply accelerative learning principles to overcome these?
- *Day 2.* Think of some examples from your own experience when 'suggestion' of an indirect nature played an important part in influencing your behaviour. How could you apply this to your current situation?
- *Day 3.* Have you ever followed any kind of 'positive thinking' programme? How effective was it? Now that you understand accelerative learning principles, can you explain why it was or was not effective? How could you use more of your mind-brain to make such a programme more effective for you now?
- *Day 4.* What could you do in your work environment to assist you and

Week 1

Figure 13.1

Day/week	Question	My reaction	My reflection
1			
2			
3			
4			
5			
6			
7			

Note: The design of this chart is developed from the 3-R Note-Taking pad developed by Keith Noble to encourage students to develop a whole-brain approach to note-taking. The lined portion is for the left brain; the blank 'Reaction' section is for the right brain's spontaneous and creative reactions; and the blank 'Reflection' section allows for mature reflection on the overall meaning.

your team members to be in the creative state of relaxed alertness more often?

Questions relating to Chapter 3, Motivation for managers

- *Day 5*. How could you increase commitment to your next project by giving your team members more scope to make decisions?
- *Day 6*. How could you adjust the 'emotional thermostat' in your workplace to increase the level of motivation? If you had to choose one limited area, which would it be?
- *Day 7*. Start a log for the next week and record every motivational suggestion you are aware of, either from yourself or from others in your workplace. Notice whether it is direct or indirect, conscious or unconscious.

Week 2

- *Day 8*. What do you find are the most common reasons given by your colleagues for why a proposed change won't work? Are these reasons based more on logic, feeling or a sense of injustice? Or all three? What creative steps could you take to persuade your colleagues to your viewpoint? Are you sure your viewpoint is really the most appropriate one?
- *Day 9*. Think of a time when either you were a coach, or you yourself were being coached. Did the coaching use more of direct or indirect suggestion? How could you combine direct and indirect suggestion to become a better coach? What advice on coaching do you give your staff?

Questions relating to Chapter 4, Personality type indicators, learning styles and accelerative learning

- *Day 10*. Recall a situation from your own experience in which a knowledge of personality type differences might have helped to smooth the way. How would you deal with such a situation now, using your understanding of learning styles and accelerative learning?
- *Day 11*. If you were the chairman in Case Study 3 in Chapter 4, handling a personality clash between right- and left-brain dominated staff, how would you use your understanding of personality types and accelerative learning to resolve the conflict situation?
- *Day 12*. If you had a Bill (Case Study 4, Chapter 4) on your staff—a person

who feels reluctant to engage in discussion with others—what could you do to increase his confidence and ability to relate informally to others?
- *Day 13*. How could you make your meetings more productive and come to better-informed decisions by allowing the different personalities of your staff more scope for input?

Questions relating to Chapter 5, Making sense of your communication

- *Day 14*. Do the words you use to talk to your colleagues tend to be visual (V), auditory (A) or kinesthetic (K)? Or are they more neutral (Aid)? Over the next week, make a note of the words that you and your colleagues use regularly. Do you all tend to use the same type of words? Who uses different types? If there is a mismatch, is this a possible source of misunderstanding?

Week 3

- *Day 15*. Visualise the next occasion when you have to make a point. Imagine how you would explain yourself using mainly visual words, then mainly auditory, and finally mainly kinesthetic. Which was the hardest? Which kind of words do you think are most likely to appeal to your colleague(s)?
- *Day 16*. Review one of your current formal or informal presentations. How might you incorporate a greater variety of kinesthetic, auditory and visual language into it to make it a more effective communication?
- *Day 17*. Think of someone whom you find very persuasive. What is it that makes them persuasive? How might you adapt some of their techniques to suit your own style?

Questions relating to Chapter 6, Accelerate your time management

- *Day 18*. Using the suggestions in Chapter 6, review and write down your visions for yourself. What is the next immediate step to achieving one or more of these visions?
- *Day 19*. What planning tools work best for you? How might you use them more effectively? What benefits would this bring you?
- *Day 20*. Review the way you organise your workspace and your work. Do you enjoy your workspace? (This is different from enjoying your work.) How could you make your workspace more interesting and relaxing? When are you going to do this?

- *Day 21*. Think of some more ways in which you might simplify your working life by organising it to suit your needs and style. Write these down where you will see them regularly.

Week 4

- *Day 22*. Review the excuses you make to yourself about why some things don't get done. How are you going to deal with these excuses now?
- *Day 23*. Is there an important task you have been putting off for one reason or another? Using the procedure suggested in Chapter 6, visualise yourself successfully completing that task. Now hear your boss congratulating you on its completion and feel that pride of achievement. (Remember, you don't need to be modest in your imagination. Have some fun!)
- *Day 24*. Review ways in which you could either make better use of your high-energy times or increase your total amount of energy. Are you doing the really important things at your high-energy times, or are you wasting them on routine tasks? How could you increase your energy by: (a) taking more exercise; (b) taking regular breaks; (c) eating differently; (d) anything else? Write an affirmation about how you use your energy.

Questions relating to Chapter 7, Team building using accelerative learning

- *Day 25*. Are you and the people you work with more like a group or a team? How could you be more like a team?
- *Day 26*. What do you consider are the six most important characteristics of a team? How could you ensure that your teams have or develop these characteristics?
- *Day 27*. Think of a dysfunctional team that you know and consider how you could apply accelerative learning techniques to make it synergistic? Take time out and visualise your ideal team as suggested in Chapter 7. After visualising your ideal team, consider whom you would like to have on your next team? What are these persons' specific contributions and how would they benefit the team?
- *Day 28*. In what stage of development would you put your present team or teams? How best can you contribute to their development? In what ways are you behaving as a good team role model for them? What else could you do to encourage good team behaviour?

Second month

Week 1

Questions relating to Chapter 8, The accelerative learning way to health and stress management

- *Day 1*. Put on some Baroque music (Vivaldi, Telemann, Bach), sit in a comfortable chair, breathe deeply and visualise your relaxed and stress-free self. If you find it difficult to make a picture of yourself relaxed and stress-free, then try either talking to yourself as you would if you were in that state, or feeling what your body experiences when you are relaxed. As you do this, let your shoulders droop and allow your abdomen and hips to relax (this is no time to worry about what you look like!) In this relaxed condition, review what you are doing on a daily basis to cope with stress and pressure when they arise, as they will. In what ways since you started this programme are you now managing your working life better? Imagine yourself doing a few degrees better in the future. There is no need to imagine yourself perfect. No one is. Just see yourself doing recognisably a bit better than your previous best efforts.
- *Day 2*. Complete the Stress Management Chart at the end of Chapter 8 if you have not already done so. If you have already completed it, review your progress. What was easy and what was more challenging? Congratulate yourself on your achievements.
- *Day 3*. Walk up some stairs instead of taking the lift. Start the day with some skipping. Go for a swim. Consider what other forms of aerobic exercise you might do on a regular basis? If exercise on your own doesn't appeal, can you talk a friend into doing it with you? The buddy system can be a great way to develop synergy and keep on track with personal goals.
- *Day 4*. Visualise yourself successfully completing your next project. Hear what your boss and colleagues are saying (make sure it is positive—you can choose, it's *your* imagination!), see your goals achieved and feel the pride of accomplishment. Take yourself further in imagination into the future and start to think about the next successful project that will follow.

Questions relating to Chapter 9, Memory for managers

- *Day 5*. Some people have extremely good recall for particular information—such as cricket statistics, popular music titles and artists'

names—yet have difficulty remembering where they left their car in the parking lot. What are the things that you are good at remembering? Think of a few things that it would really benefit you to remember better. What could you do to improve your memory?
- *Day 6*. Do you find that you have a 'good memory for faces but a poor memory for names'? What will you do to remember names of clients and customers?
- *Day 7*. Sometimes we find we have something we're trying to recall on the 'tip of the tongue'. When does this happen to you? What might you do to bring the item into your conscious awareness?

Week 2

- *Day 8*. Think over any experience you have of learning a second or foreign language. How could you apply what you know about accelerative learning to make learning a second or foreign language easier?

Questions relating to Chapter 10, Memory and graphs

- *Day 9*. Try using both right- and left-brain techniques to memorise and recall a diagram or chart you use at work. Which techniques do you find most effective?
- *Day 10*. Devise a verbal mnemonic (use either 'first letter cuing' or an 'image chain') to recall at least eight points from a speech or newspaper article that you've heard or read recently.
- *Day 11*. Think of a graph in which you need to recall the trend. Translate the trend into a line and create a memory graph. What does the line remind you of? What associations can you give it?
- *Day 12*. Shut your eyes and recall the details of a meeting room at work. What colour are the walls? How many windows are there? How large is the table? How many chairs? What shape and colour? Now think of some important decision that was made while you were in that room and for which you need to remember the details. Find an association between the decision and some aspect of the room. It can be as bizarre as you like. The more unusual, the more likely you are to remember the details.
- *Day 13*. Take your shopping list or a list of points you want to bring up at a future meeting. Make the items into a vivid and bizarre picture or story. What outrageous associations can you make? What is the funniest thing about the picture(s) you have created in your mind?

- *Day 14.* Take a set of instructions that you need to remember or information about a product or service that you offer and make the words fit a simple and familiar tune like *Jingle Bells* or *Twinkle, Twinkle*. How could you use this technique in other areas of your work?

A final word: Keys to successful change

Keys to successful change

1. Recognise that your mind-brain is running your life, whether you like it or not! Your choice is whether or not to take more control of the process by applying accelerative learning principles. What have you got to lose? Some of your hangups? Some of the guilt trips you have allowed to interfere in your life for years? Some of your limitations? Is it not worthwhile to give some thought to and take some action to reduce, or at least limit, some of these energy sappers?
2. Anticipate resistance—from yourself and from others. Be positive about resistance. Think of the changes in your workplace that you have experienced and the resistance that you or others put up to these changes. Why the resistance? Because you were threatened. You could see how certain valuable elements in the situation were going to be lost in the new arrangements. Expect the same thing now. It is as if your unconscious suddenly feels threatened—'Hey, what's happening! I've been running this show quite satisfactorily for years. If there's nothing wrong, don't change it. I'm not going to stand for any of this!' The way to get around this resistance is to acknowledge that there *has* been a lot of good in the past and that many of the strategies that you are now considering changing have worked well for you in the past. So realise that what you are experiencing is a conflict between your conscious and your unconscious mind. Like a good negotiator, don't get bogged down in one or the other alternative. Look for points of common interest. In this case, it is your well-being that is at stake. So tell your unconscious mind, 'Thanks for looking after me so well. I realise that you've had my well-being at heart. However, I'm taking a closer look at myself now and I would like your cooperation in finding more creative ways to look after my well-being from now on. Please give me a hand by using your creativity to find better ways of taking care of me.' The answers will come.
3. Use sound and music to tune your brain to its most synchronised and creative states. Music down the ages has been used to soothe and balance

the mind. Nowadays there is a vast amount of recorded music and sound, both new age and classical. Look for names like Vivaldi, Telemann, Bach, Mozart (particularly flute and wind music) and sounds of surf and water. Keep the volume soft and unobtrusive. It is the quality of the sound that matters, not the volume.

4. Expect the unexpected. When people tune into themselves and start relying more on their own creativity, somehow the universe often seems to cooperate. As the Chinese saying has it, when the student is ready, the master appears. Practise relying on your intuition. Review a problem before you go to sleep and let your unconscious dream up a solution for you in the morning. When you are faced with a seemingly impossible project, take the view that an interesting piece of learning is coming your way and that your unconscious intuitive mind knows how to do this. Plan conscientiously and calmly, and as fully as you can, and then trust that the remaining pieces of the puzzle will fall into place.

5. Be grateful. This is extremely important. There does not seem to be a logical explanation but maybe it is because gratitude, enthusiasm and encouragement evoke similar positive emotional responses and a positive emotion will displace a negative emotion. When you're feeling up, you can't feel down at the same time, at least not about the same thing. So gratitude seems to be a response to life that attracts energy to you, whereas resentment, frustration and depression all deplete your emotional reserves.

6. Look for the second right answer. In these days of rapid change, many new possibilities are continually presenting themselves. How long does a right answer last? Maybe the first right answer simply points you in the best direction and the second right answer gives you better fine tuning of your direction. So be flexible and stay tuned into your state of relaxed alertness.

7. Be prepared to adjust. Remember that you are acknowledging yourself to be a system in action. Any reasonably complex system includes a number of feedback mechanisms and the human system is probably the most complex around. Expect to be continually adjusting your behaviour and remember that seemingly trivial and insignificant changes can sometimes have unexpectedly large and significant consequences. So be happy if you are making a series of small changes. You are the best judge of where to start.

8. Break it into manageable chunks. Tackle your working life systematically. Change a bit at a time. Remember the familiar wisdom—the journey of a

thousand miles begins with a single step—and the answer to the question of how you eat an elephant is one bite at a time.

9. Listen to your intuition. Your intuition is your unconscious mind speaking to you. Remember that the conscious mind is only the tip of the iceberg. When you access your unconscious you have more energy and a greater ability to perform. This is not to say that you should downplay or neglect your conscious mind. After all, the conscious mind, like the tip of the iceberg, is the 'visible part' of our mind-brain. It is the starting and the finishing point. But there is a great deal in between! One of the most important ways of influencing this part of us is through positive suggestion and a crucial way to make powerful positive suggestions to ourselves is through affirmations. There are certain techniques for writing affirmations:

- Always put them in the present tense or you may end up like the Red Queen in *Alice Through the Looking Glass* with 'jam yesterday, jam tomorrow, but never jam today'.
- Always put them in the positive or you risk attracting your mind and feelings to what you *don't* want. For example, rather than saying 'I am no longer late for meetings'—if that is what you want to achieve—try 'I arrive at meetings with enough time to gather my thoughts and review the agenda items carefully'. Or, 'I arrive at meetings with enough time to chat with other members and ascertain their views on key items', if that is more reflective of your personality style.
- Make them *artfully vague*. For example, instead of saying 'I have a tidy, well-organised office' when you know from past experience that you generally do not, you could try 'I am well organised at work whenever I need to be'. Or again, if you are aiming to manage your life with less stress through doing regular exercise, instead of saying 'I swim three times a week', when you know that, although you have the opportunity, you don't really enjoy swimming, you might try 'I make the most of every opportunity to become fitter through regular exercise'. In other words, don't tackle your objections head on. Take the higher ground and use an affirmation with which you totally agree.

Remind yourself regularly and passionately of these affirmations—every morning when you wake up and every evening before you go to sleep—and also remind yourself that you are the kind of person who can make such changes. For example, you might have an affirmation 'I am the kind of person who likes to be fit' which you say while visualising yourself fit and full of energy, making the most of all the challenges that come your way. As this affirmation takes root in your subconscious, you may find that exercise—whether it be regular swimming, skipping, or climbing the stairs more often at work—takes on a more attractive aspect.

10 Take time out and make space in your life for new things to happen. While you are still totally immersed in your current way of managing your work and yourself, you have no 'space' to sow the seeds of change. You can use the five-minute programme to enjoy this essential space. Once you have sown the seeds, nourish and care for them. Switching on your brain is not just a once and for all happening. Once switched on, your brain can develop all sorts of interesting and creative ways which will enhance your life and make it more productive and satisfying. But you must encourage yourself as you would a colleague, by creating the internal learning environment.

This book has been about managing our work using accelerative learning techniques. But you will have noticed that, because accelerative learning is a holistic and systematic approach, it also has a personal application. Work—important as it is—is still only a *part* of life. The first and most important priority is to manage our personal lives in a way that makes best use of our abilities and potential. Your mind-brain is by far your most important asset. So switch it on, cherish and enjoy it!

Switching on your brain: Personal manifesto

Here is another chart you may find helpful to photocopy and complete each week as you progress through the programme. At the end of the six-week period, or sooner if it is appropriate, switch on your music, relax your mind, review what you have written and create a blueprint on a single new sheet for the next six weeks.

Vision statement for myself

- I am the kind of person who _____
  _____
  _____

- Areas of my life I am switching on are _____
  _____
  _____

> - Potential ways of switching on in these areas are _____
>   _____
>   _____
>
> (List each area you have identified and jot down whatever comes to mind as a possible way of using more of your mind-brain in your endeavours in this area. Don't worry about consistency at this stage. This is a chance to let your creative unconscious guide you.)
>
> - Specific and particular things that I could do in these areas are
>   _____
>   _____
>
> (List the areas again and jot down what comes to mind. There may be some overlap with the previous category but focus on the specifics here.)

Recapping the key points

- What is your unique style? What is it that makes you special as a person?
- How do you anticipate that a whole-brain approach will enhance your personal style and qualities?
- What personal goals do you have that a whole-brain approach will assist you to achieve?
- What are the priorities for change? Which 20 per cent of your life is most likely to yield 80 per cent return if you focus on making specific changes to it?
- What support can you invoke from others in making changes? Family? Friends? Colleagues? Team members? What benefit(s) are there for these people in supporting you in making these changes?
- How can you improve your own environment to make it more conducive to refreshing, motivating and inspiring you to creative enjoyment of what you do?
- What can you do to improve the environment for those around you, remembering that you are yourself part of the environment for these people?

Bibliography

Agor, W. (1984) *Intuitive Management: Integrating Left and Right Brain Management Skills*, Prentice Hall, Englewood Cliffs, New Jersey, USA
—— (ed.) (1989) *Intuition in Organizations: Leading and Managing Productively*, Sage Publications, California, USA
Armstrong, T. (1987) *In Their Own Way: Discovering and Encouraging Your Child's Personal Learning Style*, Jeremy P. Tarcher Inc., Los Angeles, USA
Baddeley, A. (1982) *Your Memory. A User's Guide*, Penguin Books, Middlesex, UK
Bandler, R. (1984) *Magic in Action*, Metamorphous Press, Oregon, Portland, USA
—— (1986) *Using Your Brain for a Change*, Metamorphous Press, Oregon, Portland, USA
Bandler, R. & Grindler, J. (1975 & 1986) *The Structure of Magic*, Vols 1 & 2, Science and Behaviour Books, California, USA
—— (1979) *Frogs into Princes: Neuro Linguistic Programming*, Real People Press, Utah, USA
Bateson, G. (1985) *Steps to an Ecology of Mind*, Ballantine Chandler, Canada
Benson, H. (1975) *The Relaxation Response*, William Morrow, New York, USA
—— (1979) *The Mind/Body Effect*, Simon & Schuster, New York, USA
—— (1985) *Beyond the Relaxation Response*, Collin Fount Paperbacks, London, UK
Bergland, R. (1985) *The Fabric of the Mind*, Penguin Books, Australia
Brown, B. (1980) *SuperMind: The Ultimate Energy*, Bantam Books, New York, USA
Brownsword, A.W. (1987) *It Takes All Types*, Baytree Publication Company, California, USA
—— (1989) *The Type Descriptions*, Baytree Publication Company, California, USA
Buzan, T. (1989) *Use Your Memory*, BBC Books, London, UK
—— (1991) *Using Both Sides of Your Brain*, 3rd edn, Plume Books, USA
—— (1993) *The Mindmap Book*, BBC Books, London, UK
Cacioppe, R. (1989) *Mind Maps*, Integra Pty Ltd, Perth, Australia
Card, C.N.W. (1993) *Discover the Power of Introversion*, Type and Temperament Inc., Pennsylvania, USA
Cook, N.D. (1986) *The Brain Code*, Methuen, London, UK
Dilts, R., Grindler, J., Bandler, R. & Delozier, J. (1980) *Neuro-Linguistic Programming: The Study of the Structure of Subjective Experience*, Meta Publications, California, USA
Edwards, E. (1982) *Drawing on the Right Side of the Brain*, Fontana Paperbacks, UK

Evans, P. & Deehan, G. (1991) *The Descent of Mind: The Nature and Purpose of Intelligence*, Paladin Grafton Books, London, UK

Gardner, H. (1983) *Frames of Mind*, Basic Books, New York, USA

Gazzaniga, M.S. (1985) *The Social Brain: Discovering the Networks of the Mind*, Basic Books, New York, USA

Grinder, M. (1989) *Righting the Educational Conveyor Belt*, Metamorphous Press, Oregon, Portland, USA

Halpern, S. & Savary, L. (1985) *Sound Health: The Music and Sounds that Make Us Whole*, Harper & Row, Sydney, Australia

Herrman, N. (1989) *The Creative Brain*, Ned Herrman/Brain Books, USA

Honey, P. & Mumford, A. (1983) *Capitalizing on Your Learning Style*, Ardingly House, Maidenhead, Berkshire, UK

Houston, J. (1982) *The Possible Human*, J.P. Tarcher Inc., New York, USA

Houston, J. and Masters, R. (1978) *Listening to the Body*, Delta, New York, USA

Hirsch, S.K. (1989) *Life Types*, Warner Books, New York, USA

Industry Task Force on Leadership and Management Skills (1995) *Enterprising Nation: Renewing Australia's Managers to Meet the Challenges of the Asia-Pacific Century*, Australian Government Publishing Service, Canberra

Isachsen, O. & Berens, L.V. (1988) *Working Together*, Neworld Management Press, California, USA

Jeffries, W.C. (1991) *True to Type*, Hampton Roads Publishing Company, Virginia, USA

Jensen, E. (1989) *Superteaching: Master Strategies for Building Student Success*, Turning Point for Teachers, USA

Klauser, H.A. (1987) *Writing on Both Sides of the Brain: Breakthrough Techniques for People Who Write*, Harper & Row, San Francisco, USA

Laborde, G. (1987) *Influencing With Integrity: Management Skills for Communication and Negotiation*, Syntony Publishing, California, USA

Lewis, D. (1987) *Mind Skills*, Grafton Books, London, UK

Lozanov, G. (1978) *Suggestology and Outlines of Suggestopedy*, Gordon and Breach, New York, USA

Luria, A.R. (1969) (translated by Lynn Solotaroff) *The Mind of Mnemonist*, Jonathan Cape Ltd, London, UK

Lloyd, L. (1990) *Classroom Magic: Amazing Technology for Teachers and Home Schoolers*, Metamorphous Press, Portland, Oregon, USA

McGee-Cooper, A. (1983) *Time Management for Unmanageable People*, Ann McGee and Associates, Dallas, Texas, USA

Mehrabian, A. (1971) *Silent Messages*, Wadsworth, California, USA

Merritt, S. (1990) *Mind, Music and Imagery*, Plume, California, USA

Moir, A. & Jessel, D. (1991) *Brain Sex: The Real Difference Between Men and Women*, Dell Publishing, New York, USA

Murray, W.D.G. (1995) *Give Yourself the Unfair Advantage*, Type and Temperament Inc., Pennyslvania, USA

Myers, I. & McCaulley, M.H. (1985) *Manual: A Guide to the Development and Use of the Myers-Briggs Type Indicator*, Consulting Psychologist Press, California, USA

Neville, B. (1989) *Educating Psyche*, Collins Dove, Melbourne, Australia

Ornstein, R.E. & Thompson, R.F. (1984) *The Amazing Brain*, Houghton Mifflin, Boston, USA

Ostrander, S. & Schroeder, L. (1979) *Superlearning*, Delta Books, New York, USA

Pritchard, A. & Taylor, J. (1980) *Accelerated Learning: The Use of Suggestion in the Classroom*, Academic Therapic Publications, California, USA

Rose, C. (1989) *Accelerated Learning*, Accelerated Learning Systems Ltd, Aylesbury, UK

Russell, P. (1980) *The Brain Book*, Routledge and Kegan Paul, London, UK

Schuster, D. & Gritton, C. (1985) *Suggestive Accelerative Learning and Teaching*, Gordon and Breach, New York, USA

Stockwell, T. (1992) *Accelerated Learning in Theory and Practice*, Druckerei AG, Liechtenstein

Storz, M.L. (1993) *Mind Body Power: The Self Help Book on Accelerated Learning*, Times Editions, Singapore

Svantesson, I. (1989) *Mind Mapping and Memory*, Swan Communications Ltd, New Zealand

Tannen, D. (1990) *You Just Don't Understand: Women and Men in Conversation*, Random House, Sydney, Australia

Tart, C. (1986) *Waking Up: Overcoming the Obstacles to Human Potential*, Shambala, Boston, USA

Teffert, D.A. (1989) *Extraordinary People*, Bantam Press, New York, USA

Tieger, P.D. & Barron-Tieger, B. (1992) *Do What You Are*, Little Brown and Company, Canada

Tufte, E.R. (1983) *The Visual Display of Quantitative Information*, Graphic Press, Cheshire, Connecticut, USA

Vitale, B.M. (1986) *Unicorns Are Real: A Right Brained Approach to Learning*, Warner Books, New York, USA

—— (1986) *Free Flight: Celebrating Your Right Brain*, Jalmar Press, California, USA

Wolman, B. and Ullman, M. (1986) *Handbook of States of Consciousness*, Van Nostrand, New York, USA

Wurman, R. S. (1989) *Information Anxiety*, Doubleday, New York, USA

Zdenek, M. (1985) *The Right Brain Experience: An Intimate Programme to Free the Powers of Your Imagination*, Corgi Books, UK

CW01102950

LIMITED EDITION!?
To buy or not to buy? It's all in the packaging design.

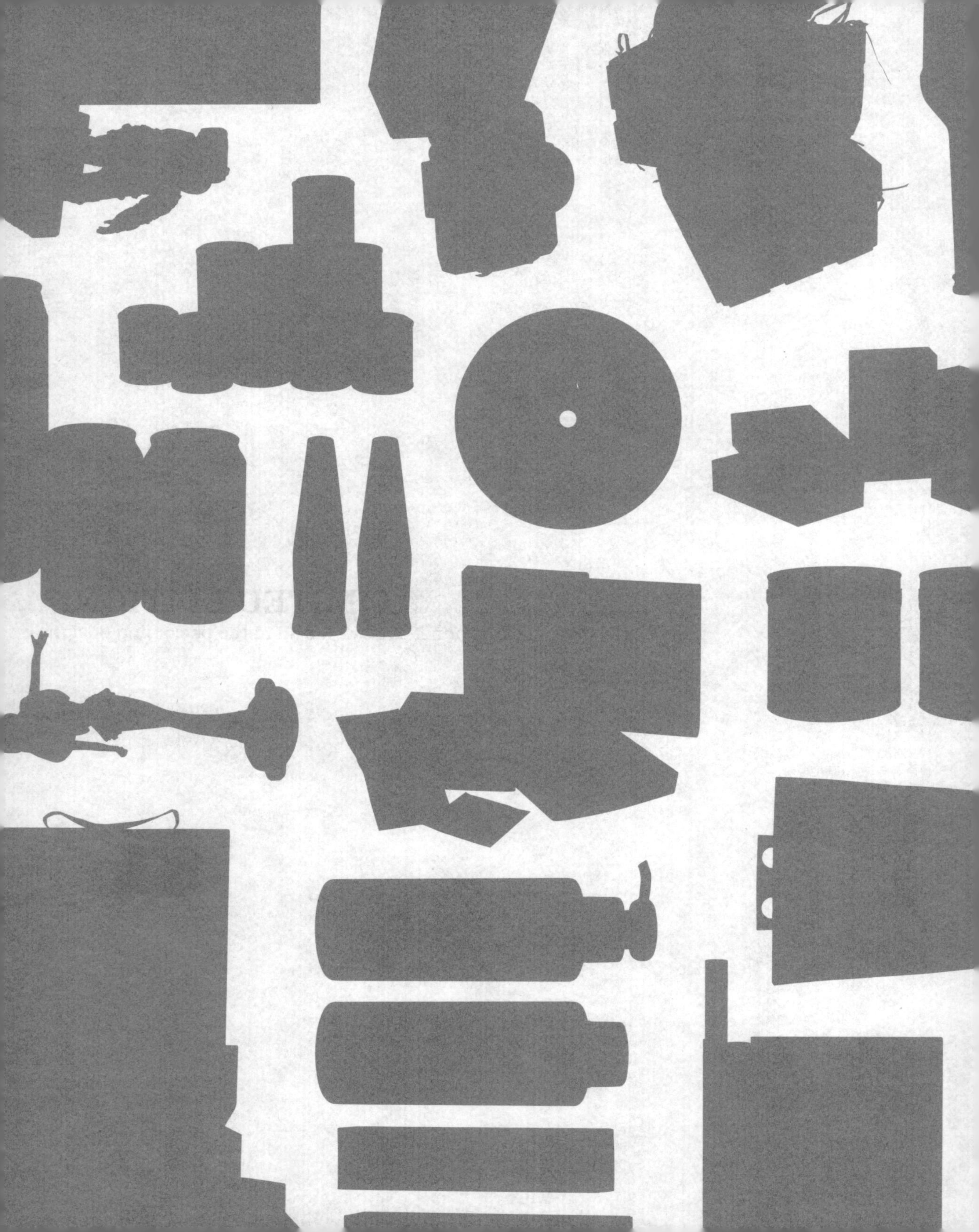

Chapter 1
008 Let's Have Some Fun
Column: Purpose of Packaging

Chapter 2
096 Things We Need
Column: Material

Chapter 3
162 Flat-out
Column: Ecology/Recycling

Chapter 4
192 Package Design?

Publisher:
AllRightsReserved Ltd.

Concept:
AllRightsReserved Ltd.

Design:
3KG

Editor:
Kazutomo Ryuko

Contributing Editors:
Daniel Mason, Takako Narita,
Naomi Hiyama

Translation:
Takako Narita, Naoko Ryuko

Proof Reading:
Ann Asano, Cherise Fong

Photographer:
Nobutoshi Kurisu, David Lo (H.K)

First Published in 2005 by AllRightsReserved Ltd.
Tel (852)2712 0873
Fax (852)2712 6701
URL www.allrights-reserved.com

For General Enquires:
info@allrights-reserved.com

For Distribution:
garylau@allrights-reserved.com

For Editorial Submission & Collaboration:
editor@allrights-reserved.com

Printed in Hong Kong
ISBN 988-97054-8-6

Editor's Foreword

This is a book which gathers all kinds of packaging around us and presents it as one collection. Later I will explain the reason why we named it "Limited Edition" – not that all the products in this book are of limited edition. We value packaging above content, and that was one of the key points when making our selection.

The key points were:
- Remarkable shape and appearance
- No similarity in the same genre
- Dynamically conveying the charm of the product
- Unconventional storage ideas
- Uniqueness and originality
- Display of strong identity

There are many people in the world who are attracted by CD covers and purchase them based on this alone. Similarly, there are many people who are fascinated by interesting binding and materials. Figuratively speaking of personal relationships, it may be similar to "love at first sight". This concept – whether we fell in love with the packages at first sight or not – was one of the assessment points to select the packages for this book. Another point was not to focus on only one country. The collections cover a wide area including Japan, UK, Hong Kong, USA and more. The contributors based in the areas searched for the most interesting packages and collected them. Foremostly, this is how we could collect such large numbers of items.

Packages are designed to convey every aspect of the product, including distribution and display. It is like people changing their dress to suit a certain situation, or following the seasons. Packaging doesn't need to be splendid all the time. Materials may change to fit purpose as the materials of a garment change: cotton for summer, wool for winter.

No effective packaging design can ignore its contents; similarly clothes can never accomplish their primary duty if no one wears them. A perishable food item wrapped only in plastic could be compared to a sumo wrestler dressed only in a loincloth. It is essential that food should be fresh, and that a sumo wrestler fights almost naked. It is not necessary for him to assert himself through clothing. Face the consumer, play the opponent fairly! Then, the "package" naturally becomes simple.

On the other hand, even sumo wrestlers dress up when they leave the sumo ring. Nowadays sumo wrestlers enjoy singing karaoke and going to parties to meet girls. On these occasions, needless to say, they must wear more than a loincloth. To attract the opposite sex, they package themselves in a kimono to distinguish themselves from their in-the-ring presence. This could be the "Limited Edition" of the sumo wrestler. If he is high-ranking, he selects the kimono which fits his character. Sumo wrestlers select their own "packaging" according to both situation and character.

So hopefully you'll look at these package designs and think about clothing. We hope this book helps you to unwrap the world of packaging.

Finally, the meaning of the title "Limited Edition": all products are created by a designer and manufactured one by one. Therefore, every package is a "Limited Edition". This is also what this book aims to be.

Kazutomo Ryuko

Contributors:

Anisa Suthayalai
Anna Sui Cosmetics
ASYL DESIGN
Atsushi Kikuchi (Blue Mark)
butterfly stroke Inc.
CAMEL Pleasure Factory
Communion W
Design Barcodes™
Design Bridge
DEVILROBOTS
D-Mop
Final Home
Furi Furi Company
fuseproject
GK Design
good design company
Goodwin Hartshorn
Graphic Thought Facility
groovisions
Happypets
THE LINCOLN GRAPHIX FAMILY
j-me
Junkie Design
Kasia Korczak
Kashiwa Sato (Samurai)
Katsu Kimura
Kenjiro Sano (Hakuhodo Design)
Mark James
Masayoshi Kodaira (FLAME)
MEDICOM TOY CORPORATION
Manabu Mizuno (good design company)
Myeong-hee Lee
Michael.Nash Associates
Naomi Hirabayashi
NBStudio
Non-Format
Norio Nakamura
Oliver Laric
onedotzero
Output
Pearlfisher
Red Design
RMC
Ryosuke Uehara (D-Bros)
Sam Hurt and Jude Biddulph
Shibusawa Kenta
Shuichi Ito
Shu Uemura
Soup Design
Stanley Wong Ping-Pui
state
Studio Dror
Surface to Air
TAKORA Kimiyoshi Futori
Taku Satoh
Templin Brink Design
Tobias Wong
Tsuyoshi Kusano
Tycoon Graphics
Yoshie Watanabe (D-Bros)
Yuki Sugiyama (Hakuhodo Design)
ZIP
3KG
AllRightsReserved

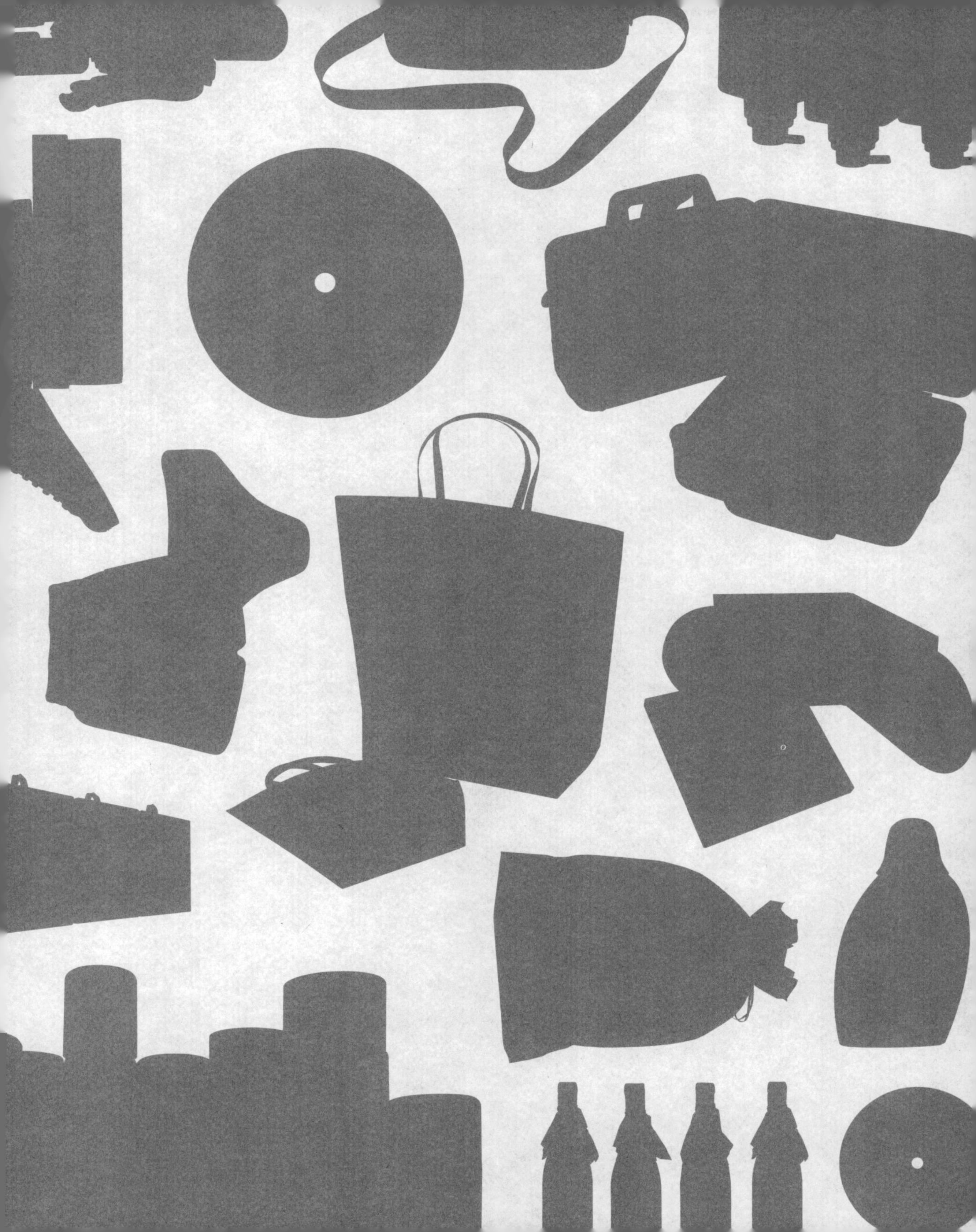

Chapter 1

Let's Have Some Fun

CD/DVD/Art Book/Toys

This chapter introduces packaging for hobbies such as CDs, DVDs, special packaged books, figure dolls and so on. The distinctive feature in this category is that most are flowery and have elements of entertainment. Some are very experimental and created beyond conventional forms. They arouse the desire for possession.

010

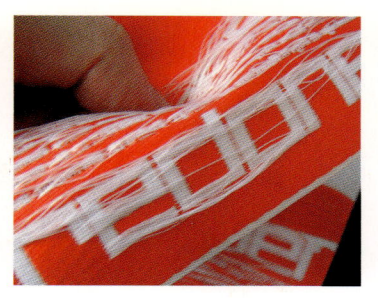

Red Snapper/Redone

The cover fold is actually a woven label inserted into clear CD jewel case with the reverse side facing out to reveal its red and white stitching, suggesting a noisy signal. Inside, the words are mirrored to reflect the bichrome pattern.

011

name:
Red Snapper/Redone
designer:
Non-Format
client:
Lo Recordings

012

'Like a spread of Marble Chocolate' – this comment from artist Ken Ishii was the starting point for the initial concept of this DVD package. The focus is the DVD itself, where visual motion blur follows the spinning movement of the disc. Although motionless, it is in fact a motion picture.

Interpretations for Ken Ishii –
Future In Light Visualized & Remixed

name:
Interpretations for Ken Ishii –
Future In Light Visualized & Remixed
designer:
Tsuyoshi Kusano
client:
70Drums All Rights Reserved.

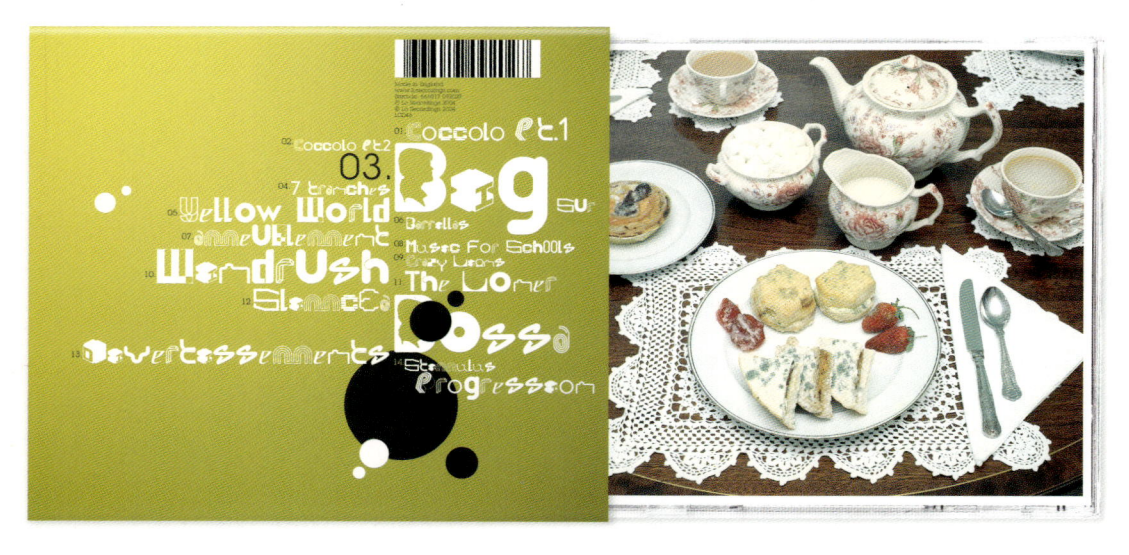

Rediffusion (King Of Woolworths)

Rediffusion's King of Woolworths slip-case album wrapper is an abstract design of crazy fonts and geometrics in black, white and beige, but the inside jewel case slides out like English breakfast in bed or tea-time, set at a very posh table.

name:
Rediffusion (King Of Woolworths)
designer:
Non-Format
artist:
King Of Woolworths
Photography:
Natalie Stevens

Lo Editions 1.2.3.

Low Editions' 3-CD box set comprises three black and white panels of faces distorted by blotches of ink, increasingly overridden by geometrical shapes.

name:
Lo Editions 1.2.3. (various)
designer:
Non-Format
artist:
various

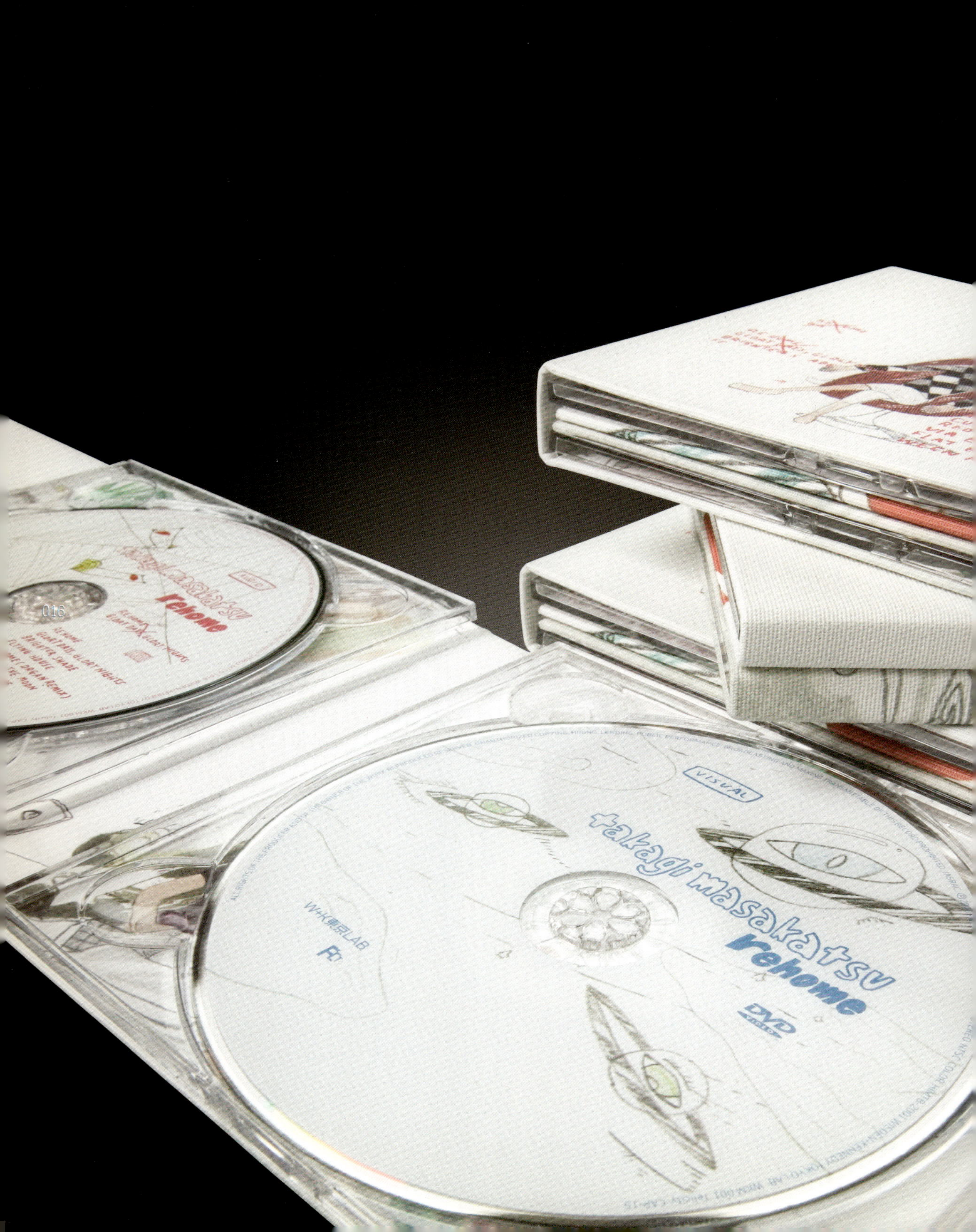
takagi masakatsu
rehome
VISUAL
W+K東京LAB
DVD
VIDEO

Takagi Masakatsu's Rehome album folds up neatly into a canvas portfolio including both audio CD and visual DVD. The illustrated cover theme and handwritten titles wrap around the entire package, just like an artist's universe contained in itself.

Takagi Masakatsu/ Rehome

017

name:
Takagi Masakatsu/Rehome
creative director:
John C Jay + Sumiko Sato
art director/producer:
+CRUZ
designer:
+CRUZ/Bryan Kestell
artist:
Kentaro Kobuke
client:
W+K Tokyo Lab

018

The prequel to the 'Another Late Night' and 'Late Night Tales' series, the 'Another Fine Mess' series aims to capture the energy and eclectic musical styles of an impromptu house party 'round your mate's house'. The concept for all four compilations in this series is a simple visual joke which, if explained, would lose its appeal. But take as your cue the premise that the album aims to capture the loud and raucous nature of a good night in.

Another Fine Mess Vol 1 & 2

019

name:
Another Fine Mess Vol 1 & 2
designer:
Red Design
client:
Whoa Music/Azuli

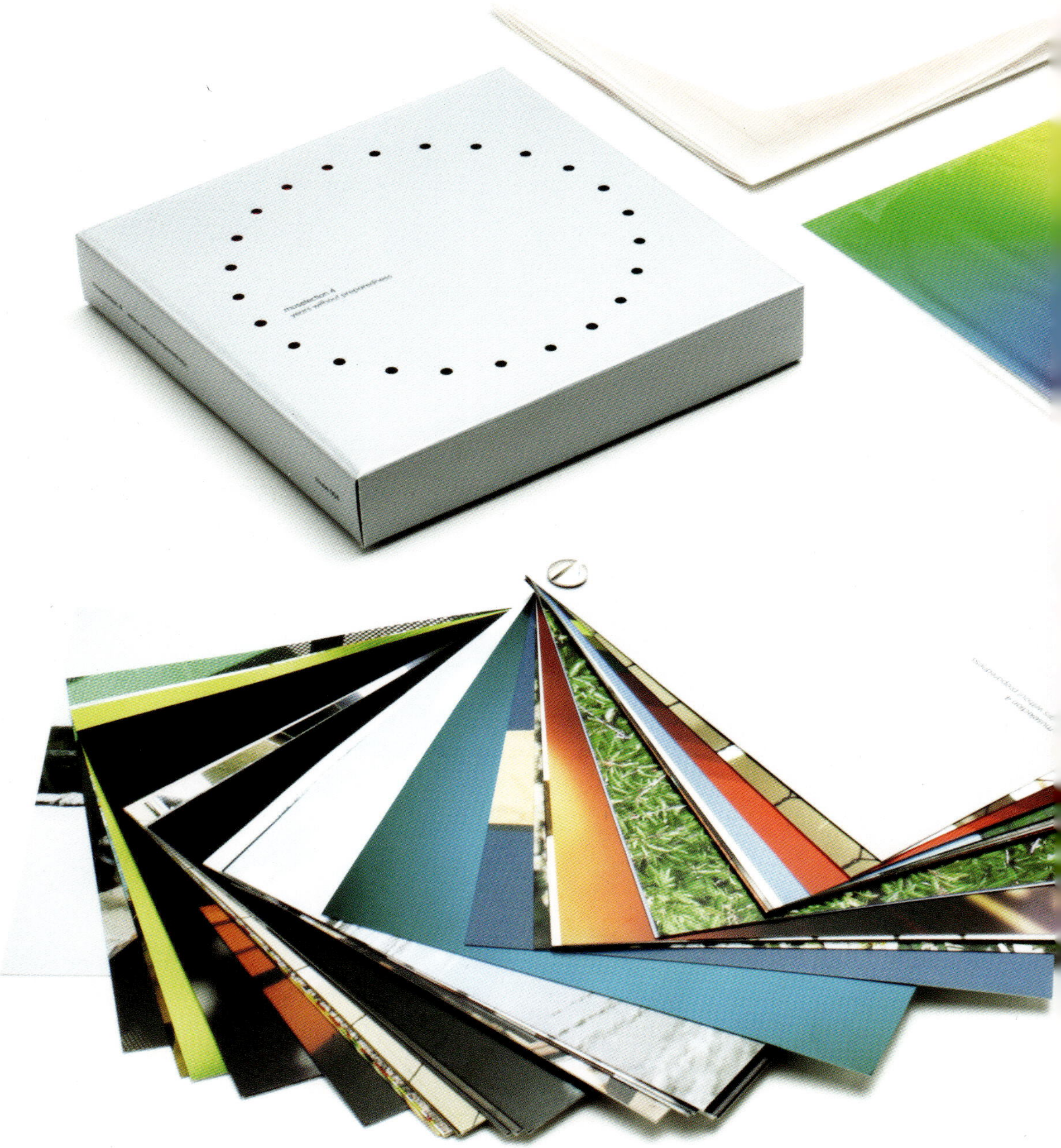

This is the fourth publication of Hiroyuki Miyata, one of the 3KG collective, who has been producing this collection of poems for the past decade as Muselecton. His book of 44 poems written in Japanese and English, plus photographs, illustrations and soundtrack, fans out like a Pantone colour sampler. Limited edition of 150 copies.

muselection 4 years without preparedness

name:
muselection 4
years without preparedness
designer:
3KG
client:
muselection
photographer:
Tsubasa Fujikura

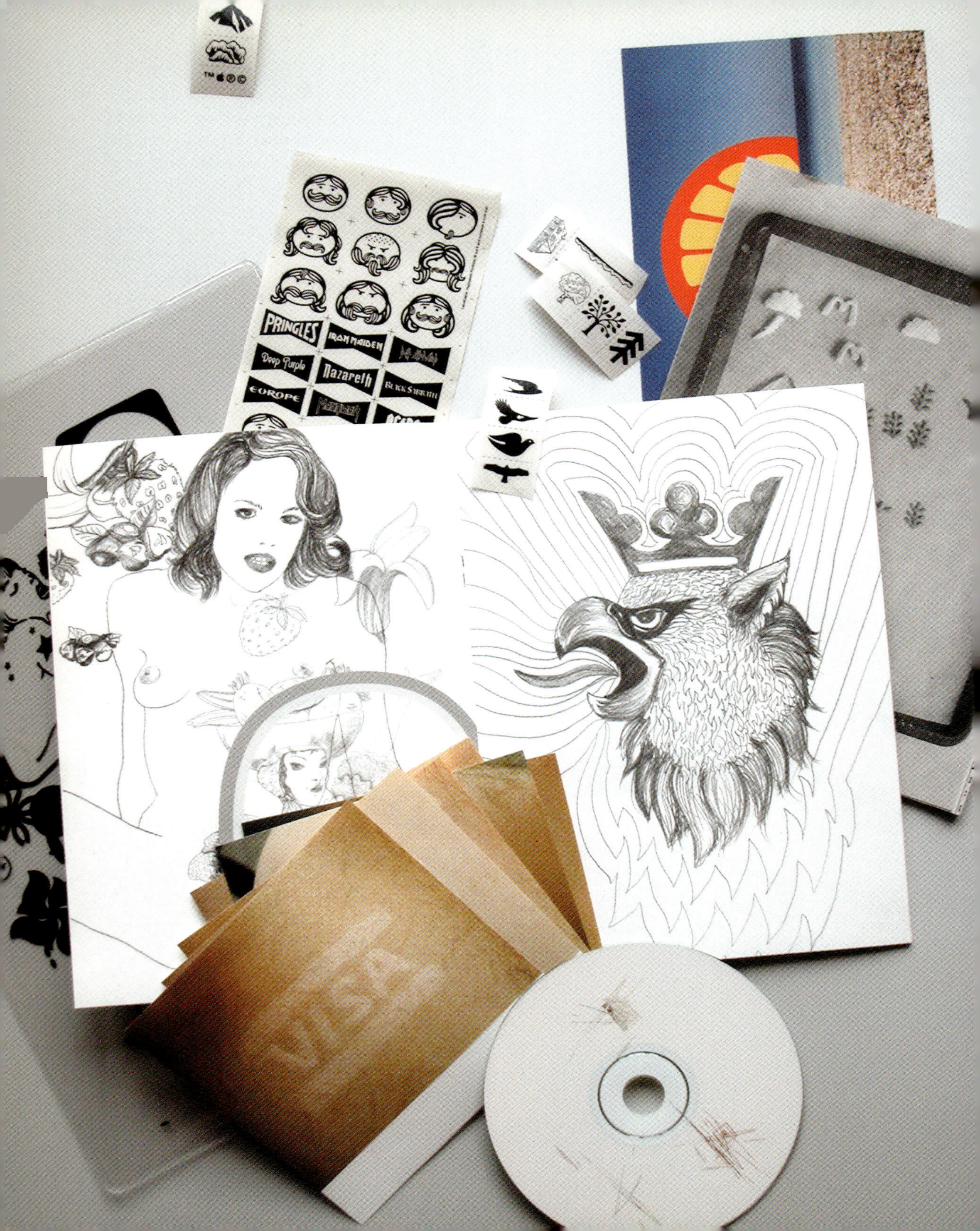
PRINGLES
IRON MAIDEN
Deep Purple
Nazareth
EUROPE
VISA

Labelusine is a virtual firm made up of a multitude of different experiences using recycled logos. The labelusine project developed itself throughout different objects: posters, a small edition wallpaper, a CD, shirts, an inflatable rubber ring, postcards... many different supports such as signs, logotypes, and trademarks which could be reappropriated and played with to create something new. The idea is that labelusine, like a small firm, can be self-financed and self-sufficient and diffuse artistic products on a small scale.

Labelusine

name:
LABELUSINE
designer:
HAPPYPETS
client:
HAPPYPETS

MOULIN-NEUF
2004-2005

The typeface used for the visual identity of this theatre is a readaptation and reappropriation of a children's rubber puzzle playing mat. This approach corresponded to the creative, playful and underground aspect of the theatre.

name:
MOULIN-NEUF 2004-2005
designer:
HAPPYPETS
client:
MOULIN-NEUF THEATRE

ÄRTONWALL

The visual identity of this album was inspired from graffiti, tattoos and typical rock'n'roll type imagery, complete with red striped Ä guitar picks. A gold sticker legitimises the group's EP.

name:
Ärtonwall
designer:
HAPPYPETS
client:
Ärtonwall

This was the first album released by Red Records, Red Design's sister company. A bespoke box contains manila envelopes holding the CD and a set of postcards, as well as a limited edition poster. It was designed to be special without being lavish, conserving an earthy organic feel akin to the music.

Lucky Jim/
Our Troubles End Tonight

name:
Lucky Jim/Our Troubles End Tonight
designer:
Red Design
client:
Red Records

Gonzo Digimation Calendar

This was a package of 500 limited edition giveaways. Since the client was a CG animation company, a calendar in the shape of a CD-R was appropriate.

name:
Gonzo Digimation Calendar
designer:
Tsuyoshi Kusano
client:
GDH K.K.

Quantic Soul Orchestra/ Stampede

For Quantic's first album with his full band, it was decided to concentrate on the album's title and the afro-beat musical influences for the illustrations. These were overlaid with details of 'wear and tear' – scratches and aged sticky tape – like you get on well-used vintage albums, to mimic Quantic's much loved early '70s funk records.

name:
Quantic Soul Orchestra/
Stampede
designer:
Red Design
client:
Tru Thoughts

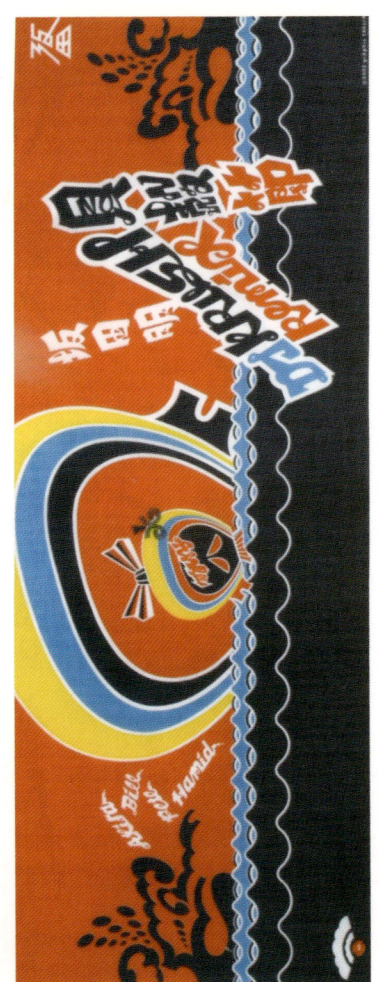

Akira Sakata/Kaigarabushi DJ Krush Remix

This CD package presents traditional Japanese folk music in a new angle. The song is an old Japanese fisherman's song, and the graphics were designed with reference to a Japanese fishing harvest flag [Tairyobata]. A special tenugui [Japanese hand towel] was also produced to become a mobile advertising medium, carried in the street.

name:
Akira Sakata/Kaigarabushi DJ Krush Remix
designer:
Takora Kimiyoshi Futori (Cheap Pop)
client:
Dogtail productions

Mara Carlyle/The Lovely

Mara Carlyle's lovely album is printed in positive/negative black and white, with a booklet of transparent pages. Each page is impressed on both sides with herbal silhouettes, giving the album a ghostly feel.

name:
Mara Carlyle/The Lovely
designer:
Non-Format
client:
Accidental Records

Nike Air Presto 2001

name:
Nike Air Presto 2001
creative director:
John C Jay + Sumiko Sato
art director:
+CRUZ/John C Jay
campaign artist:
ROSTARR
client:
Nike Japan

Presto [6:46]

Ken Ishii
A side

Nike Air Presto 2001

033

name:
Nike Air Presto 2001
creative director:
John C Jay + Sumiko Sato
art director:
+CRUZ/John C Jay
campaign artist:
ROSTARR
client:
Nike Japan

034

Another characteristically hybrid album of audio CD and visual DVD, DJ Uppercut's Pieces opposes two faces in a duel between the western cowboy and the eastern ninja, on two booklets which slide together into a slitted square package.

DJ UPPERCUT/ PIECES

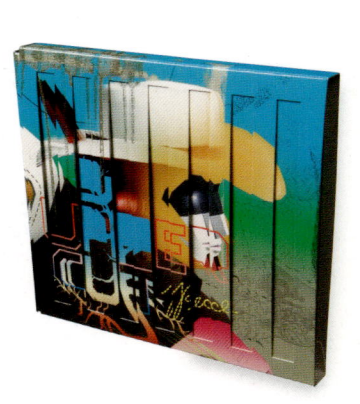

name:
DJ UPPERCUT/PIECES
creative director:
John C Jay + Sumiko Sato
art director / producer:
+CRUZ
designer:
+CRUZ/WOOG
illustrator:
JUSTIN WOOD
client:
W+K Tokyo Lab

Pre-School/
Masterpiece Album

This rainbow pre-school themed album is a cheerfully coloured CD carrying case. Its soft, waterproof cover with rounded edges is perfectly safe and suited to little hands. Pre-School's featured CD is the first in this portfolio, which can be used to hold all your favourite CDs.

name:
Pre-School Masterpiece Album
designer:
Hikaru Kawahara/TLGF
client:
Toy's Factory

This album is designed like a square children's picture book featuring the illustrations of Takashi Murakami/ Kaikai Kiki. Each hard cardboard page displays the lyrics and the book tells a story that connects all the songs into a concept album. The last page holds YUZU's latest CD.

YUZUMORE
Limited Edition

name:
YUZUMORE Limited Edition
designer:
Hikaru Kawahara/TLGF
©2002 Takashi Murakami/Kaikai Kiki.
client:
Senha&Co.

Mr. Children/ SHIFUKUNO OTO

After overcoming various incidents, Mr. Children released the album SHIFUKUNO OTO after a two-and-a-half year absence. The album was themed 'the bliss of creating music and musical bliss'. For the designer, bliss was found through drawing and so the cover illustration for the album was born – SHIFUKUNO.

name:
SHIFUKUNO OTO/Mr. Children
designer:
Kashiwa Sato
client:
TOY'S FACTORY

HIFANA/
FRESH PUSH BREAKIN'

This time the double CD/DVD audio/visual album opens up into two sides of a fantastic and colourful scene, while the outer paper packaging is a sober copper and black. The discs reprise the copperplate, distinguished by red or green.

name:
HIFANA/FRESH PUSH BREAKIN'
creative director:
John C Jay + Sumiko Sato
art director/producer:
+CRUZ
designer:
+CRUZ/WOOG
illustrator:
HIFANA, MAHARO
client:
W+K Tokyo Lab

040

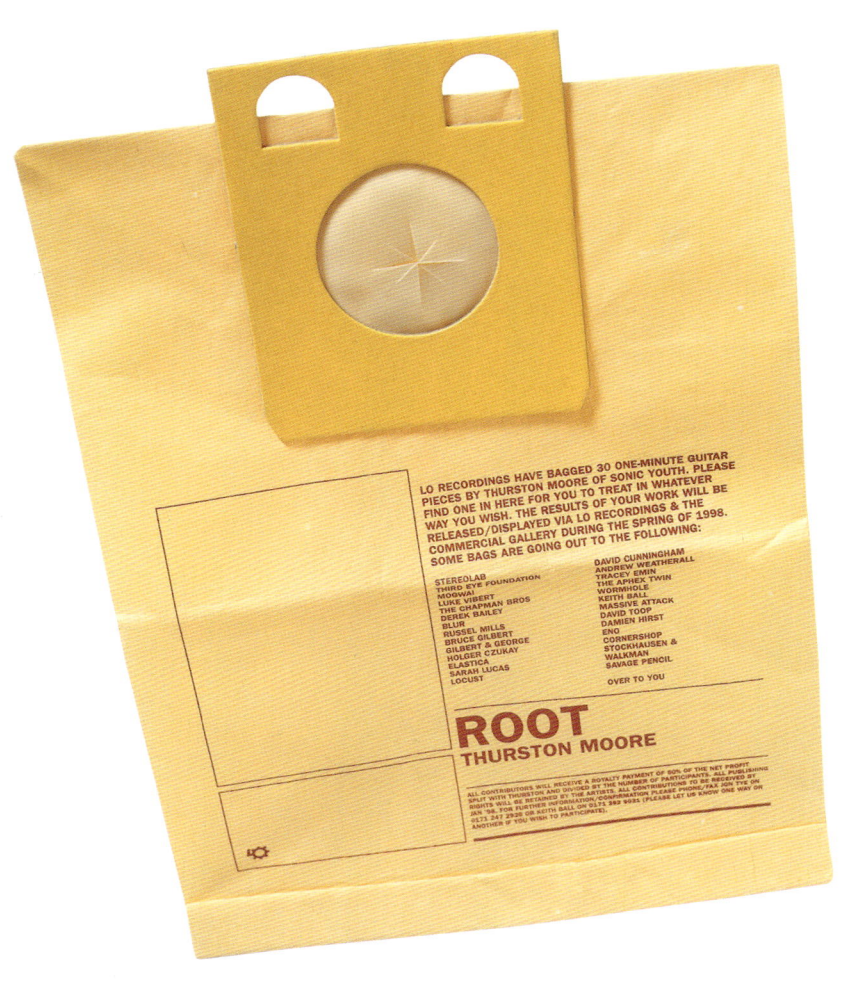

Root Thurston Moore

name:
Root Thurston Moore
designer:
Non-Format
client:
Lo Recordings

FULLMETAL ALCHEMIST 1

As the ultra-transparent plastic DVD box opens up, our forceful anime hero punches out with a steely fist at the extremity of an iron-armoured arm. In the full colour edition, his heroic force of movement is highlighted by a flowing red cape, blond hair and muscular torso.

name:
FULLMETAL ALCHEMIST 1
designer:
Tsuyoshi Kusano
client:
Aniplex Inc. All rights reserved.

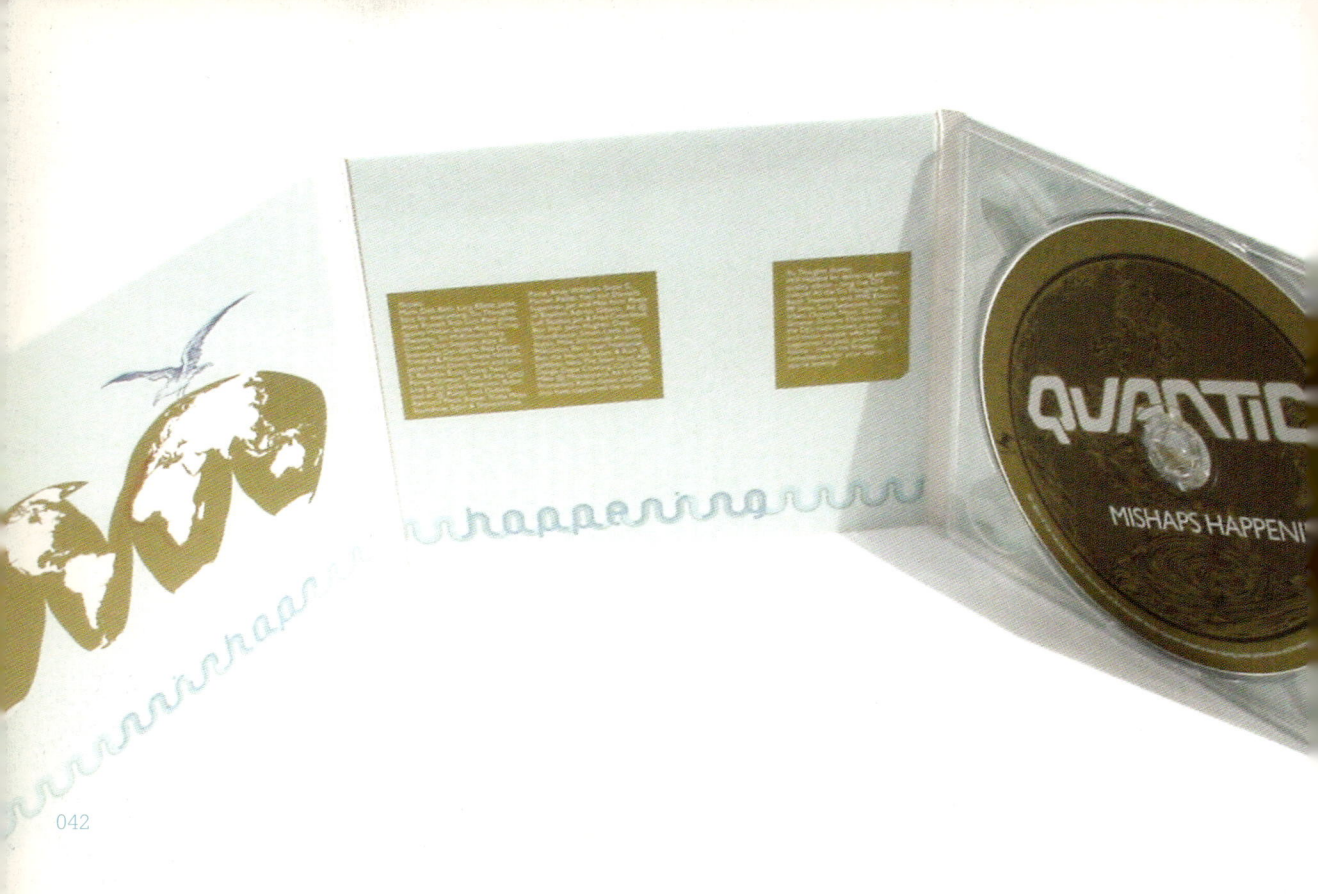

Quantic/
Mishaps Happening

The artwork concentrated on the international influence of the album both from Will Quantic's DJ gigs around the world and the music itself, interpreting Quantic's jet-set lifestyle through the more genteel travel mode of the Ocean Liner.

name:
Quantic/
Mishaps Happening
designer:
Red Design
client:
Tru Thoughts

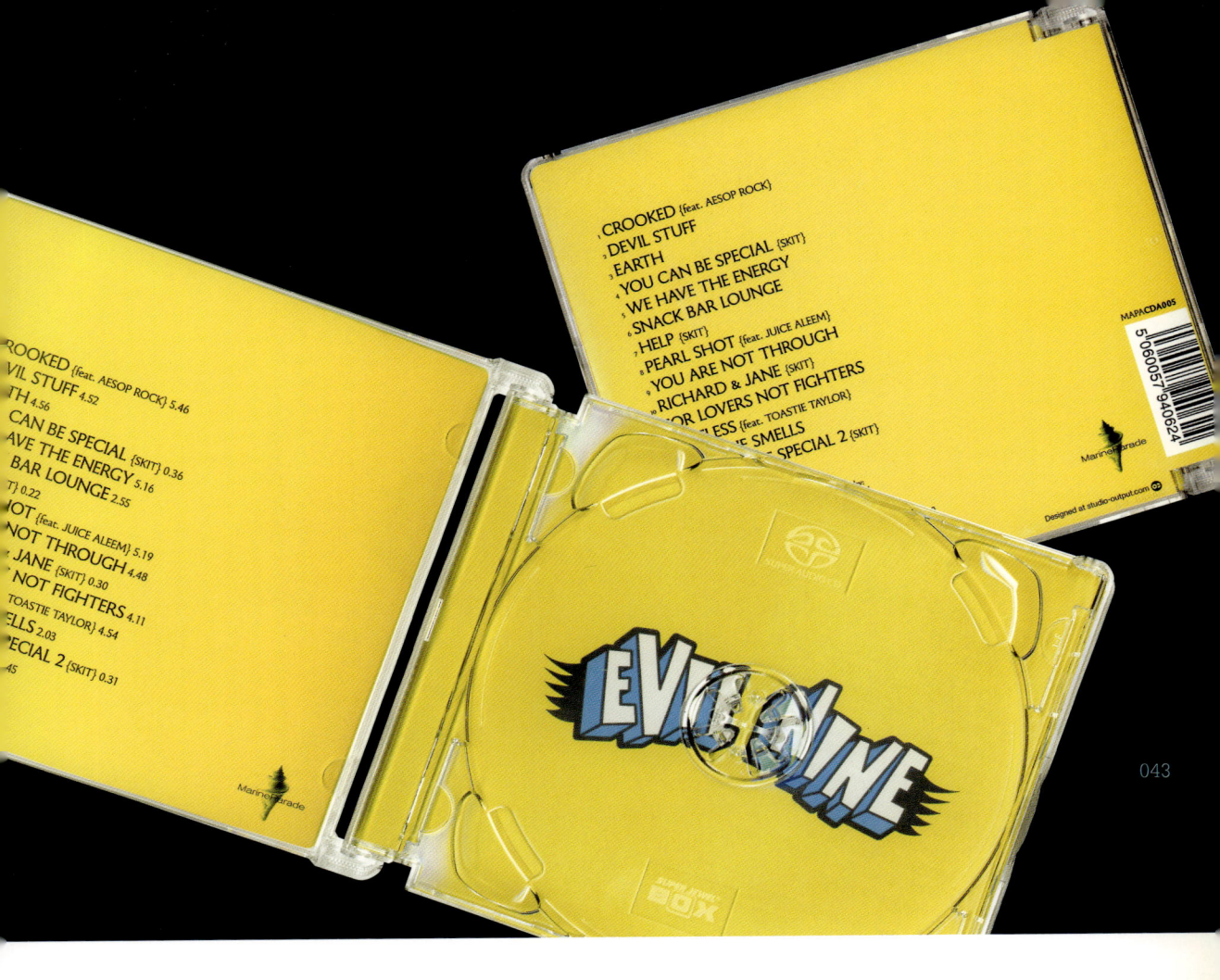

Evil Nine/
You Can Be Special Too

The sleeve and campaign for Evil Nine's CD, 'You Can Be Special Too', features illustrations of the band based on a sketch by the artists themselves. As well as the sturdy new super jewel case format, the album is also available in a luxurious double gatefold vinyl, which includes stickers and masks of the characters, allowing you to 'be evil' while listening!

name:
Evil Nine/
You Can Be Special Too
designer:
Studio Output
client:
Marine Parade

onedotzero
motion blur

book   dvd   graphic moving imagemakers

motion blur: onedotzero   graphic moving imagemakers

This design balances three elements – book, DVD and slipcase. The case houses both book and DVD in a durable, luxurious and eye-catching parcel. A special stencil version of the onedotzero house font was made to puncture the case, and is used throughout the contents. The book, which features interviews with motion graphics artists, uses a flexible grid to accommodate a wide variety of content, and a mixture of stocks to separate areas of content. A colour code identifies each artist and is used across book and DVD, where examples of their work can be viewed.

onedotzero motion blur

name:
onedotzero motion blur
designer:
state
client:
onedotzero

046

The Infernal Affairs Trilogy of Hong Kong undercover cop and robber films is already so popular and dear to Hong Kong people that the DVD box-set special edition merits a respectfully solemn treatment. The entire package is shrouded in black and illustrated in shades of grey, while the movies and all their audiovisual extras are expanded onto eight individual discs, with distinctive character portraits to label each CD. The hard cardboard box also includes two black and white posters and a mini binder of collectible character cards to complete the story. Standing on its own outside the box, the inside plastic container doubles as a display rack for the seven DVD cases and binder, true to cult.

Infernal Affairs Trilogy DVD Boxset

name:
The Infernal Affairs Trilogy DVD Boxset
designer:
AllRightsReserved
client:
MegaStar Distribution (HK) Limited

Since these three VHS tapes contain episodes of the same series, a parallel theme of greyed couple portraits was used for the cover, with the outer binding in three primary colours of pink, green and blue to distinguish FLAT, home and news, echoed respectively by symbols of shadow, liquid drop and bird. Very deadpan, as " The box filled with laugh."

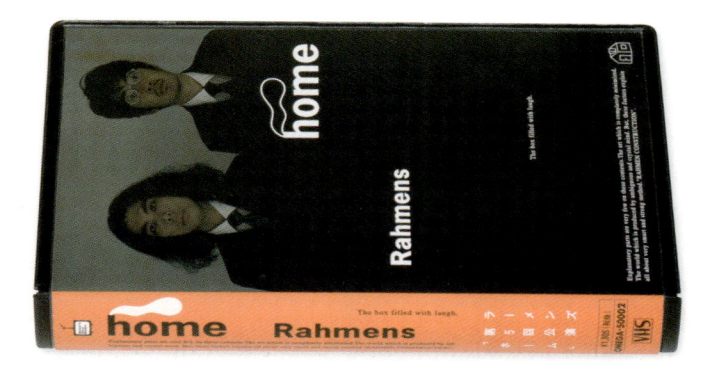

Rahmens/FLAT, home, news

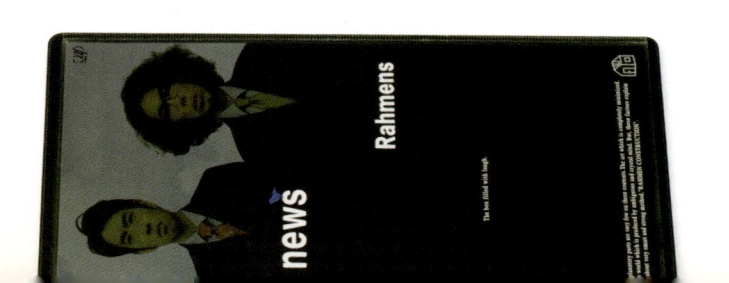

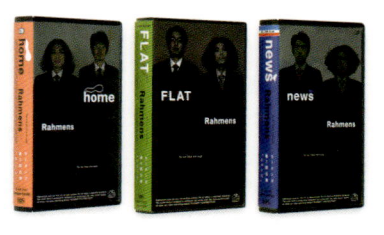

name:
Rahmens/FLAT, home, news
designer:
good design company
client:
PONY CANYON

Kamoncho (Crest Book)

This paulownia box packaging was designed for the book KAMONCHO, containing a selection of excellently designed and modern Japanese crests. Rubber stamp printing presents the title in a simple, tasteful manner. When the book is removed from the box, a rabbit print is revealed on the inside.

name:
Kamoncho (Crest Book)
creative director:
Yoko Omori
art director:
Atsuki Kikuchi (blue mark)
designer:
Atsuki Kikuchi (blue mark)
client:
PIE Books

Groovisions Van Lines is a moving truck in a book, which contains a history of of Groovisions gadgets and knick-knacks stored and displayed on square shelves. Chappie, the girl with the blond pigtails, is the omniscient witness of all this accumulated stuff over time, traversing the colourfully varied inventory of the eight-wheeled lorry as a stationary passenger, the three-dimensional figurine incrusted into each page of Groovision graphics.

Groovisions Van Lines

name:
Groovisions Van Lines
designer:
Groovisions
client:
Korinsha Press & Co., Ltd

GRV0946

Nike needs no introduction, and basketball player Lebron James is perfectly cast as the movie star lead of a Chinese action ghost story. Since the campaign is built around the B-movie metaphor of Chamber of Fear, the hardbound book is a portfolio of 1970s themed martial arts and horror film posters which open out on each overleaf. On the right is a photo album and graphic novel of the fictional film, with all the end credits to balance out the package.

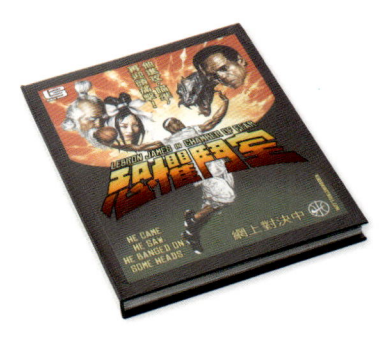

Nike LeBorn James Posterbook

name:
Nike LeBorn James Posterbook
designer:
SK Lam/AllRightsReserved
client:
Nike

Gardenergala Book

This Gardenergala book-in-a-box is a true collector's item, including a figurine, a CD-rom and a full-colour booklet detailing the frontal views and profiles of all 101 characters in the Gardenergala collection, featuring one character per page. The Gardenergala boxed book set is available in two contrasting editions, one black and one white.

name:
Gardenergala Book
designer:
Junkie Design
client:
Michael Lau

Materials are used in combinations that result in visually dynamic effects. On the Nagoya facade, a 'moiré' effect arises from the blending of two offset layers of pattern between the exterior glass facade and the opaque wall within. What is fascinating about the moiré phenomenon is that it combines otherwise ordinary materials into something special and Nagoya comes up!. This blurry, blurred mystical effect reinforces the aura of transparence Louis Vuitton. Other materials that combine to create this cinderella-like transformation include woven metal mesh against polished-like, pixellated images against a dumber film woven metal mesh against its own reflection in polished steel panels [19, Osonooke pixellated image]. Another pile on perception occurs on the Kobe parking facade through the articulation of a series of vertical louvres. Similar to typical vertical Japanese street signage, groups of individual louvres with fragmented graphics are angled perpendicular to approaching pedestrians so as to compose a series of complete images.

The effects created by the skins and their combination of different materials have become the medium that connects a series of buildings designed by different architects. This is a unique situation, while each project is distinct, taken together they have a recognizable continuity of form of architectural branding. For example, the Nagoya main glass facade by Jun Aoki inspired our design for the woven metal and mosaic tile facade for Seoul, which in turn inspired Aoki's design for the woven metal mesh and polished metal facade in Omotesando, and so on [19. Sapporo Jenner LV/flower].

LOGIQUE/VISUELLE: THE ARCHITECTURE OF LOUIS VUITTON

055

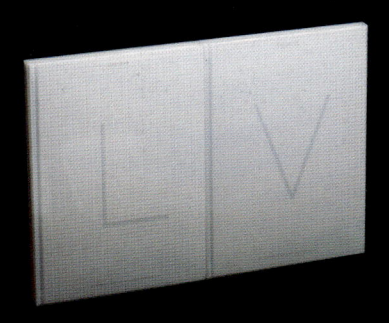

name:
LOGIQUE/VISUELLE:
THE ARCHITECTURE OF
LOUIS VUITTON
designer:
Masayoshi Kodaira
client:
LOUIS VUITTON JAPAN

056

Strangely enough, Valeria Golino has never been compared to Greco-Roman architecture. She should be: both are at home in random locations around the world. Both bring a dimension of cool mystery and nostalgia for something great yet forgotten to their spectators. Both emerge rugged and steadfast yet often are found devastated and beautiful. From the fluffy, Olympic skies of *Hot Shots* to the disturbingly warm, rocky earth of *Respiro*. The only difference is maybe that Valeria is not exactly a monument, rather what monuments are made for…

Cross Magazine

Cross Magazine's style unfolds lengthwise, beginning with a cover photo which opens out into a cover feature, which wraps around the whole magazine. The top inside flap bookmarks the article with a textual header in large typography as the story unfolds.

name:
Cross Magazine
art direction:
Kasia Korczak
edior:
Velimir Hoveyda McCauley
client:
Cross Magazine

Takashi Matsumoto presents KAZEMACHI ZUKAN

This seven CD boxed set was designed for songwriter Takashi Matsumoto's 30th anniversary, like a cubicle coloured barcode.

name:
Takashi Matsumoto presents KAZEMACHI ZUKAN
designer:
groovisions
client:
Sony Music Entertainment (Japan) Inc.

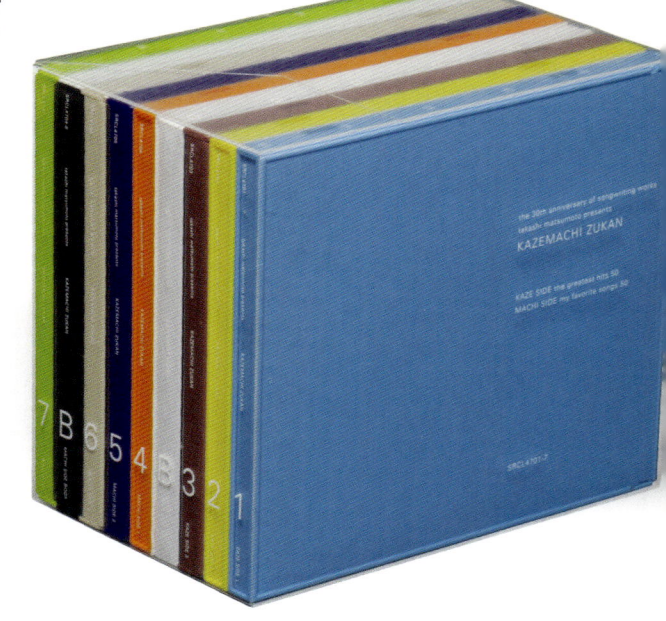

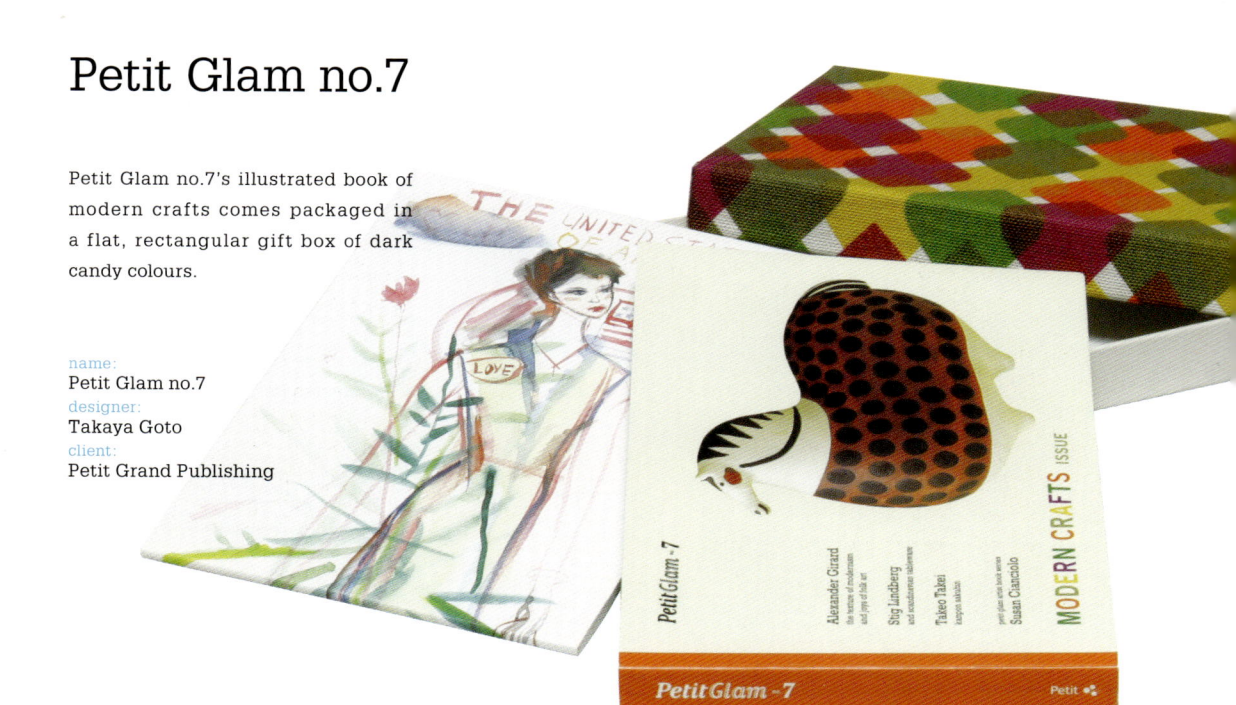

Petit Glam no.7

Petit Glam no.7's illustrated book of modern crafts comes packaged in a flat, rectangular gift box of dark candy colours.

name:
Petit Glam no.7
designer:
Takaya Goto
client:
Petit Grand Publishing

Diesel's 'Lost Paradise'

Diesel's 'Lost Paradise' is cast on-shore with a sandy message in a bottle and a DVD movie to show for it. The two castaway items are boxed into a crate and nestled in ribboned hay, a found treasure indeed.

name:
Diesel's 'Lost Paradise'
designer:
Diesel's Creative Team and Lobo
client:
Diesel

Scandinavian Design Series

The Scandinivian Design Series is a boxed set of three RGB-coloured books in an elegant grey cardboard holder. Playing cards fit neatly into a bright yellow box.

name:
Scandinavian Design Series
designer:
Soup Design
client:
Petit Grand Publishing

Cheburashka/
Welcome to the Happy House

Cheburashka lives in a happy house that pops open and up to welcome you inside. Striking cartoon characters and decors stand at odd angles as Cheburashka emerges from the blue drawer.

name:
Cheburashka/
Welcome to the Happy House
designer:
Takaya Goto
client:
Petit Grand Publishing

Pre-school/"no title"

This little black box contains more than meets the eye: not only Pre-School's" no title" album on a limited edition CD, but also a black and white illustration portrait poster and a black bite-sized booklet. No title required – the 'p' says it all, proving that big things come in small packages.

name:
Pre-School/ no title"
designer:
Hikaru Kawahara/TLGF
client:
Toy's Factory

062

LowFat Graphics is a fat little book and a spinning CD about graphics in motion, so its visual journey is reflected in its cosmopolitan packaging. Squared like a suitcase and complete with boarding pass and ID card, the boxy album sports stickered souvenirs of your 96 hot motion graphics destinations for a colourfully bon voyage.

LowFat Graphics
A Visual Journey Taking You To
96 Hot Motion Graphics Destinations

name:
LOWFAT GRAPHICS
A Visual Journey Taking You To 96 Hot Motion Graphics Destinations
designer:
3KG
publisher:
AllRightsReserved

All You Need Is Sticker Graphics

StickerGraphics brings back the childhood delight of opening up a box and sifting through all its individual contents, just like your very own collection of stickers. On one side, the sticker book itself; on the other, the stickers, loosely displayed under a transparent lid. The StickerGraphics box and book come in two more special editions, designed especially for AAAA and Colette.

name:
All You Need Is Sticker Graphcis
designer:
SK Lam, Yan/AllRightsReserved
client:
AllRightsReserved

Junkie x LamDog

Junkie has packaged LamDog into a little black puddle which opens like a capsule and hugs the raggy bundle like a single Russian doll. LamDog is wrapped in shrouds of grey, so it's only fitting that his rounded domicile should be perfectly pitch black for maximum protection. His shadow is outlined for precision like a corpse on the site of the crime.

name:
Junkie x LamDog
designer:
Junkie Design
client:
Michael Lau

S.M.P. Ko2 STRIKES BACK!

This colour spectrum box contains three collaboration figures created by artist Takashi Murakami and Kiyodo, and a T-shirt designed by groovisions.

©2000 Takashi Murakami/Kaikai Kiki.
All Rights Reserved.

name:
S.M.P. Ko2 STRIKES BACK!
designer:
groovisions
client:
Kaikai Kiki Co., Ltd.

067

GRV2000

This groovisions omnibus was published in late 2000, with a life-size picture of their mascot rabbit in an acrylic case.

name:
GRV2000
designer:
groovisions
client:
Exceed Press Co.

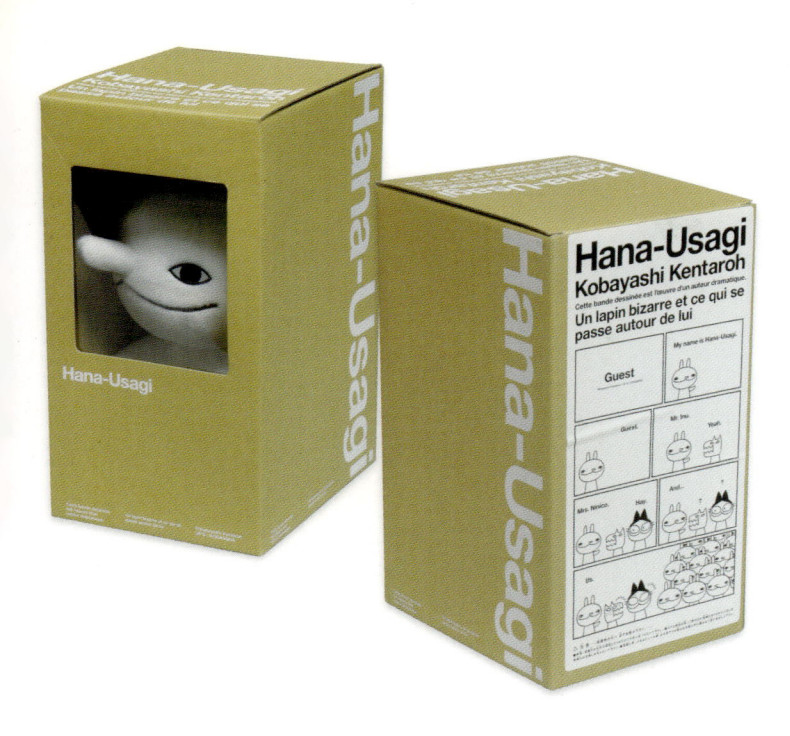

Hana-Usagi

Hana-Usagi is treated with all the due respect given to a popular manga character, transported and displayed like a living creature looking out the window of his temporary domicile. This domotics inspired capsule is dyed in subdued tones of beige and white, with handle-with-care fonts used to label its contents. On the back side, a newspaper comic strip gives some anecdotal context.

name:
Hana-Usagi
designer:
good design company
client:
KODANSHA

MAYWA DENKI/ Na-Cord Strap

Maywa Denki's spiny power cord connects the sockets like a glowing fish in the water, as flexible as cartilage. The bristly bones bring the cord to life when it's traversed by an electrical current.

name:
MAYWA DENKI/Na-Cord Strap
designer:
Norio Nakamura
client:
Yoshimoto Kogyo

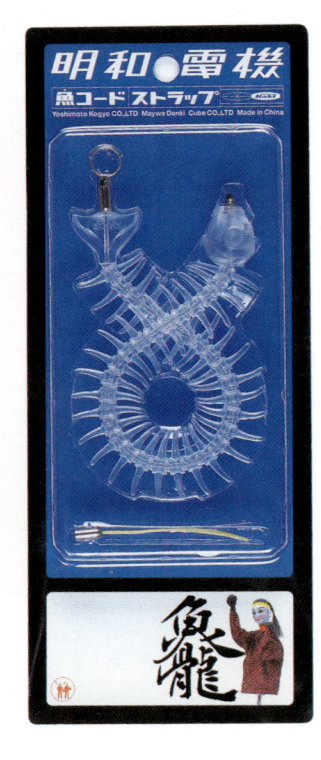

CardBoy

Inspired from the manufacturing of vinyl toys, came the idea of a series of flat pack figures entirely made out of cardboard. Once the final character had been designed, the flat pack grid with all its components fitting onto an A4 sheet was packed into a cardboard box. Not to waste, the box is part of the actual figure. A reversible head is printed on the box, and after hooking up with Playbeast, attached to a vinyl body.

name:
CardBoy
designer:
Mark James
client:
Self-generated Project

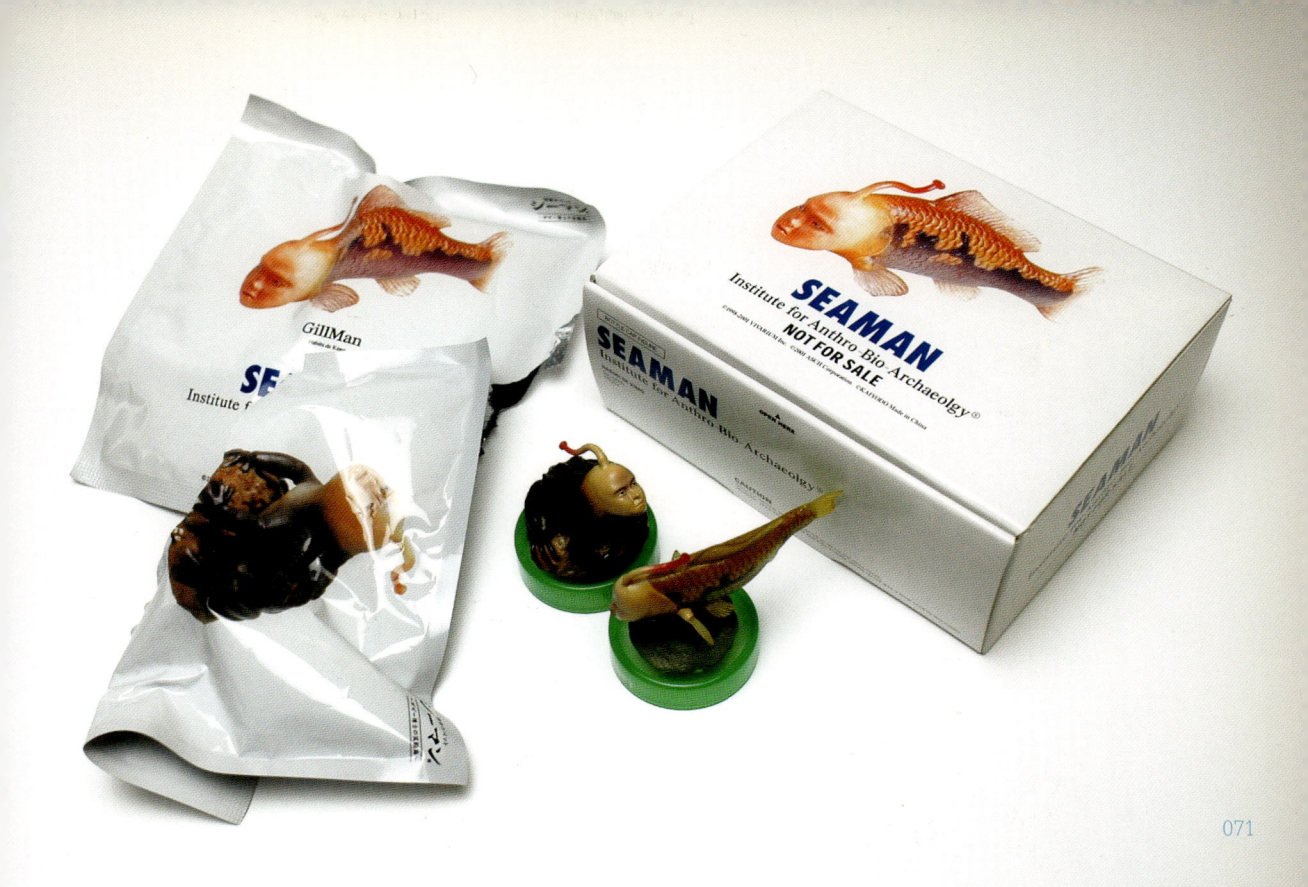

SEAMAN Institute for Anthro-Bio-Archaeolgy

The design concept was to resemble a Smithsonian Museum novelty item. It aimed to have the feel of an imitation organism, like the ones often seen in Japanese candy stores.

name:
SEAMAN Institute
for Anthro-Bio-Archaeolgy
designer:
Tsuyoshi Kusano
client:
VIVARIUM Inc.

TO-FU 34/102 PK is the packaging for the TOFU OYAKO catalogue, presented with a cute KUBRICK toy robot gift. The sequel TO-FU 69/102 was also designed in the same style.

TO-FU 34/102 PK

name:
TO-FU 34/102 PK
designer:
DEVILROBOTS
client:
FUSO Publishing Inc.

TO-FU Kubrick PK

TO-FU Kubrick packages a total of 30 editions. This series of packages is designed not to be thrown away, but collected along with the products. The front of the boxes features a TOFU illustration, and on the back, a framed cartoon.

name:
TO-FU Kubrick PK
designer:
DEVILROBOTS
client:
Medicom Toy

EVILGOLD PK

This is DEVILROBOTS' first published DVD package. The set comprises a DVD, Kubrick model and keychain presented as a treasure chest of fun.

name:
EVILGOLD PK
designer:
DEVILROBOTS
client:
Now On DVD

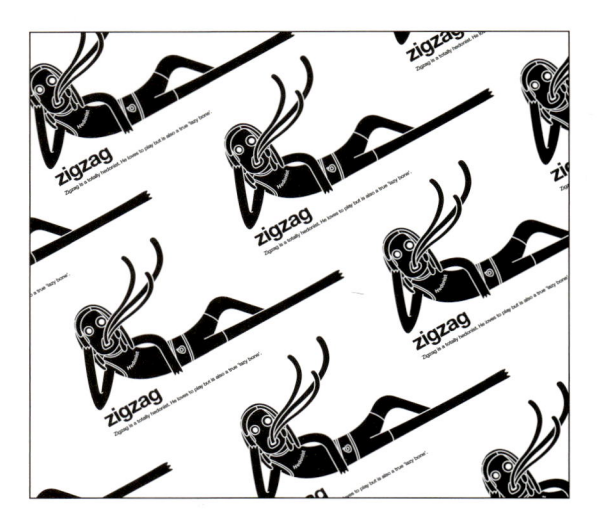

Agnès b x Cava Slipper

Agnès b's black and white slippers blow with the flow of Shya La La's Cavalulu character, whose round and rubbery eyes and mouth are right at home in the bathroom. The equally contrasted goodie packs, decorated like black cut-outs, hold mobile phone straps to extend the word-of-mouth.

name:
Agnès b x Cava Slipper
designer:
Shya La La
client:
Agnès b

Lamdogstar

Lamdog series, including Lamdog figures. The concept was to salute Adidas and the 1980s. The Adidas black and blue shoebox is the star of the Lamdog series, containing Lamdog figurines wrapped in bold, brash plastic – a sporty salute to the '80s.

name
Lamdogstar
designer
Junkie
client
Crazysmiles co.

SONY
MEMORY STICK DUO
32MB
MAGICGATE
VALUE PACK
SONY
VALUE PACK
PSP-1000 K
SONY
SONY
VALUE PACK
HOME
VOL
SONY
POWER
HOLD
HOME
VOL
SELECT
START

Playstation PSP introduces its new UMD (Universal Media Disc) format for game cartridges, packaged in a compact plastic casing. At 60 millimeters in diameter, the UMD is smaller than a DVD but larger than a mini-disc. Its rounded shape recalls the aerodynamic form of a UFO but matches the futuristic curves of the PlayStation Portable (PSP) console and headphone accessories. The game discs are protected in transparent plastic DVD-sized boxes with ample cover illustrations, so they fit right into your game box collection. The games on the discs in the boxes, plus white and silver remote-control headphones, are all included in the standard PlayStation Portable value pack.

PlayStation Portable (PSP)

name:
PlayStation Portable (PSP)
client:
© 2004 Sony Computer Entertainment Inc, All Rights Reserved.

Intermission, W.W
(Madsaki x Jun Takahashi)

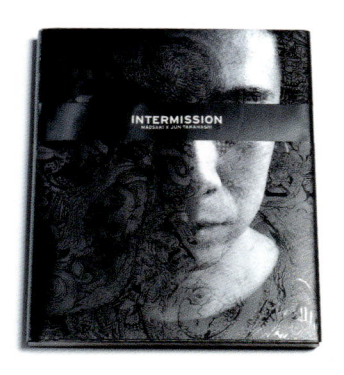

For the Intermission Exhibition held in Hong Kong, an art book was published presenting Madsaki & Jun's art pieces with shots of behind the scenes preparation, mysteriously enveloped in black plastic.

name:
Intermission, W.W
(Madsaki x Jun Takahashi)
designer:
Communion W
client:
Communion W

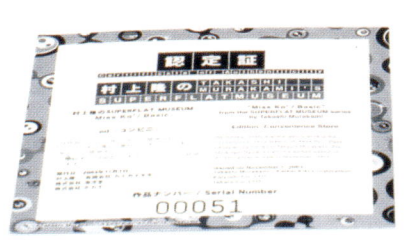

Takashi Murakami's SUPERFLATMUSEUM: Convenience Store Edition "Miss ko2"

This small box is a special limited edition of Takashi Murakami's SUPERFLATMUSEUM. Inside the box are a hand-painted figurine based on the artist's original sculpture; two pieces of chewing gum; a certificate of authenticity; and a brochure describing the figurine. In this Convenience Store edition, the shokugan, or 'snack-toy,' is based on Murakami's first life-size bishojo (beautiful girl), Miss ko2. The purpose of this shokugan series is to make miniature versions of Murakami's work widely available to the public at a reasonable price, which is consistent with the artist's belief that art should be made more accessible.

Name:
Takashi Murakami's
SUPERFLATMUSEUM:
Convenience Store Edition "Miss ko2"

Figurative Planning and Production by:
Takashi Murakami, Kaiyodo Co., Ltd.,
Kaikai Kiki Co., Ltd.

Released by & Distributed by:
TAKARA Co., Ltd.
Dreams Come True, Co., Ltd.

Juice x Tamagotchis

Don't count your tamagotchis before they hatch. Juice tamagotchis are delivered two-by-two straight from the egg carton, safely nestled in a finely finished wooden box, complete with sliding door to insure privacy. Grade A security for the young'uns.

name:
Juice x Tamagotchis
designer:
Juice
client:
Juice & Bandai

Fly Me To The Moon

In 2002, NASA collaborated with Dragon Model to produce a series of 12" action figures, saluting the first man to land on the moon. A black colour limited edition was designed by Eric Kot using his own body to model the figure. A limited edition of 100 were available worldwide. An even more rare edition produced by Eric Kot, with only 50 boxes produced, included a T-shirt of" Fly Me To The Moon" produced by A Bathing Ape.

name:
Fly Me to The Moon
designer:
Double X WorkShop
client:
Dragon Model

Edison Chen "PAL" CD Album + "the Wonder Ed" Figure

Japanese Illustrator Katsura Moshino was invited to create Edison portraits and illustrate backgrounds to match Edison's CD album "Peace and Love". An Edison figure, "the Wonder Ed", was thus produced based on Katsura's design with his illustrations of bombs and blasting images on the box to contrast with the peace and love theme.

name:
Edison Chen "PAL" CD Album + "the Wonder Ed" Figure
designer:
Communion W
client:
Edison Chen - EEG Music

KAWS BENDY

This package was designed by KAWS, and manufactured by MEDICOM TOY. The PC case with embossed KAWS' unique characters was prepared in six colours, and assigned according to the color of figure inside. The package itself immediately makes its majestic presence felt.
© KAWS..04

name:
KAWS BENDY
licenser:
KAWS
produced by:
MEDICOM TOY

Rez
Ladies and Gentlemen, open your senses.
Go to Synaesthesia.
You can transform the world into your original Sounds, Lights and Vibrations just by locking and shooting the enemies.
You will discover the brand new time full of rhythm as well as ecstasy
The instinct "Rez" is now finally being released.
Can you really tear yourself from the sense of trance?
Contents
Rez / Trance vibrator / Vibration headphone
Eye drops / T-shirt / Wristband / Sticker
TAPEX
Vibration headphone
Ladies and Gentlemen, open your senses.
Go to Synaesthesia.
Rez

This sturdy cardboard box contains a PlayStation2 game, headphones and T-shirt, to be opened in that order. Printed in two colours and branded with an unmistakable logo, it reflects the straightforward nature of the products while suggesting the experiential possibilities of their combined use through sensory, synaesthetic copy: "Can you really tear yourself from the sense of trance?"

REZ Limited edition

085

name:
REZ Limited edition
designer:
Tsuyoshi Kusano
client:
United Game Artists

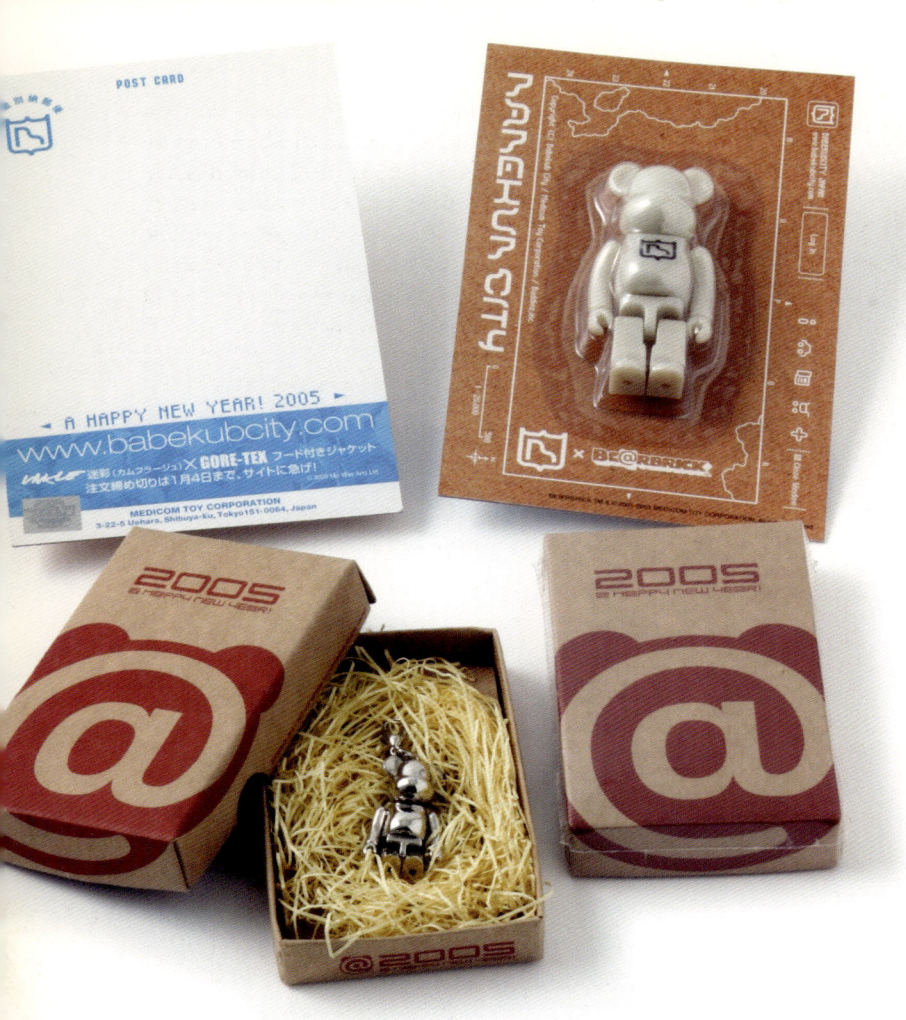

(Top) - This was mailed to members of BABEKUB CITY as a New Year's card for 2005. A BE@RBRICK in a blister pack was directly attached to the postcard. It delivered the first delight of the year to its recipients.

(Bottom) - Mailed to clients and business connections as MEDICOM TOY's New Year's card for 2005. The package with BE@RBRICK logo contains a 50% scaled BE@RBRICK key-chain inside, and was mailed as shown. Those who received the box were pleasantly surprised by the gift as the exterior of the package displayed no indication of contents.

BE@RBRICK TM & © 2001-2005 MEDICOM TOY CORPORATION. All rights reserved.

BABEKUB CITY x BE@RBRICK New Year's Card (Top)

BE@RBRICK New Year's Card (Bottom)

name:
BABEKUB CITY X BE@RBRICK New Year's Card/
BE@RBRICK New Year's Card
licenser:
MEDICOM TOY
produced by:
MEDICOM TOY

The Package was printed with FUTURA's paint which was previously prepared for an UNKLE record jacket. Along with 25 KUBRICKs that are designed based on characters from the FUTURA MAGNET FONT, the whole package gives a feeling of a limited edition music album.

©2004 Mo Wax Arts Ltd
KUBRICK TM & © 2000-2004 MEDICOM TOY CORPORATION. All rights reserved.

Name:
Never, Never Land/25 Piece
designer:
James Lavelle, Ben Drury & Kazuki based on drawings by Futura 2000
Client:
Mo'Wax Arts
Licenser:
Unkle/MEDICOM TOY
Produced by:
MEDICOM TOY

Never, Never Land/25 Piece

Unkle Pyramid Set

JAMES(UNKLE)'s idea of making a triangle package had been realised by Skate-Thing's design. When you open these triple layered triangle flaps, you will find KUBRICK and die-cut picture single record are placed neatly in a blister tray.

name:
Unkle Pyramid Set
Designer:
Skate Shin
Client:
Mo'Wax Arts
licenser:
Unkle/MEDICOM TOY
produced by:
MEDICOM TOY

LICENSED FROM UNKLE ENTERTAINMENT
KUBRICK TM & © 2000 - 2003 MEDICOM TOY CORPORATION. All rights reserved.

BE@RBRICK TOKIO

This package was designed by Taichi Kokubun (Keyboardist of TOKIO), and manufactured by MEDICOM TOY. Its motif is a bus which is a fundamental element for a traveling band. The case is transparent so that the figures can be displayed as packaged. With a driver sitting in the driver's seat and moving-part wheels, the package doubles as a vehicle.

© 2004 M. Co.
BE@RBRICK TM & © 2001 - 2004 MEDICOM TOY CORPORATION. All rights reserved.

name:
BE@RBRICK TOKIO
licenser:
M.Co./MEDICOM TOY
produced by:
MEDICOM TOY

BE@RBRICK Series 1 to 9

Uniformly designed blind individual boxes contain a variety of BE@RBRICKs and trading cards, which the customer can enjoy collecting in a luck-of-the-draw style. The display box is designed so retail shops can place it on their shelves as is. The style has been unchanged from series one to nine, and continues to attract fans from all over the world.

name:
BE@RBRICK Series 1 to 9
licenser :
MEDICOM TOY
produced by :
MEDICOM TOY

BE@RBRICK TM & © 2001-2004 MEDICOM TOY CORPORATION. All rights reserved.

BE@RBRICK NIKE BE@RFORCE 1

This project was based on the 20th anniversary of the Nike AIRFORCE ONE shoe. It was created paying homage by designing a lace up box to represent the actual shoe, with very simple graphic elements taken from the AIRFORCE ONE, put together in a modern way. MEDICOM TOY developed the design and made it work. Even the laces were printed and designed to be a collectible piece. The collaboration project with MEDICOM TOY was certainly a new area and a great medium to celebrate NIKE design.

name:
BE@RBRICK NIKE BE@RFORCE 1
licenser:
NIKE/MEDICOM TOY
produced by:
MEDICOM TOY

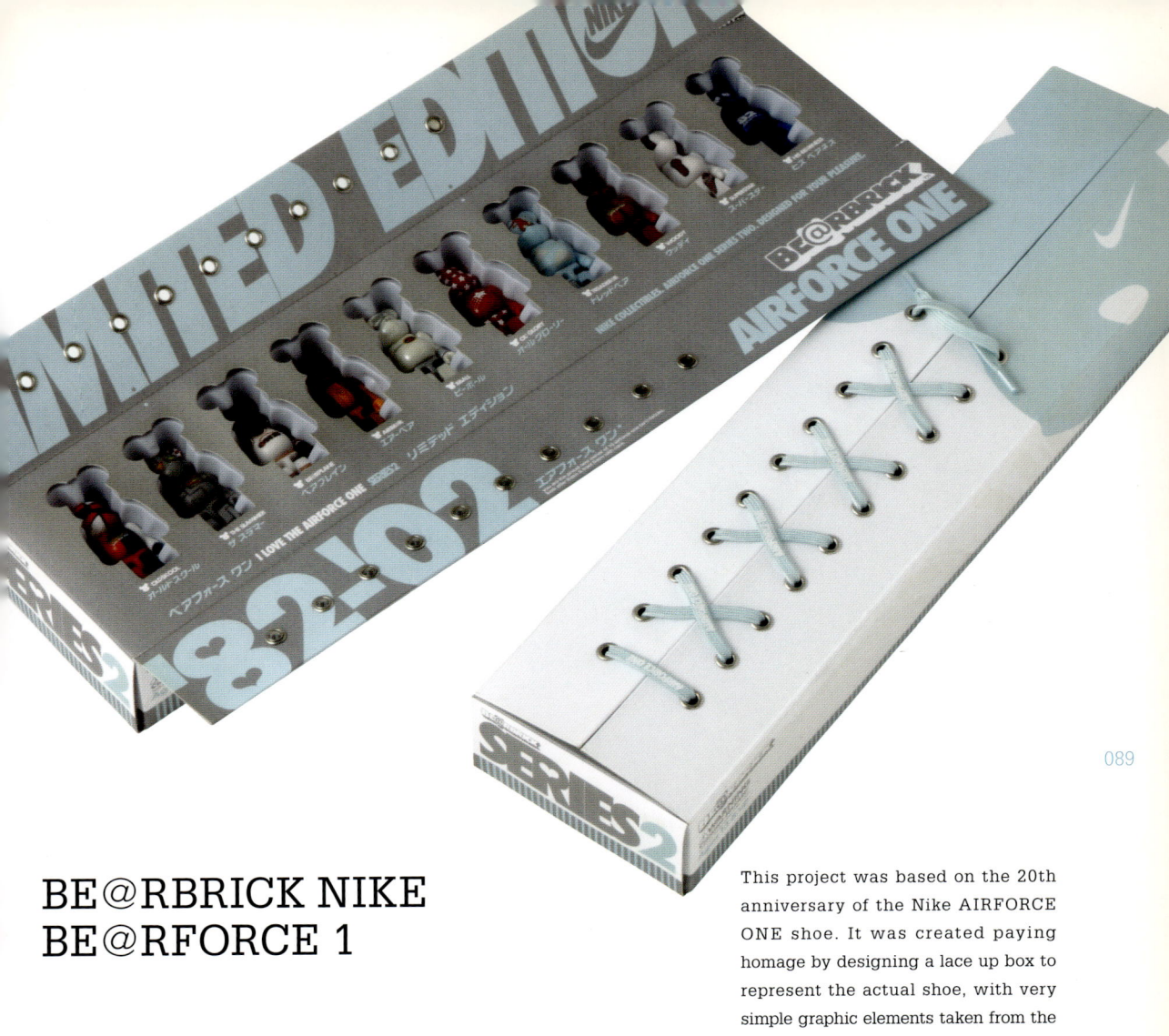

NIKE, the Swoosh Design, the composite NIKE AIR & Swoosh Design and AIR FORCE 1 are trademarks of NIKE, Inc.
BE@RBRICK TM & © 2001-2002 MEDICOM TOY CORPORATION. All rights reserved.

Kinnikuman Generations

This year marks the famous anime character Kinnikuman's 25th anniversary. Kinnikumann is hatched from an egg, along with a comic strip ribbon. Compactly interlocked inside the box, the figurines spring into individual positions as soon as they escape.

name:
Kinnikuman - Generations
clients:
© 2004 Sony Computer Entertainment Inc, All Rights Reserved./ © 2002 Yudetamago/Shueisha, Toei Animation Co., Ltd.

Happy Water DVD

The Happy Water DVD box set contains not only a complete wakeboarding lesson taught the Chinese way on DVD, but also a useful fashion accessory for strutting your stuff on the beach – a white and orange HiMo Dudes T-shirt, just to remind the surfers where you're from.

name:
Happy Water DVD
designer:
Junkie Design
clients:
HiMo Dudes productions

MISSING LINK (Left) & BUNYIP (Right)

name:
PAMTOY/MEDICOM
MISSING LINK (Left) & BUNYIP (Right)
designer:
P.A.M.
clients:
PAMTOY/MEDICOM TOYS

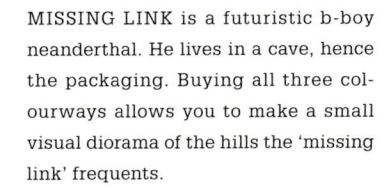

MISSING LINK is a futuristic b-boy neanderthal. He lives in a cave, hence the packaging. Buying all three colourways allows you to make a small visual diorama of the hills the 'missing link' frequents.

BUNYIP is a fictional Australian creature, apparently living in billabongs. The packaging represents his home and environment. He prefers the surrounding areas of Uluhru, or Ayers Rock.

KITTY EX.
30 YEARS OF HELLO KITTY
ANNIVERSARY EXHIBITION
NAKAYOKU PROJECT 2004-2005
ARTISTS: KATSUHIKO HIBINO KASHIWA SATO+ICHIRO TANIDA TAKU TADA NAGI NODA NAOHIRO UKAWA HIROKO SHIMIZU TETSUYA NAKAMURA HAJIME TACHIBANA KAZUNARI HATTORI GROOVISIONS TYG _ S TYG _ M SUNDAY-VISION KENTARO KOBUKE KATSUKI TANAKA KEIJI ITO TSUWAKI ED
SEKI YURIO HIROSHI FUJIWARA OSAMU TEZUKA TADASHI MOCHIZU
+MASAFUMI SANAI+KYOKO KOIZUMI FUKUMIMI+MATALLY
KUROSAKI ALFREDO MARTINEZ AS FOUR BOB PARTINGTON
DEGRAW DAN COLEN DAVID ELLIS DAVID KOMUREK DONALD BAECHL
JEAN CHARLES DE CASTELBAJAC JEFF BURTON JENNIFER HERRE
JEREMIAH CLANCY&ALEXIA STAMATIOU JEREMY SCOTT JESS HOLZWOR
BRANDS&SHOPS: LOREE RODKIN LUCIEN PELLAT-FINET
EX.
OFF

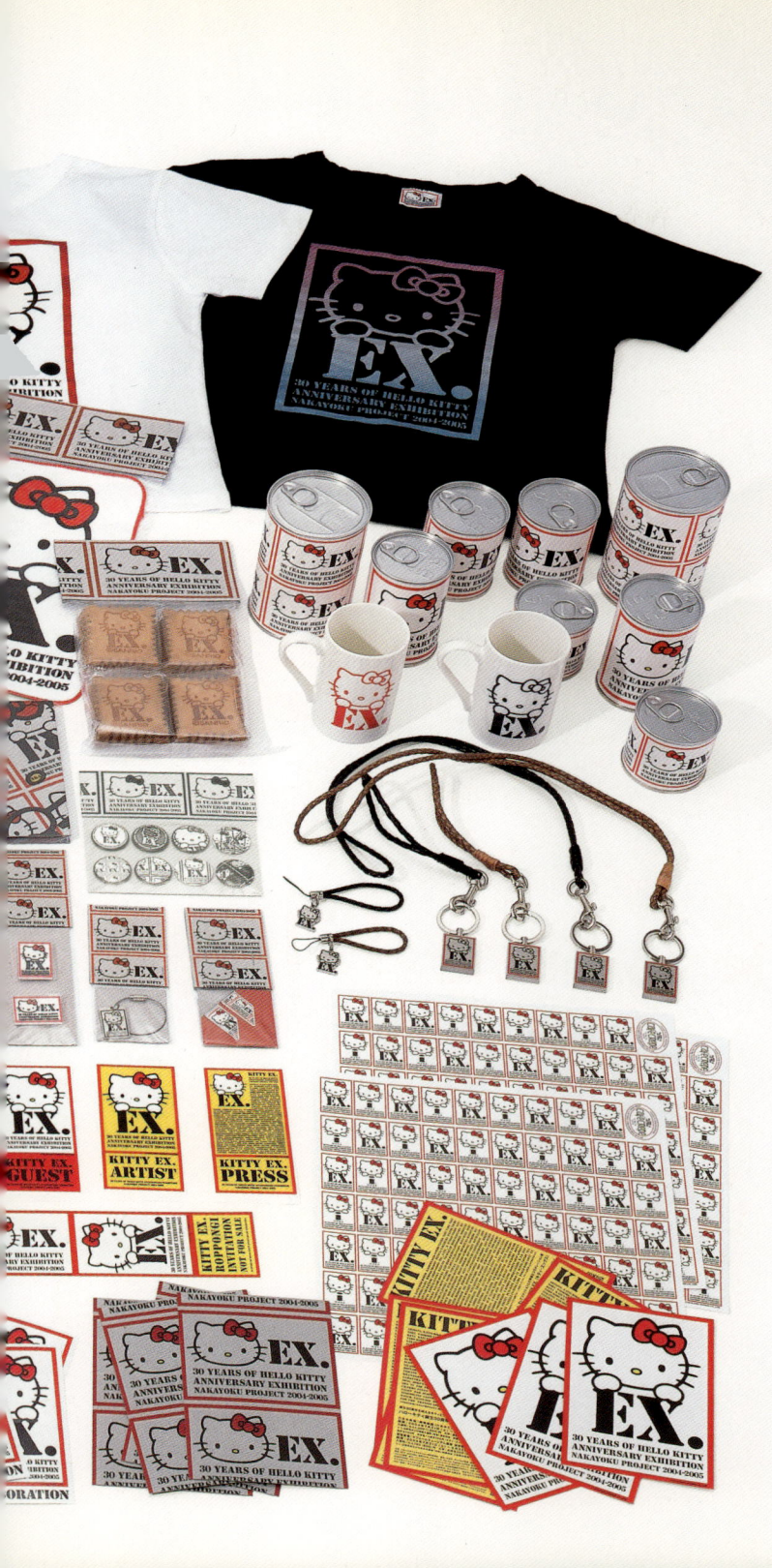

KITTY EX. was an exhibition for Hello KITTY's 30th anniversary commemoration, in which artists from around the world contributed new expressions of Hello Kitty. To reflect this concept in the museum souvenirs, various practical and adult-friendly items for home and leisure such as tote bags, T-shirts and mugs were created, all bearing the immediately recognisable KITTY EX. logo.

KITTY EX. MUSEUM GOODS

name:
KITTY EX.
designed by:
KASHIWA SATO
client:
SANRIO CO., LTD.
©1976, 2004 SANRIO CO., LTD/
KASHIWA SATO

Purpose of Packaging

Pushing the possibilities of form and function

Daniel Mason

Packaging has many purposes. These purposes have been derived through its historical development. In the past we had no need to house the items we produced. It was only when a surplus of the food stuffs we grew, or other products we produced, needed transporting to market, that some kind of receptacle was needed to put them in. When we realised that others had produced a surplus, we had to differentiate what we had produced compared to others, so we put our name on it. Even then that wasn't enough, so we started applying descriptions to the packaging. And so history took its course and printing methods took over, along with the development of materials to create the packaging form.

Currently, packaging has to perform a number of purposes. Some of these purposes derive from its origins, others are a direct result of the demands of human-kind's need for innovation.

Packaging has to be dependable, an important aspect in areas such as food packaging. But dependability should be regarded as a flame to be extinguished if new ideas are to be explored.

Packaging has to be functional. Convenience products, in particular, utilise built-in devices to make them work, like the ring-pull mechanism on a soft drink can. Without functionalism packaging is redundant; however, there are a myriad of opportunities for packaging to subvert widely held precedents in a bid to create something new. There is every possibility that the norms of packaging from one area can be subverted and used in another with dramatic results. It's all about knowledge and a willingness to be open to new ideas. Functionalism is where protection is an important component. Protection is needed for storage and transit, the ability for products to be stacked neatly in multiples and not fall over in-store. Maybe this is the area that needs exposing and where decoration should be applied.

Packaging has to be immediate. The relationship with the purchaser must be immediate and a bond has to be created in a split second. Where a buyer is in two minds about spending money, the packaging may be the one moment where the choice is swayed in its favour.

Packaging has to be informative. Whilst advertising and marketing are key to any new or existing product, it is only packaging that creates the final interface with the outside world. Instructions which are sometimes a necessary component, have always proved a stumbling block to the realisation of a packaging idea. How do you include so much information without compromising the idea? How do you print this information to maximise its effect and potentially add to the overall aesthetic? In this instance, perhaps the manipulation of this information is the key component to the packaging, at the expense of everything else.

Packaging has to be recognisable. Nowadays a great deal of time, money and effort is invested into product development through its advertising, marketing and distribution. It has to have an immediate effect on the consumer to secure a purchase. It should also remain in the purchaser's memory if a sale is not happening immediately. Its recognisability can be maximised through graphics, shape, material and construction. A combination of these may create a desire for something they may have never wanted before. It may also re-introduce them to a product that has not been consumed for a long time.

Packaging has to be textural. Budget permitting, this is the one aspect where the use of materials, print process and construction can be used to augment the design. This area provides the greatest enjoyment for client, designer, retailer and customer alike. In this area a number of the senses can be stimulated. Decoration is a term that is used in this area, but decoration can be physical in its use of blocking or embossing. A logo or decoration can be metaphorical in that it is being used to mask or hide the true nature of the product. Decoration can be used to augment an essentially valueless and redundant product. The term 'added value' is employed at this point. This implies that there was no value in the first place and that the consumer is being sold a lie.

In conclusion, packaging is a multi-faceted component of the created world we live in. We could just as well live without it, but it has the ability to clad our existence and offer support to our desires. It gives beauty to the ordinary and feeds our desire for new and existing objects. Whilst it is inanimate, it is imbued with a number of human characteristics. For the designer it provides exciting possibilities for experimentation, not only in material, print process and construction, but also in allowing its creator the chance to cheat the consumers to buy or lull them into a false sense of security that the choice they have made is the right one.

Chapter 2

Things We Need

**Bottles/Sweets/Clothes/
Cosmetics/Cigarettes**

This chapter introduces essential goods for daily use such as bottles, sweets, clothes, cosmetics and cigarettes. The dominating feature of these packages is not only sophistication but also flexibility to merge into our daily lives. Moreover, many of them have a shapely appearance which reflects the inside of the product.

/arc-en-ciel
HIP
HOLISPA
holi-gloss
ONCTION CORPS
allège, tonifie, stimule le désir
BODY UNCTION
to lighten, tone up and sex appeal

/arc-en-ciel
HIP
HOLISPA
holi-gloss
ONCTION CORPS
hydrate, illumine, anti-age
BODY UNCTION
to moisturise and enhance, anti-aging

/arc-en-ciel
HIP
HOLISPA
holi-gloss
ONCTION CORPS
purifie, apaise, astringent
BODY UNCTION
to purify and soothe, astringent

/arc-en-ciel
HIP
HOLISPA
holi-gloss
ONCTION CORPS
hydrate, rafraîchit
BODY UNCTION
to moisturise, refresh

HIP's new line of beauty and hair products is natural and holistic. The outside container is translucent, allowing the contents and colours to be easily viewed, and bright colours silk-screened onto the outside call attention to the airless inside pocket. The container is packaged inside a starch foam outer box, which is entirely soluble in water and is certified non-transgenic. Within the container is an internal pocket, which protects the product in a vacuum seal. Placing the product inside the pocket, inside the container, demonstrates the preciousness and naturalness of the product as a whole.

HIP Bottles and Packaging

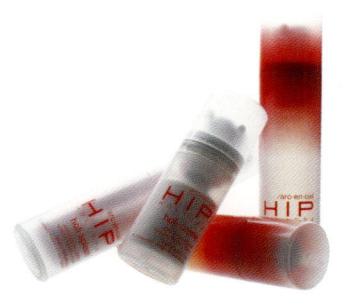

name:
HIP Bottles and Packaging
designer:
fuseproject
client:
HIP

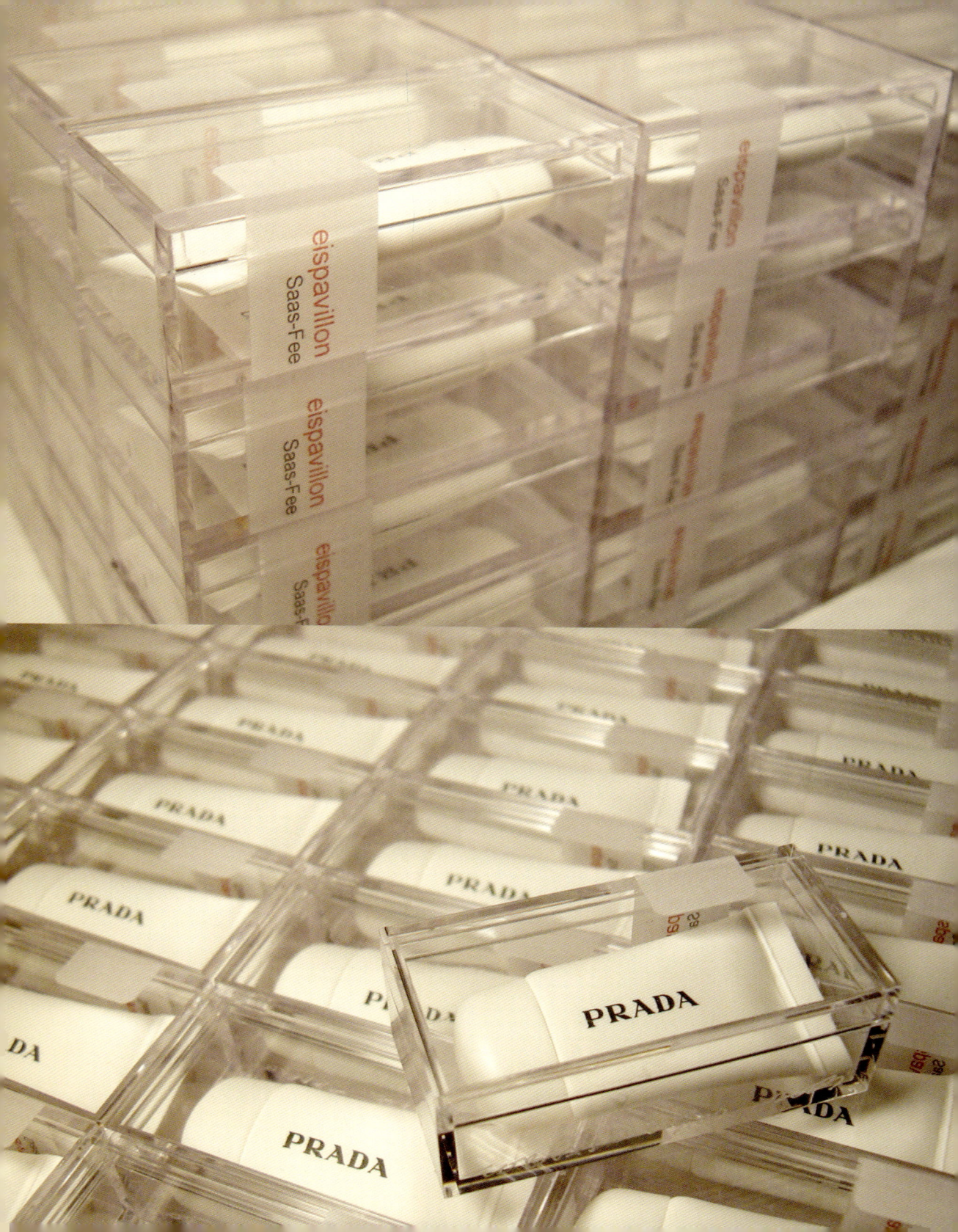

eispavillon Saas-Fee

PRADA

Tobias Wong of New York has designed custom enclosed cases of Prada lip balm. The product is already an indulgent, one-time use luxury, but Wong takes it one step further by enclosing it inside a clear plastic capsule that emphasises the organisation of the Swiss lifestyle. To be used, the seal of the artist must be broken. The object becomes suspended in the choice of the recipient – is it a necessity, a luxury, an art object or all three?

Pradada, 2003

name:
Pradada, 2003
curated by:
Rachel K. Ward and Eveline Notter.
designer:
Tobias Wong
photography:
Jose Lau
client:
Eispavillon Exhibition – Sassfee, Switzerland.

Philou Shampoo and Conditioner Bottles

These shampoo and conditioner bottles are designed to exude a sense of nascent purity and sensuality of preteens. The simple silhouette of the fluidly transformed egg emotionally resonates with teens and adults alike, capped with a budding nipple.

name:
Philou Shampoo and Conditioner Bottles
designer:
fuseproject
client:
Philou

Anna Sui Cosmetics

Anna Sui's cosmetics range reprises the dark floral theme of her mirror-on-the-wall frame. The boxes are patterned with deep faded hues of red, purple and yellow rose blossoms and soft petals against a foundation of solid ebony. Long, slender and sultry characterise the dramatic forms of elegant handles, containers and covers – sometimes budding, always brooding.

name:
Anni Sui Cosmetics
brand:
Anna Sui
company:
Cosmoplitan Cosmetics China Ltd.

Anna Sui Fragrances:
(Left to Right) Sui Dreams/Dolly Girl/Anna Sui/Sui Love

Anna Sui's line of perfume bottles employs four distinctive shapes and colours to suggest the essential elements of a dolly girl's lifestyle: a liquid blue round purse, a pink heart-shaped head and neck, a long black framed mirror and a candy orange butterfly.

name:
Anna Sui Collection (left to right): Sui Dreams/Dolly Girl/Anna Sui/Sui Love
brand:
Anna Sui
company:
Cosmopolitan Cosmetics China Ltd.

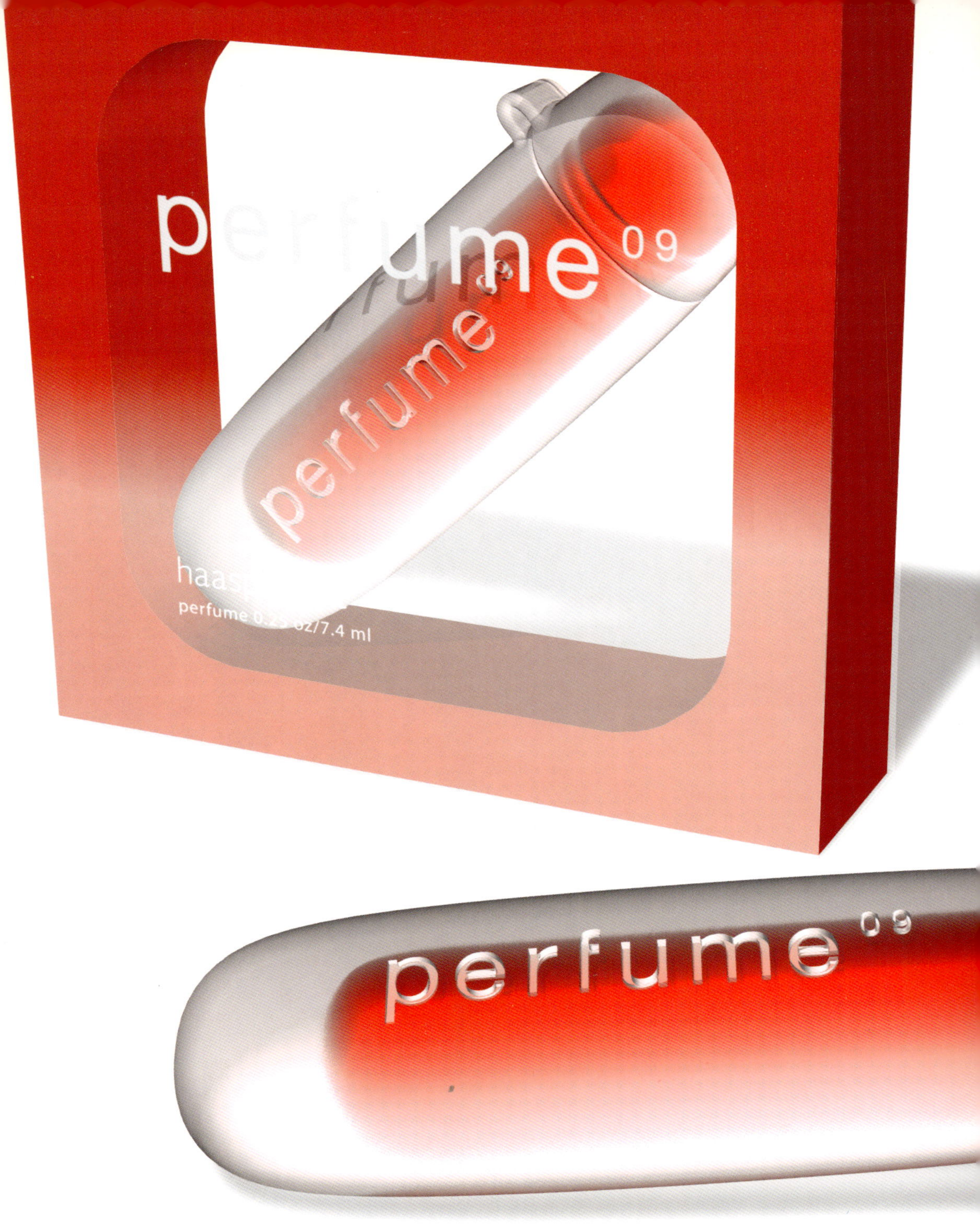
perfume 09
perfume
perfume 09

Perfume09 builds on spacescent's fusion of modern life with the tradition of perfume, and goes one step further to address the modern need for a durable travel version. A soft clear rubber body encases the small red perfume vial, making the container more portable and resistant to shock and falls, elegantly addressing the hazards of modern travel.

Perfume09

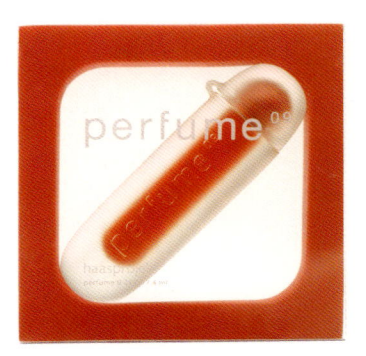

name:
Perfume09
designer:
fuseproject
client:
haasprojekt

Yuskin
Bruna Skin Care Series

The character Miffy is the motif of this skin care series for babies and children, designed to be attractive skin care items for parents as well as their kids. The design represents Bruna's interpretation of the world.

name:
Yuskin Bruna Skin Care Series
designer:
Kashiwa Sato
client:
Yuskin Pharmaceutical Co., Ltd

Purebase Soap

Purebase Soap is a vegetable soap made of pure rapeseed. It is designed to present the product in a new light, by focusing not only on its substance, but also on the enjoyment of its use. The simple original typography organises the series through the use of colour, designed for integration in future products.

name:
Purebase Soap
designer:
Naoki Sato + Yuu Sato (ASYL DESIGN)
client:
Miyoshi Soap Corporation

high
performance
balancing
cleansing oil
enriched
SHU UEMURA SKIN PURIF
art work by ai yamaguchi

high
performance
balancing
cleansing oil
light
SHU UEMURA SKIN PURIFIER
art work by ai yamaguchi

Shu Uemura's Cleansing Oil
(Limited Edition)

Transparent pump bottles tinted by the colour of the liquid they contain are decorated by artist Ai Yamaguchi. Her young, partially-clad girls with long hair and large eyes, each posing against a vivid, delicately contoured background, radiate an intense expression, blending manga subculture with the planar, highly decorative traditional Japanese art of ukiyoe. The characters have an aura of eroticism about them, evoked by their pure hearts and immature bodies.

name:
Shu Uemura Cleansing Oil
(Limited Edition)
artist:
Ai Yamaguchi
client:
Shu Uemura

U*MO PIG MUG

U*MO adds a little humour to your everyday life. To present the concept of low cost but good functional design, the package includes an instruction sticker on an ordinary cardboard box which shows how to use the mug. The boxes are designed so that a pattern forms when two boxes are placed beside each other.

name:
U*MO PIG MUG
art director:
Kenjiro Sano
designer:
Kenjiro Sano, Yuki Sugiyama
photographer:
Tetsuya Morimoto
client:
BALS/FRANCFRANC

Cobella Professional Haircare

Design cues were taken from fashion, fragrance and cosmetics. Instead of complex colour-coding usually associated with shampoos and conditioners, simplicity was opted for – black text and lids, and clear plastic substrates, with the product reminiscent of cosmetic products in pink skin tones. The Avant Garde typeface made use of the alternative characters to add an individual and sophisticated feel. A foil silver ring hints at the luxury pampering element of the product.

name:
Cobella Professional Haircare
designer:
Ben Stott, Nick Finney & Alan Dye
client:
Boots the Chemist & Cobella

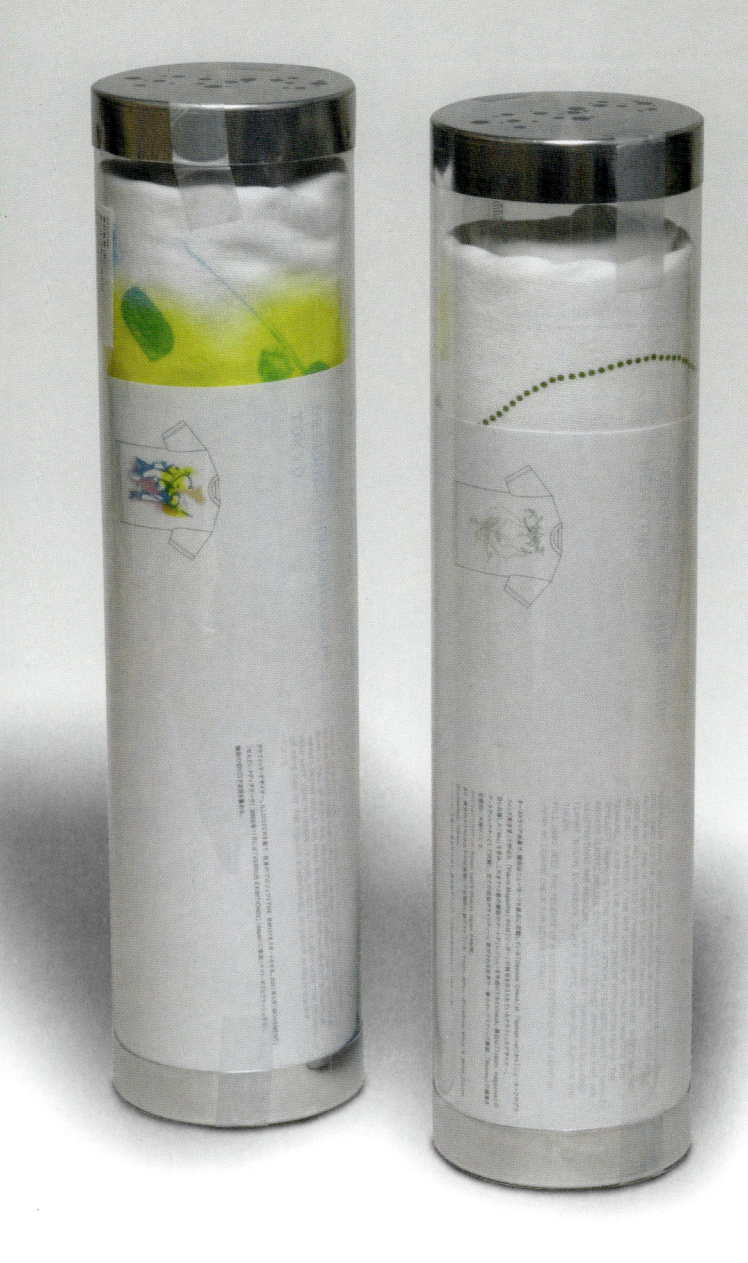

GAS Shirt

Anti-gravity is the concept of this package constructed using magnets. The packaging, fixtures and fittings, and shop space were considered as a unit for this project, which is used as a communication tool. Customers should feel they are taking a part of the store away with them.

name:
GAS Shirt
designer:
Myeong-hee Lee
client:
GAS As Interface CO., LTD.

DEVO
Underwear Packaging

In the store, each package communicates information about the product inside by taking the shape of the contents. The tank-top packages are shaped like tank tops and the boxer short packages look like boxer shorts. The outer wrapper is made entirely of corn based starch material, which dissolves quickly and completely in water. After you've made your purchase, just drop the entire package into the washer as a small amount of detergent is added to the cornstarch mix. When it's done, the underwear will be clean, and the package will be gone – perfectly efficient from beginning to end.

name:
DEVO Underwear Packaging
designer:
fuseproject
client:
DEVO

RMC Jeans Packaging

Martin Ksohoh, RMC's principal leader and designer, not only focused on their jeans product and exquisite quality, he also insisted on high quality and control in packaging. All of RMC's high quality jeans line would have to be packed in a wooden box for protection. For special individual designs, a cloth bag was added for further protection to help the owner collect and manage their cherished jeans.

name:
RMC Jeans Packaging
designer:
Martin Ksohoh
client:
RMC (Red Monkey Company)

© 2005 ISSEY MIYAKE INC.
Graphic Design - Takeshi Fukui

Issey Miyake knows there's more than one way to package a T-shirt. Chiho Aoshima and Aya Takano have designed pink and blue boxes silhouetting the detailed illustrations on the white fabric inside. On the plastic front, the splashy beach ball bag bubbles the cotton tee into a transparent, waterproof pillow.

Chiho Aoshima & Aya Takano T-shirt Box Beach Ball Packaged T-shirt
(Opposite Page)

name:
Chiho Aoshima & Aya Takano
T-shirt Box
Beach Ball Packaged T-shirt
designer:
Takeshi Fukui
client:
ISSEY MIYAKE INC

ISSEY MIYAKE BY NAOKI TAKIZAWA ROPPONGI-HILLS
© 2003 ISSEY MIYAKE INC. Chiho Aoshima / Kaikai Kiki.

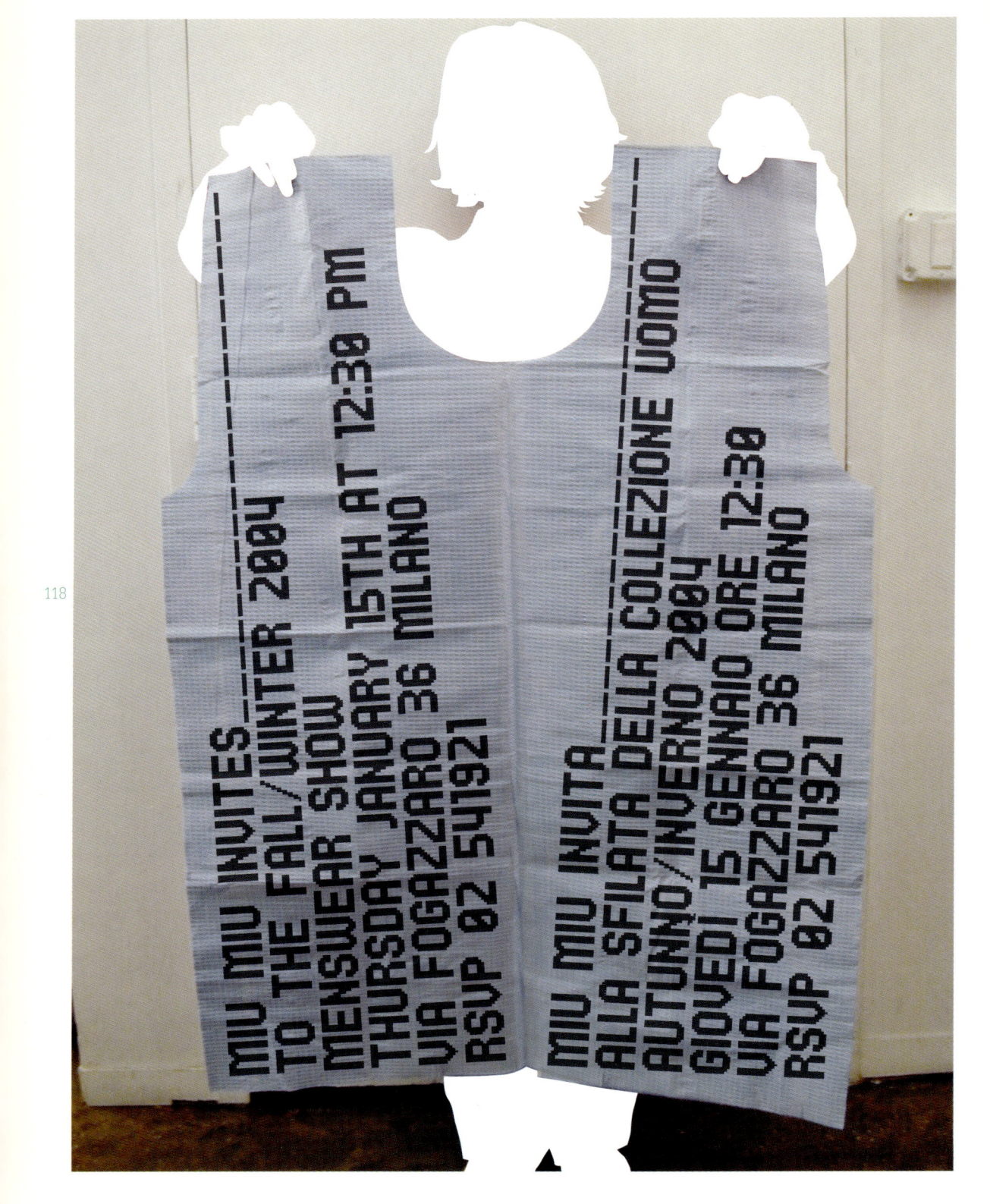

MIU MIU INVITES
TO THE FALL/WINTER 2004
MENSWEAR SHOW
THURSDAY JANUARY 15TH AT 12:30 PM
VIA FOGAZZARO 36 MILANO
RSVP 02 541921

MIU MIU INVITA
ALLA SFILATA DELLA COLLEZIONE UOMO
AUTUNNO/INVERNO 2004
GIOVEDI 15 GENNAIO ORE 12:30
VIA FOGAZZARO 36 MILANO
RSVP 02 541921

Miu Miu Menswear
Fall/Winter 2003 Invite

Miu Miu's fashion show invitation comes wrapped around the metal frame of a common coat hanger, formally introducing the nature of the event. Once unwrapped from the hanger, the cloth becomes a giant calling card on which is clearly printed the event name, time and venue. The 'garment' then fully unfolds and opens up into a larger-than-life-size singlet displaying bilingual information.

name:
Miu Miu Menswear
Fall/Winter 2003 Invite
creative director:
Michael Rock
art director:
Anisa Suthayalai
designer:
Anisa Suthayalai
client:
Prada Milano

120

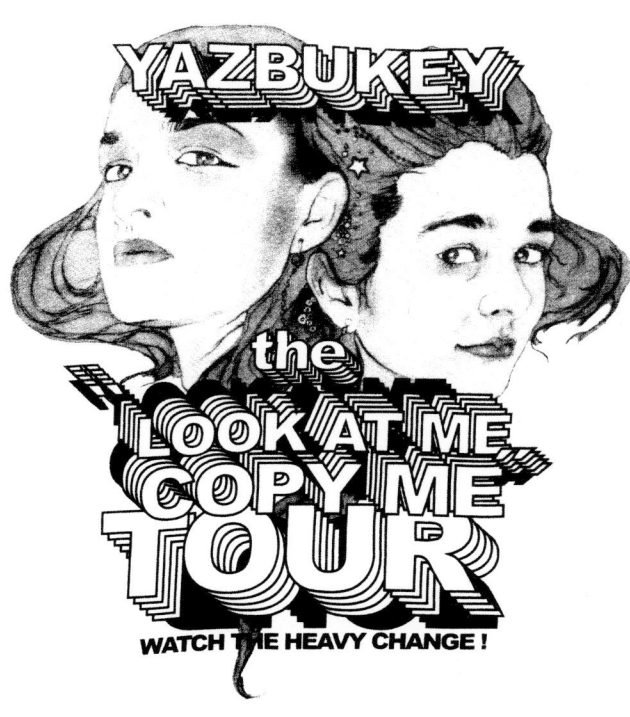

This 10-page portfolio exhibits a different T-shirt on each plastic page, displaying 10 unique designs by 10 different artists. All the T-shirts are white; all the artists had carte blanche to design their own frontal statement. The book is an example of artwork on a commercial product repackaged as an art object that's wearable, washable and framable. A T-shirt collector's delight, where one size fits all.

Surface to Air vs D-Mop T-Shirt Book

Top: Art by Cédric Rivrain & EEM for Yazbukey
Bottom: Art by Naohiro Ukawa

name:
Surface to Air vs D-Mop T-Shirt Book
designer:
Surface to Air
client:
D-Mop

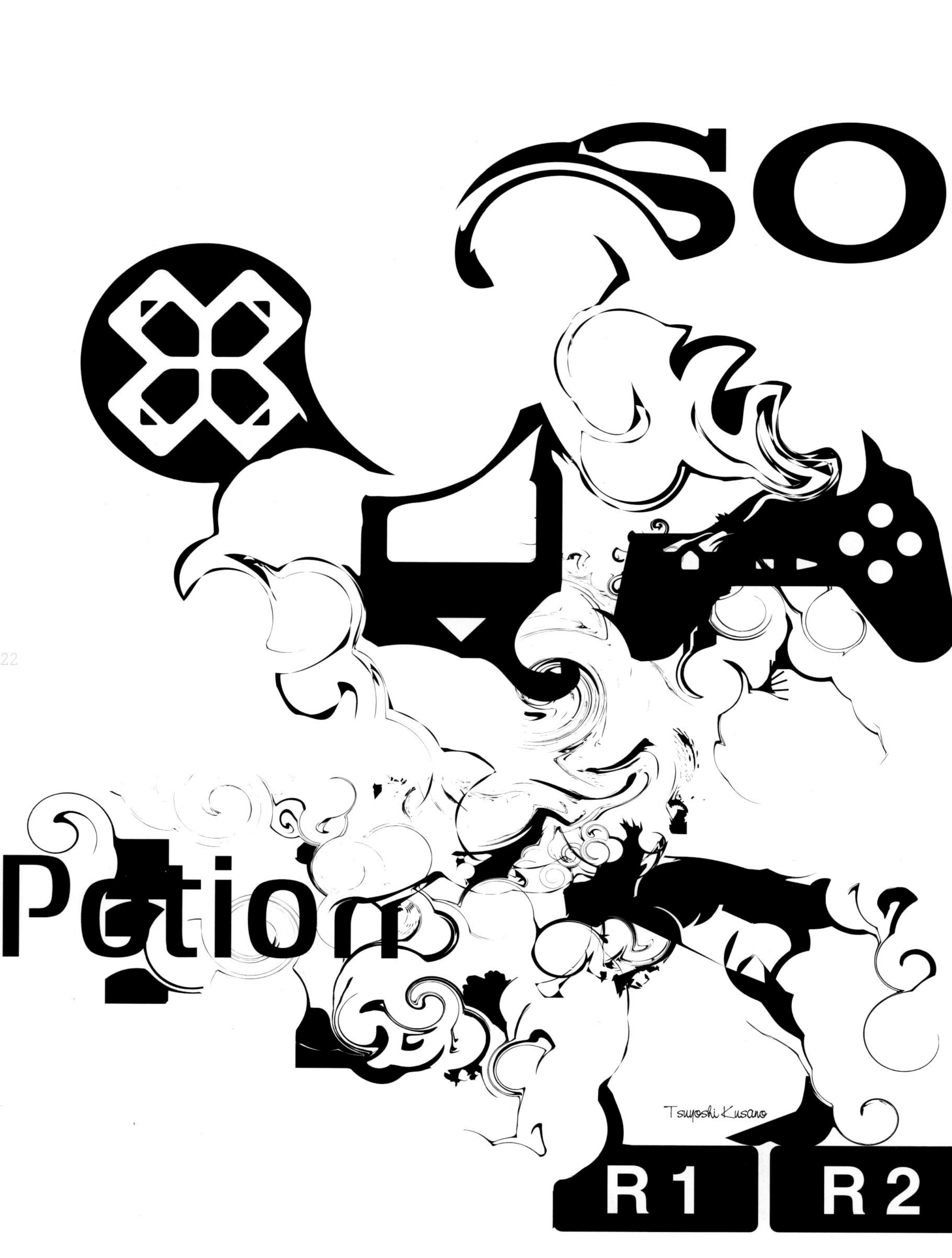
SO
Tsuyoshi Kusano
R1
R2

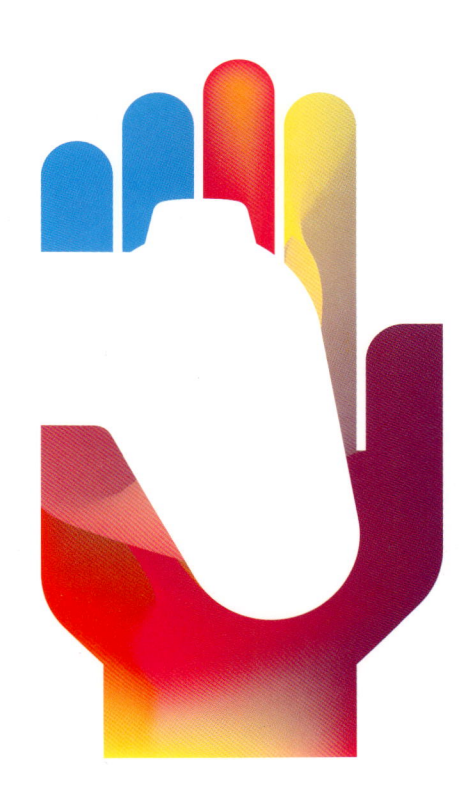

Five distinct T-shirts designs were created to celebrate Play Station's 10th anniversary in Hong Kong, but they were packaged with a poster in the same black and white plastic pouch. Sealed shut by a ziploc at the top, the white bag features a black ink-blotted collage of the five different illustrations by Tsuyoshi Kusano.

PlayStation 10th Anniversary T-Shirt Package

name:
PlayStation 10th Anniversary T-Shirt Package
designer:
AllRightsReserved
illustartor:
Tsuyoshi Kusano
client:
© 2004 Sony Computer Entertainment Inc, All Rights Reserved.

evirob KIT PK

Like a silver-plated pizza box, the special edition evirob kit opens up like a treasure chest of grey-maroon goodies, from sporting wristband, to fashionable tee and pin, plus the obligatory evirob Kubrick symbolising "the essence of weird life", courtesy of DEVILROBOTS.

name:
evirob KIT PK
designer:
DEVILROBOTS
client:
Medicom Toy & Intel

TyGun BOX

TyGun BOX is a T-shirt product concept created for sale in vending machines. The box shows a sticker of the character on the T-shirt inside. This clean design features a printed specification column showing size and colour. A type of cardboard was selected for the box material which is normally used as a backing paper. Gold and silver foil blocking was used, and a mismatch printing method highlighted the originality of the concept.

name:
TyGun BOX
designer:
Tycoon Graphics
client:
B's INTERNATIONAL

GRV1982

Believe it or not, the design cooperative Groovisions owns the Japanese copyright to the word " copyright". So it was only fitting that they boast their trademark on a T-shirt. Boxed into a typically limited edition numbered cardboard package.

name:
GRV1982
designer:
groovisions

126

adidas 35th Anniverisary Campaign

For adidas' Superstar 35th anniversary, a number of artists were commissioned to design a skin for the famous striped sports shoe. Captain Tsubasa, the character originally drawn by Youichi Takahashi over 20 years ago, lends his anime icon status as Japan's world champion football player to this white leather shoe as part of the Expression series. On the outside, the colour team portrait catches the eye and reflects the golden adidas logo on the heel; on the inside, carefully shaded drawings of the Captain in action flash scenes from the hero's life story. Limited edition of 4,000 pairs.

name:
adidas 35th Anniverisary Campaign
client:
adidas
special thanks:
D-Mop

Nike/Gran Turismo Limited Edition

This suitcased special edition of Playstation's new GT4 game gangs up with Nike to bombast its players with a whole new fashion in gaming experience. Pop out the cartridge and put on the shoes, but be sure to wear the ITOY techonology engineered T-shirt if you want to drive the Nike car featured in the game. For all you boys in black.

name:
GT4 Nike Edition
client:
© 2004 Sony Computer Entertainment Inc, All Rights Reserved.

Nike Brasil
The Rhythm and
Art of Movement

This five-tier shoebox is a small tribute to the great Brazilian sports tradition where Os Gemeos, twin artists Octavio and Gustavo Pandolfo from São Paolo, illustrate the richness and variety of Brazil and its people. Their artwork conveys Ginga, an untranslatable yet crystal clear expression of living in a constant state of dance - the artful, seductive language of movement.

name:
Nike Brasil
The Rhythm and Art of Movement
client:
Nike

Anzen Senshi Condom Series 4 Types

To ease the dull image on sexual protection products, Surprise Co. Ltd bring the joy and fun into condoms by applying the hottest and coolest japanese animations. Now, we are protected from sexual disease and AIDS in colourful anime style.

name:
Anzen Senshi
Condom Series 4 Types
designer:
Peaches Brand
client:
Surprise Co., Ltd.

FH Chocolate Candle

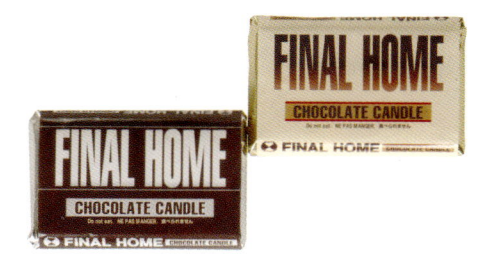

Final Home's chocolate candle challenges the tasteful imitation of wax. Remember the good old-fashioned, all-American Hershey bars? This candle moulded from chocolate was inspired by the story of a person in distress who survived by eating chocolate. Can be used as survival goods or as party goods.

name:
FH Chocolate C andle
designer:
Kosuke Tsumura
client:
FINAL HOME/A-net Inc

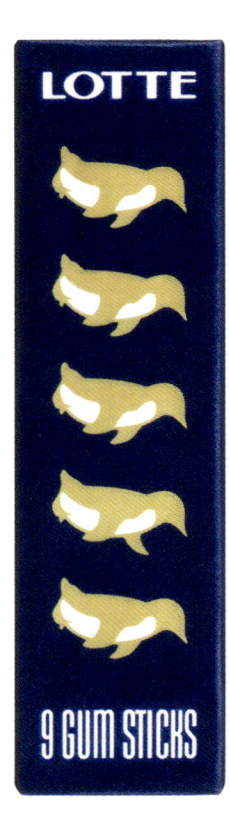

Lotte, Mint Series

Every gum flavour has its mascot, and Lotte's Mint Series of Cool, Green and Blue respectively uses stencil-like penguins, trees and dolphins to mark the difference across each stick.

name:
Lotte, Mint Series
designer:
Taku Satoh
client:
Lotte

Lotte, XYLITOL Series

Each minty flavour of Pink, Fresh or Lime is chromatically highlighted by shiny metallic packaging to distinguish the long sticks of sweets. Sugarless Cool Herb is another shape altogether.

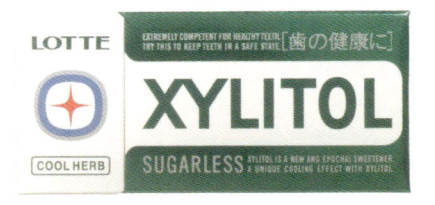

name:
Lotte, XYLITOL Series
designer:
Taku Satoh
client:
Lotte

A box of pre-perforated chocolate plates, each representing a character, to be created by the consumer to express a personal message. Each box comes with instructions and an alphanumeric reference chart along with a special peg to punch out the desired characters. "Chocolates have always been given as gifts to express oneself. Here's an opportunity to take it one personal step further..."

Photographer : Jeff Miller

name:
Six Chocolates, 2004
designer:
Tobias Wong
photographer:
Jeff Miller
client:
The Conduit Group, NYC

Six Chocolates, 2004

37 Degrees

37° is a new company that was created from the need to solve the problem of temperature regulation for newborns. Using smart textiles developed by NASA for use in spacesuits, this beautiful range of clothing works by encapsulating and storing heat from the baby's skin, releasing it only when necessary, thus maintaining the baby's optimum body temperature of 37 degrees celsius.

name:
37°
designer:
Karen Welman
client:
Pearlfisher

Broken Heart Valentine Cookie, 2004

Hopelessly romantic and self explanatory. This type of vacuum seal packaging is nothing aesthetically new in the design world, but what's most important is its function as it holds the broken cookies in place.

name:
Broken Heart Valentine Cookie, 2004
designer:
Tobias Wong
client:
Self work

TOHATO Caramel Corn

Tohato Caramel Corn's packaging was dramatically overhauled after 32 years since it was first released. It is designed to give pleasure to anyone, anywhere, anytime, so the package itself became a character based on Caramel Corn's original red pack. A number of additional characters in various colours were also developed and released with seasonal and flavor changes.

name:
TOHATO Caramel Corn
designer:
Yuki Sugiyama
client:
TOHATO INC.

137

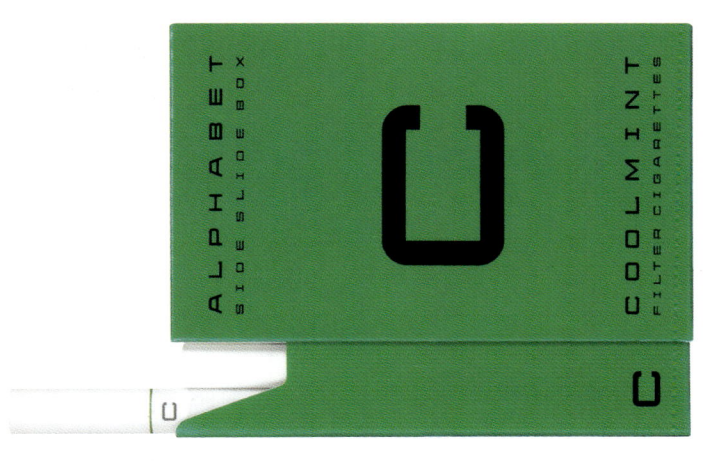

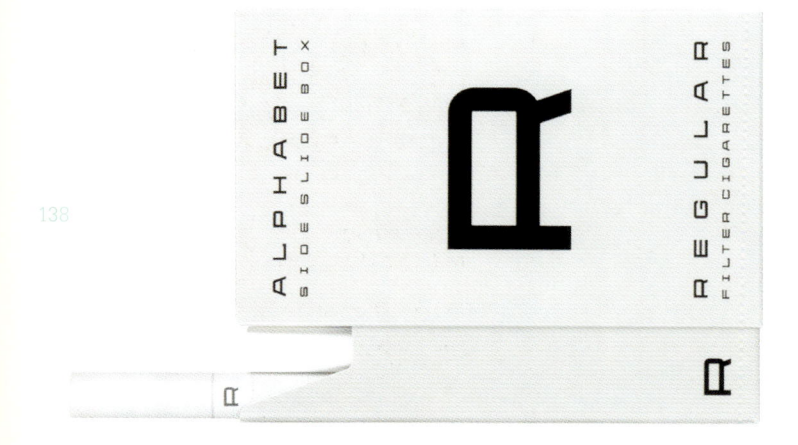

Alphabet H/R/C

ALPHABET H/R/C refocuses the character of the cigarette as a lifestyle choice, with aspirations toward "a new standard" through the box's simple eyechart design and sliding opening.

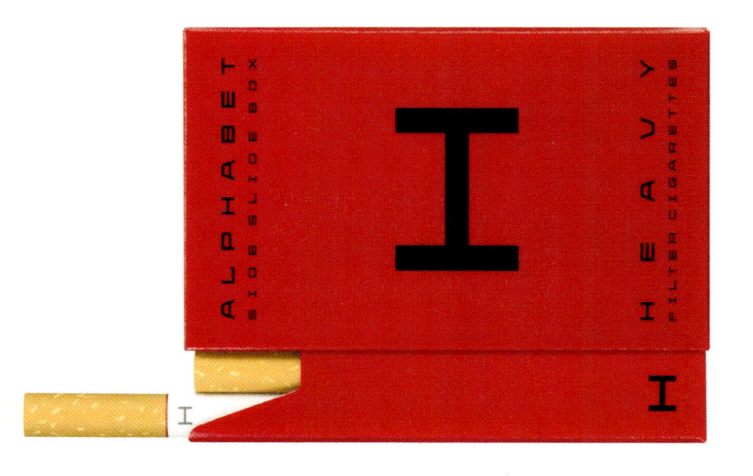

name:
Alphabet H/R/C
designer:
Naoki Sato (ASYL Design)
client:
JT

GOLDEN BAT/
SWEET & MILD,
SWEET & COOL

A sleeping golden bat, suspended from the 'S' of Sweet & Cool and Sweet & Mild cigarette packs weights the sweetness with a gilded mascot. At the stem of each of the branded cigarettes inside, a miniature graphic representing one of various poses of the bat or tree adds a distinctive golden touch.

name:
GOLDEN BAT/
SWEET & MILD, SWEET & COOL
designer:
Masayoshi Kodaira
client:
Japan Tobacco Inc.

140

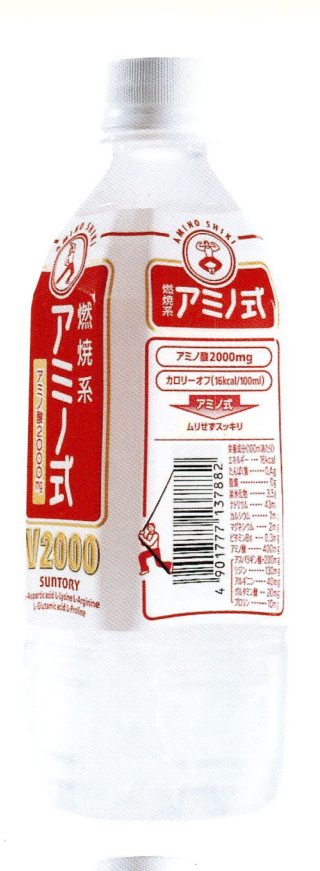

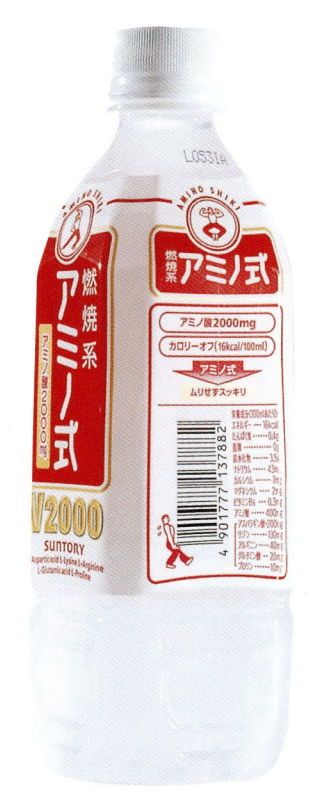

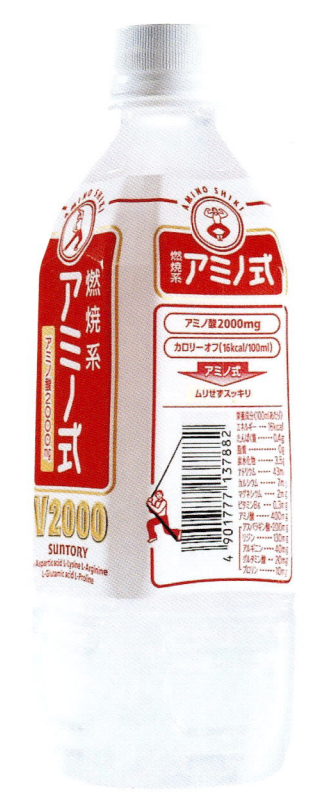

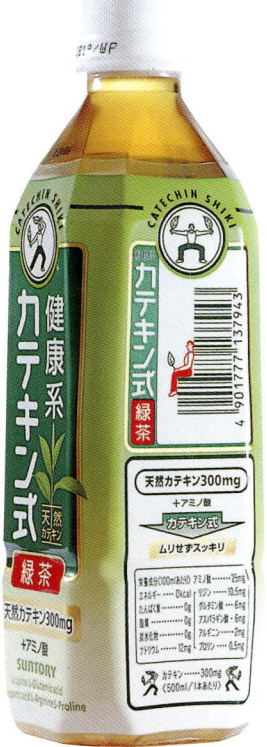

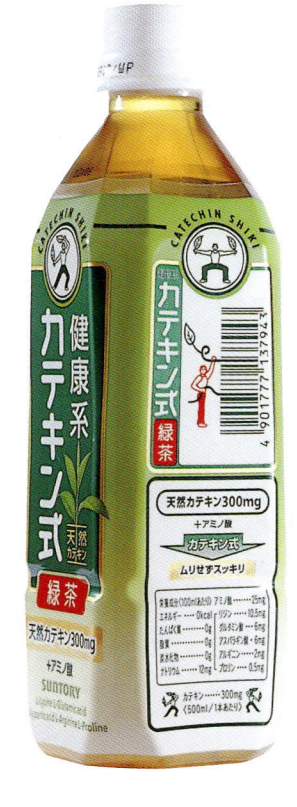

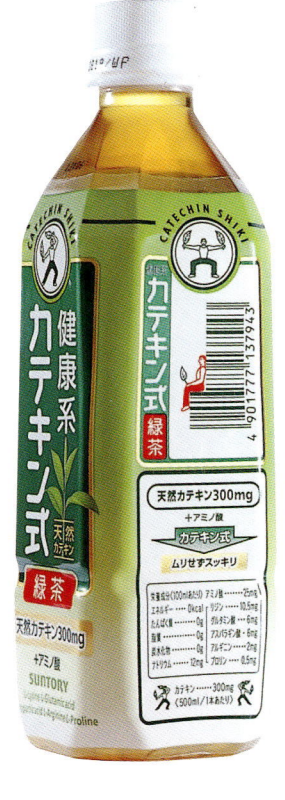

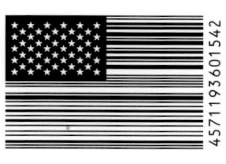

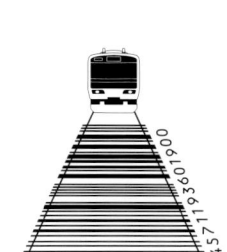

Design Barcodes™

Design Barcodes™ are barcodes that have a high element of design, yet can be put to practical use. Each barcode is designed specifically for the product it describes, using the dense, straight black lines as the key element in a black and white logo illustration.

name:
Design Barcodes™
designer:
Design Barcodes™
client:
Suntory

The package was designed with a large Kirin Kylin mark to express the company's confidence in the product, and to show in one glance that it is a premium beer. The bottle's label features just the Kylin mark, while the name of the beer is printed only on the neck. The prominence of the Kylin mark suggests this is a beer fit for sacred beings. Although only three colours were used to print the labels onto metallic paper, they were executed delicately and richly.

HOUJUN BOTTLE

name:
HOUJUN
creative director:
Kenjiro Sano
art director:
Kenjiro Sano
designer:
Kazuki Okamoto, Rikako Nagashima
client:
KIRIN Brewery Co., Ltd.

name:
Goku Nama TANK
designer:
Kashiwa Sato
client:
KIRIN Brewery Co., Ltd.

Goku Nama,
Goku Nama Tank,
Nama Kuro

By the request of the Kirin Brewery, the designer was involved in the art direction for the complete Goku Nama project: product concept, direction of taste, product naming, package design, publication and finally advertisement strategy. To present the 'more economical and easier-drinking taste than beer' character of the product to the world, all packaging, cardboard boxes and advertising visuals were printed with a simple mono-colour graphic of Kirin's Kylin mark, expressing the refreshing taste of low-malt beer.

name:
Goku Nama, Goku Nama Tank, Nama Kuro
designer:
Kashiwa Sato
client:
KIRIN Brewery Co., Ltd.

KIRIN
生黒
NAMAKURO
Kirin's passion combined with its brewing
technology brings you th
of Happo-shu. Bittersw
never tasted. Enjoy it
〈生〉
発泡酒
RE-NEW!
¥140
WITHOUT TAX
〈消費税別〉
www.gokunama.com

生黒
NAMAKURO
極生
GOKUNAMA
〈生〉

http://www.yamagishi.or.jp/

KIRIN
ムズムズする季節の春対策!!
KW乳酸菌を知ってますか？
特定アレルゲンフリー

KIRIN
KW乳酸菌配合
KW乳酸菌配合
体質水（たいしつすい）
KW乳酸菌配合
KW乳酸菌配合

KIRIN
KW乳酸菌を知ってますか？
ムズムズする季節の春対策!!
特定アレルゲンフリー

BAR 美弥子 TEL 3209-7607
スナック ディオール 2F 女性アルバイト募集 TEL 3236-2335
白梅 2F
Joy倶楽部 2F

ランチ 創作オムライス

KIRIN
ムズムズする季節の春対策!!
KW乳酸菌を知ってますか？
特定アレルゲンフリー

KIRIN
KW乳酸菌配合
KW乳酸菌配合
体質水（たいしつすい）
KW乳酸菌配合
KW乳酸菌配合

Taishitsusui Bottle

"Do you know KW lactic anti-bacterium?" The question is the catchphrase for a beverage developed by Kirin Brewery and Koiwai Dairy Products; the answer is a special liquid balance with highly beneficial medical properties. But since Japanese law is strict about the labelling of such products, the bottle was designed with the words "KW lactic anti-bacterium" surrounding the telling product name, TAISHITSUSUI, all in black on white, so that the drink stands out as a functional remedy on a convenience store shelf full of multicoloured drink packaging.

name:
Taishitsusui
designer:
Kashiwa Sato
client:
KIRIN Brewery Co., Ltd.

KIRIN

KW乳酸菌配合

体(たい)質(しつ)水(すい)

KW乳酸菌配合

KIRIN

KW乳酸菌配合

体(たい)質(しつ)水(すい)

KW乳酸菌配合

KIRIN

KW乳酸菌配合

体(たい)質(しつ)水(すい)

KW乳酸菌配合

Kirin 903

This smartly dressed sports drink is the hybrid child of Kirin Brewery beverages and adidas sports shoes; hence the trademark three stripes. Both can and bottle are a packaged in a sober black and white, where water condensation drops perspire like fresh beads of sweat.

name:
Kirin 903
art director:
Manabu Mizuno
designer:
good design company
client:
KIRIN Brewery Co., Ltd.

Shousei Inryou

Good medicine tastes bitter, and these coffee and sugar packages were derived from Japanese pharmaceutical paper bags. On the front of the bags, essential information including the roast date and grade of the coffee beans are printed to give the consumer accurate information as to the freshness of the coffee. Matchbox designs were also created to entertain the consumer visually during the few minutes it takes to enjoy the taste and aroma of a good cup of coffee.

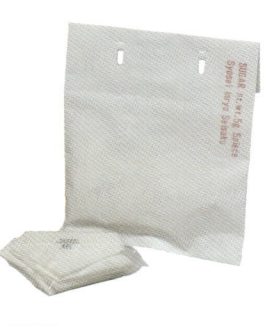

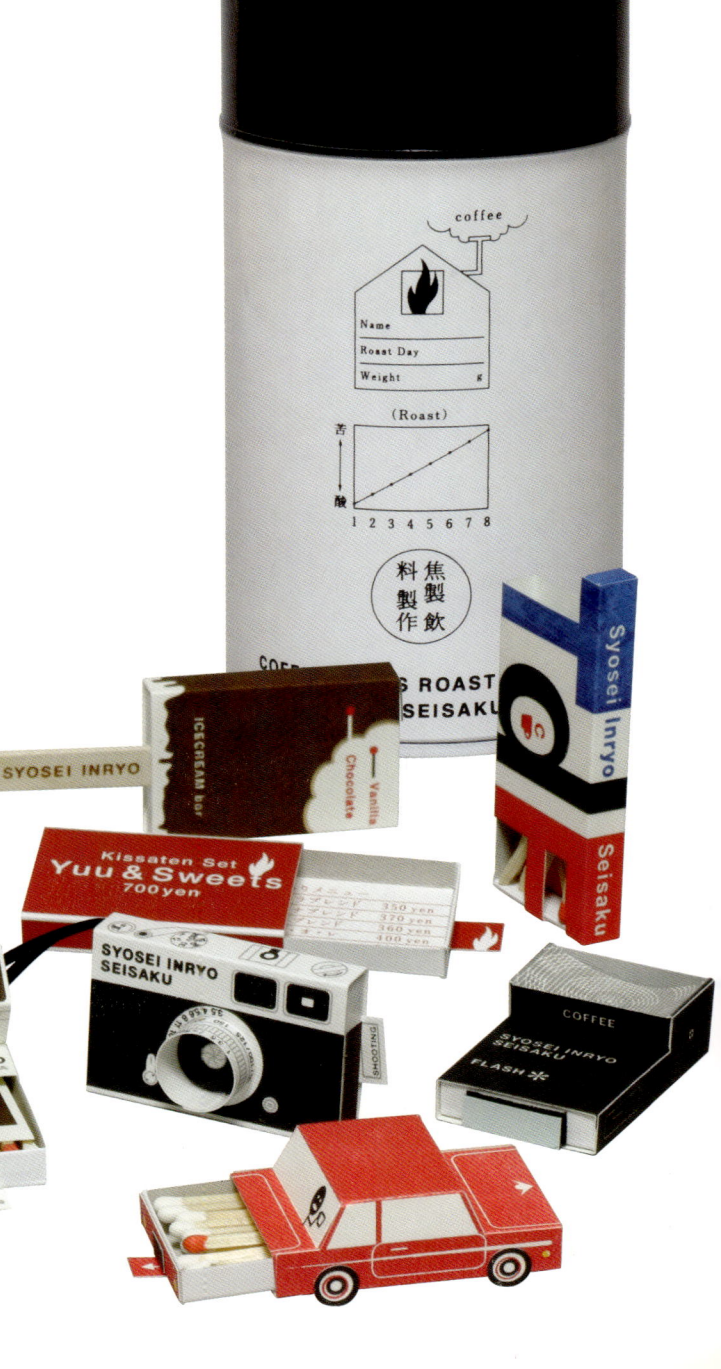

name:
Shousei Inryou
designer:
Shuichi Ito
client:
Shousei Inryou

Happy Colors Fragrance Paints

These cheerfully sweet-smelling acrylics come in a pastel array of tempered shades with simple and subdued labels suggesting the purity of colour and fragrance within.

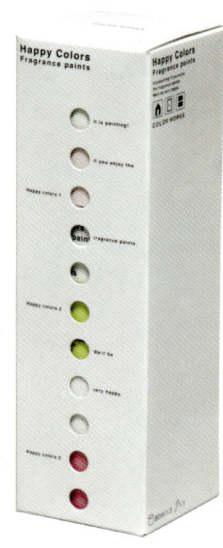

name:
Happy Colors Fragrance Paints
designer:
good design company
client:
Color Works

U*MO FACE MEMO BLOCK

U*MO adds a little humour to your everyday life. This low cost but good functional design features a silver sticker of an emoticon-like face on vinyl packaging.

name:
U*MO FACE MEMO BLOCK
art director:
Kenjiro Sano
designer:
Kenjiro Sano
client:
BALS/FRANC FRANC

Tea & Crumpets...
You make me feel like Dancing!
John
Galliano
Time Out, Time In
Gossip... Woodie's A handbag!
Wardrobe Whispers
Let Uncle Send-Me-The-
Bill explain all...
The Show Must Go On...
Mirror Mirror
Letters
D.I.Y Couture
Tea and T-shirts

John Galliano
Shopping Bag, Box & Sunglasses Case

John Galliano makes headlines on every front page of his bags and boxes, but then his gothically typefaced title brands the newspaper itself. Never again just a brown paper bag, a plain cardboard box, or even a newspapered sunglasses case, John Galliano is always the cover story scoop.

name:
John Galliano
Shopping Bag, Box & Sunglasses Case
designer:
Stephanie Nash & Anthony Michael
client:
John Galliano

Ztampz Packaging
Shopping Bags, Accessories Pack, VIP Card & Name Card

Two different artists, Fumio Tachibana and Kabo, were introduced for the summer and winter season. Their work was applied to the stamp-shaped stickers of the shopping bag, matching with other plain coloured stickers. Stamp elements were included in the design so that all corporate identity packaging items correlated with the shop's brand name "Ztampz".

name:
Ztampz Packaging
Shopping Bags/Accessories Pack/
VIP Card/Name Card
designer:
Communion W
client:
Ztampz

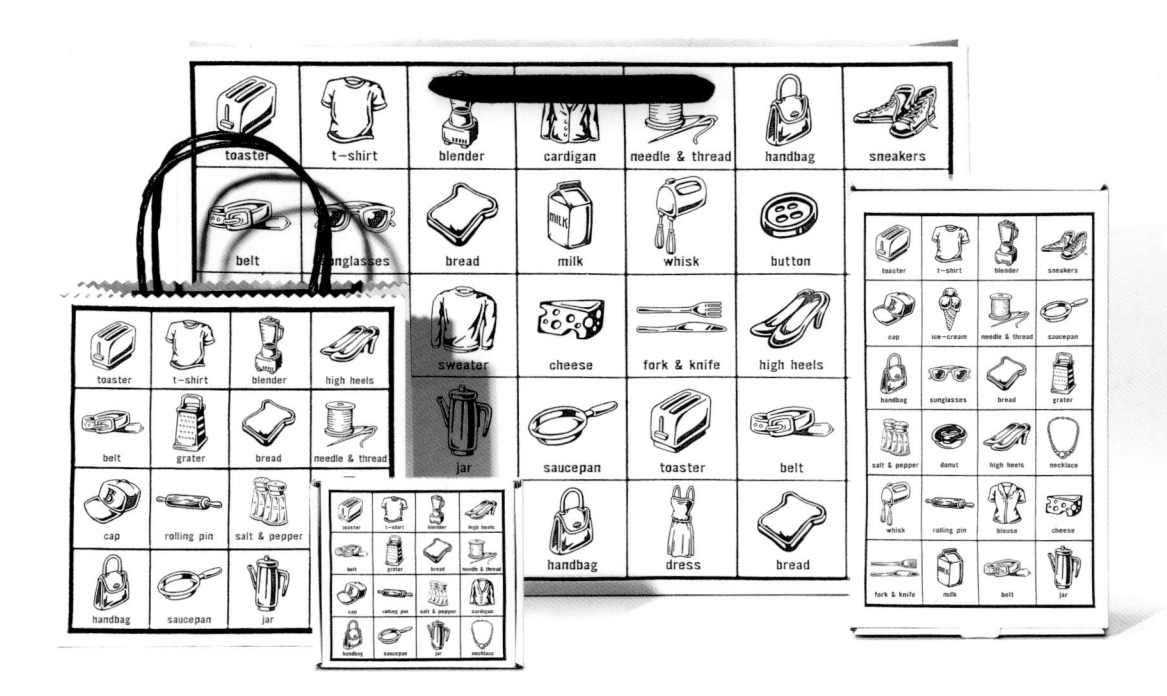

Bread n Butter Packaging
Shoe Boxes, Shopping Bags & Accessories Box

Since the name "Bread n Butter" evokes food, it was introduced as a fashion brand by mixing kitchen utensils and food icons with fashion related icons. The simple design of squarely framed line-drawn illustrations on a plain white background gives a European touch to the patterned package.

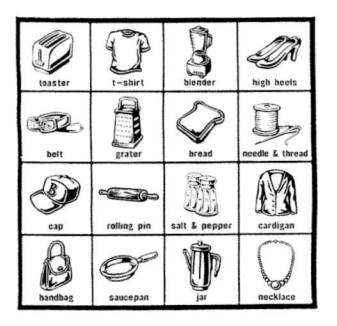

name:
Bread n Butter Packaging
Shoe Boxes/Shopping Bags/
Accessories Box
designer:
Communion W
client:
Bread n Butter

www.house-styling.com
Shopping Bags

Paper or plastic, handles or holes, these shopping bags exhibit seamless portraits of happy families in candy-land suburban homes. Landscapes are printed front and back, where no surface is wasted.

name:
**www.house-styling.com
Shopping Bags**
art director:
Manabu Mizuno
designer:
good design company
client:
www.house-styling.com

Minä Perhonen Coaster

This set of coasters is packaged in a slide box with 10 individually designed coasters in 10 different fabrics. As you slide off the slipcase it looks as if someone is drinking from the glass-shaped die-cut on the front of the package.

name:
Minä Perhonen Coaster
designer:
Atsuki Kikuchi (Blue Mark)
client:
Mina Co., Ltd.

·LOVELESS·

·LOVELESS·

LOVELESS
Shopping Bags

Trendy Paris fashion collective Surface to Air have art directed every aspect of the new luxury fashion clothing boutique Loveless in Aoyama, from its My Bloody Valentine-inspired name to the collage artwork which adorns its faux-brick walls and extends to all its merchandise bags and boxes.

name:
LOVELESS
Shopping Bags
designer:
Jeremie Rozan & Santiago Marotto
for Surface to Air. Paris
client:
LOVELESS

Material

An unexpected response to sourcing

Daniel Mason

It is not enough just to consider materials in isolation when discussing packaging. Both print process and construction are equally important.

The most intriguing area is sourcing materials that, on first investigation would appear to have no direct relation to any type of packaging. For instance materials used in heavy industry for lagging pipes or packaging machinery have certain textural values that convey the emotions of a more conventional project.

If one were to examine the packaging of the Prada cosmetics range, the look and feel is not one normally associated with this type of product. The packaging has appropriated the functions of the plastics used to minimise damage from light, heat and bacteria. Products are sealed in thermo-formed plastic trays with heat sealed foil lids (like pharmaceutical packaging). This single dose pack is then heat sealed into Tyvek pouches. The inference is entirely medical but is never overt. It also subverts the look of cosmetics packaging by becoming de-sexualised.

Playing with perceptions is where packaging can come alive. It is the unexpected that is the key to successful packaging.

The use of traditional processes can add considerable value to packaging. Processes such as foil blocking or rigid box packaging conveys a feeling of style and tradition. Both processes, by their very nature, have a significant manual component. One has to realise that production lead times are increased if these processes are selected. The results bear all the hallmarks of quality. Rigid boxes in particular, can be covered in all manner of materials. Even a traditional book cloth is now available in a mind-boggling array of colours and finishes, some of which add a futuristic twist to the devoutly traditional. Even the array of iridescent foil colours is far greater than it has ever been if you take the time to research it.

As long as you are aware of the logistical framework you are working within, then any material print process or construction can be utilised. The overall graphic design of the packaging may have to take a back seat in ascertaining the quantity needed, and the time frame in which it has to be delivered. Armed with this knowledge the designer can employ any manner of materials and constructions.

Materials divide themselves in clearly definable areas. They are: Paper & Board, Plastics & Synthetics, Book Cloths & Covering Materials and the Uncategorisable. All areas are very broad and take in all manner of sources to create a custom categorisation system.

Paper & Board varies across the world. In some cases international clients will demand certain papers from The United Kingdom or America because of the traditions associated with them. Packaging for Scottish whiskey will always be made from uncoated, coloured papers because it adds a notional feel of traditional values. There are a myriad of suppliers offering their variant of what the market demands. When it comes to more industrial feeling materials, such as Grey board, one has to dig a little deeper to find suppliers that supply another industry altogether (see above).

Plastics & Synthetics is even broader in its scope. The production of paper is similar from supplier to supplier. With plastics, different patented processes are used to create different colour shades and textures. PVC (Polyvinyl Chloride) can be clear, opaque, mark resistant or flexible, depending on its use. Some PVCs cannot be used for packaging because they are too brittle, whilst others can be heat bent or welded into all manner of shapes. Perspex is material rarely used in packaging. It is possible to heat bend it into shapes, however it really needs to be glued to form a box.

I have mentioned Book Cloths & Covering Materials previously, they can be employed to cover board sheets, die cut and shaped into cartons as opposed to rigid boxes.

The Uncategorisable is an area that can only be created through your own personal research. A great deal of time needs to be devoted to this research to reap any type of reward as it is all about information gathering. The mesh used to filter light in industrial greenhouses could be fashioned into pouches or mounted to plastic then thermo-formed. The Black Polystyrene used for car bumpers could be formed into CD packaging or shoe boxes. It is all about illumination of the ordinary and taking it from unexpected sources and exploiting it.

Another area is to celebrate the physical construction of packaging. The way a tab works or how something glues together should become the key component of packaging. Why not try to create packaging with no gluing at all? The journey in attempting it may prove exciting and fulfilling.

Chapter 3

Flat-out

**Promotional Materials/
Character Design/Merchandise Series**

Using unconventional colours, unusual materials
and eye-catching form, this chapter exposes
cases of exceptional merchandise: promotional
souvenirs, exclusive side-products and character-
based merchandising, all supporting the very
backbone of business and branding.

Nike Park
Invitation Kit

The scorpion-sealed portfolio opens into a package of postcards and flyers boasting movie poster attraction. The interior flickers with a limited edition invite. Come see the team Cerberus or Equipo Fuego, or watch your favourite star soccer players in action. At Nike Park, everybody is invited to be a hero.

name:
Nike Park Invitation Kit
art director:
Shintaro Tanabe
designer:
Shintaro Tanabe, Daisuke Kokubo
client:
Nike Japan

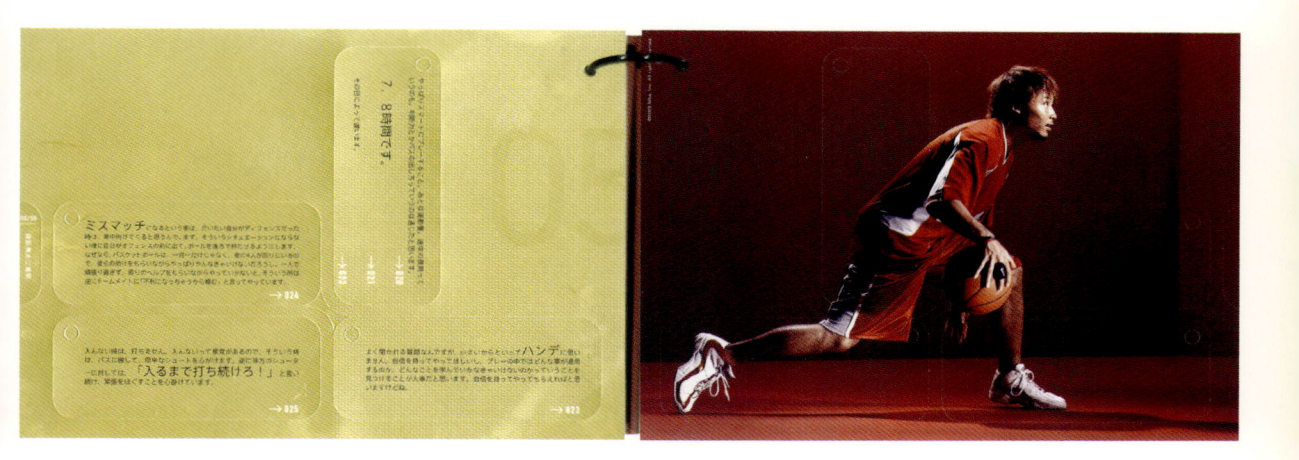

Nike Basketball Book 3 (Tabuse+Nike Basketball)

The Tabuse flipbook is already bound by a ring - but just punch out the tags on the pages to make a brand new key-ring of Nike basketball moments in a colourful mosaic of patterns and close-ups, with a multi-branching story told on the reverse side of each tag.

name:
Nike Basketball Book 3
(Tabuse+Nike Basketball)
creative director:
John C Jay, Sumiko Sato,
Kounosuke Kamitani
art director:
Shintaro Tanabe
designer:
Nao Tamura
client:
Nike Japan

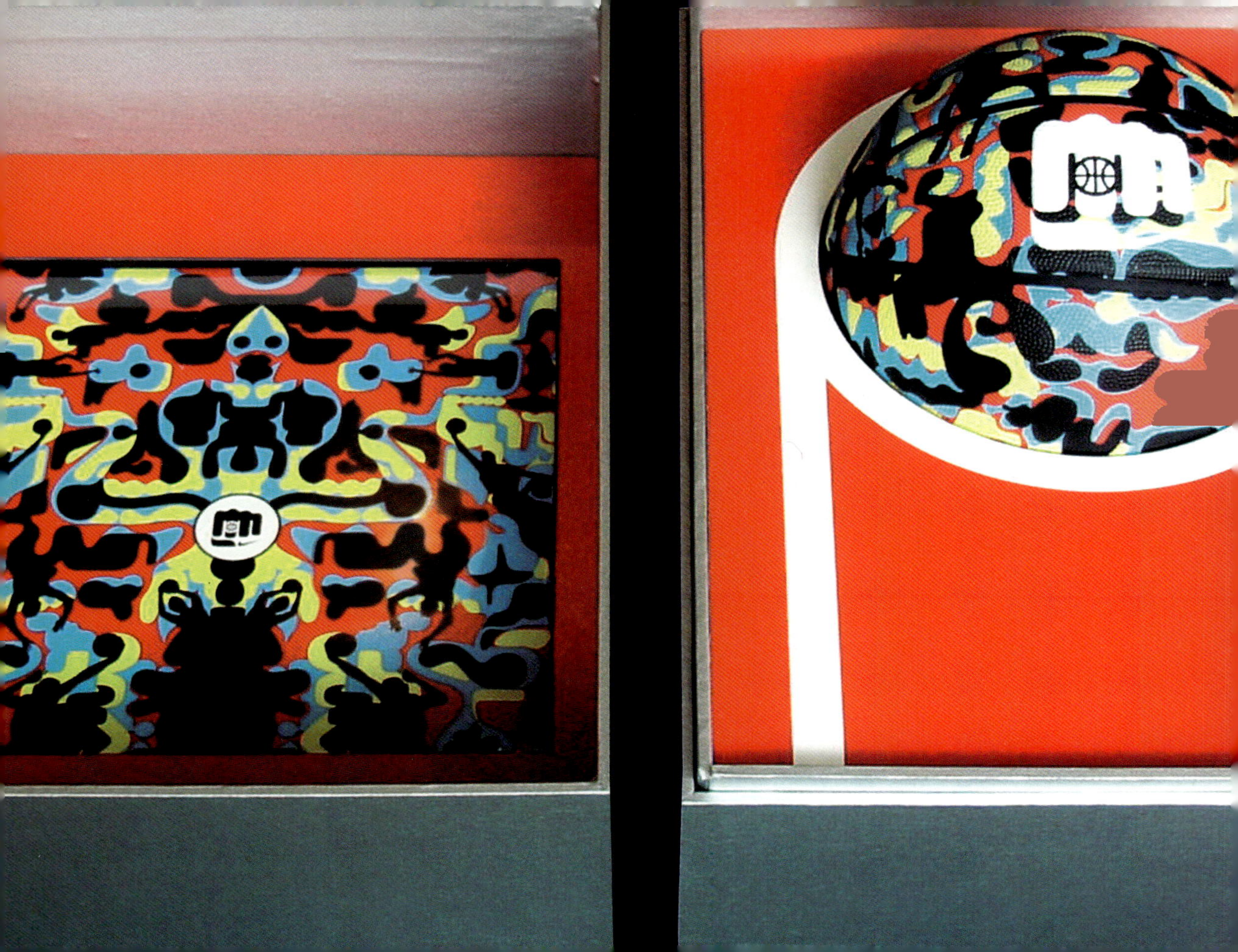

Nike Basketball Asia 2003 Flow

The brash multi-coloured hip-hop Nike basketball bursts out of its basket like a red-handed slam dunk in an embossed silver box. ROSTARR's liquid mosaic pattern warps around the sphere, just as it envelops the enclosed CD of Jurassic 5. Punch them through the centre and take them for a spin.

name:
Nike Basketball Asia 2003 Flow
creative director :
John C Jay + Sumiko Sato
art director:
+CRUZ, John C Jay
campaign artist:
ROSTARR
client:
Nike Asia

TO-FU OYAKO 2005 CALENDAR
to-fu oyako
coletto-fu
Everybody wants to eat more TO-FU!!
TOFUOYAKO 1000MEMO
TO-FU OYAKO SPECIAL DVD
TO-FU DX
DELUXE LIMITED EDITION
Everybody wants to eat more TO-FU!
TO-FU OYAKO
Eco-To
To-Fu2
Everybody wants to eat more TO-FU!!
X'MAS EXHIBITION SPECIAL
STICKER
TO-FU DEVIL
TO-FU ANGEL
MECHA TO-FU X
HOT TO-FU
TO-FU AMERICA
TO-FU BROS

TO-FU OYAKO

DEVILROBOTS' most famous character is the square white head of variable expressions, named after the 'oyako' relationship between mother and son. From the smiling face to the furrowed brow to a family of blockheads in disguise, TO-FU OYAKO is everywhere from comic books to keyrings to cubic puzzles to chocolate cookies.

name:
TO-FU OYAKO
designer:
DEVILROBOTS
client:
DEVILROBOTS

TO-FU DX
Everybody wants to eat more TO-FU
TO-FU OYAKO SPECIAL DVD
TO-FU
DX
トーフデラックス 限定版
DELUXE LIMITED EDITION
included!!
DELUXE TO-FU
OYAKO-CUBE
Everybody wants to eat more T
Pioneer
TO-FU
DX

Everybody wants to eat more TO-FU OYAKO CHOCO!!
Kabaya
TO-FU
OYAKO
CHOCO
トーフオヤコチョコ
トーフファミリーの
かわいいマスコット
1体入り！
10種 + 2種
チョコレート菓子
©2004 DEVILROBOTS
TO-FU
OYAKO
CHOCO
OPEN
LIVE THE HEALTHY LIFE!
AGENT FROM THE FAR EA
HEY! BOSS! BORN IN THE U.S.A.
BE CAREFUL OF MOUTH
TO-FU BROS

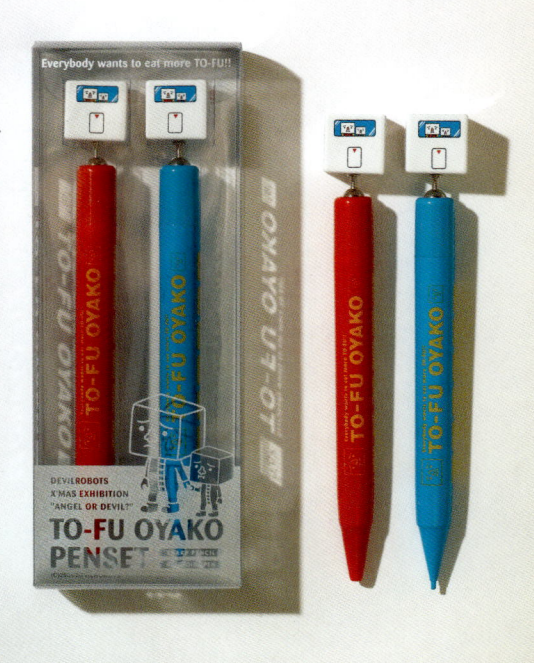

This page: (top left) TO-FU OYAKO Figure Keyholder, (top right) TO-FU OYAKO Strap for Mobile, (bottom left) TO-FU OYAKO Mobile Phone Shell for P900i, (bottom right) TO-FU OYAKO Pen Set
Opposite page: (top) TO-FU OYAKO Special DVD Deluxe Limited Edition, (bottom) TO-FU OYAKO Choco

Gold Boys, Kaizoku, Cracle & Other Characters

DEVILROBOTS strikes again with its distinctive large-pupilled characters, including the powerful Gold Boys on a golden mobile phone strap and the cross-boned Kaizoku and Cracle Cra Cra keychains.

name:
Gold Boys, Kaizoku, Cracle & Other Characters
designer:
DEVILROBOTS
client:
DEVILROBOTS

Soft Marshmallow [maffy]

Maffy's soft and spongy marshmallow head, like a billowy white shower cap falling over deep black eyes, is the perfect spokescharacter for everything sweet and soft, from the marshmallow treats to the round white mug containing the complementary cocoa.

name
Soft Marshmallow [maffy]
designer:
DEVILROBOTS
client:
DEVILROBOTS

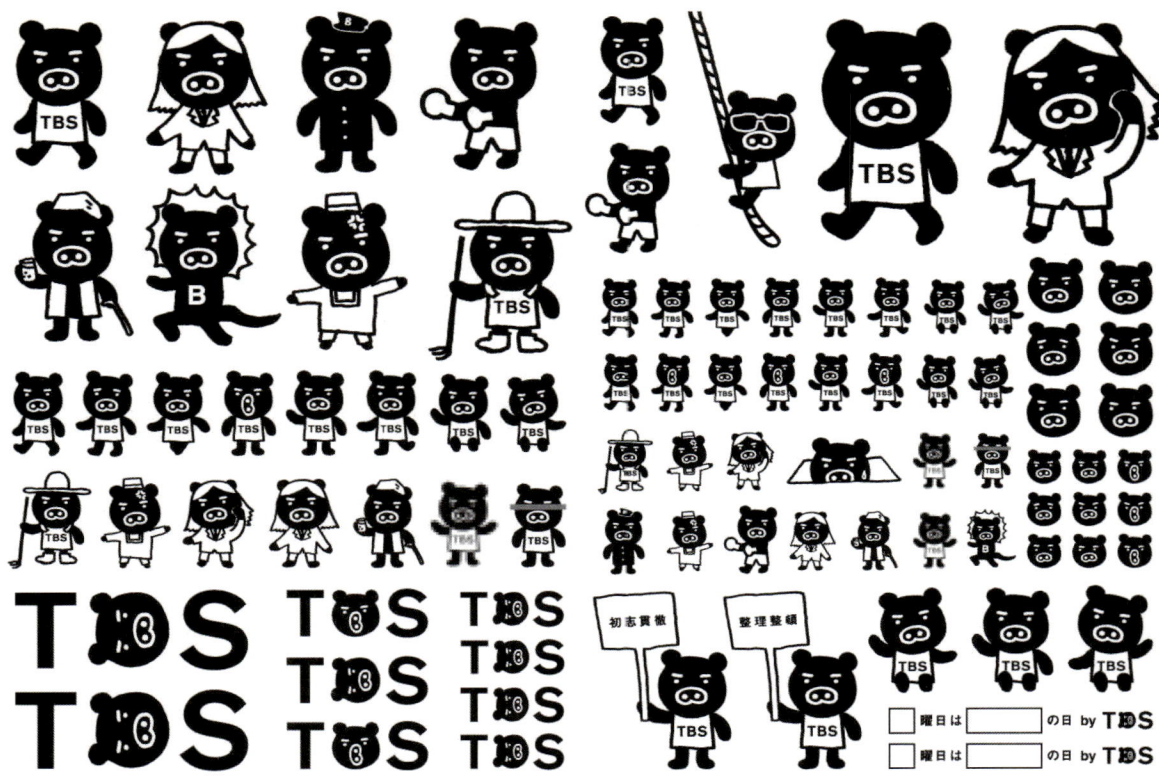

174

TBS TBS TBS
TBS TBS TBS
TBS TBS TBS

初志貫徹　整理整頓

□曜日は□の日 by TBS
□曜日は□の日 by TBS

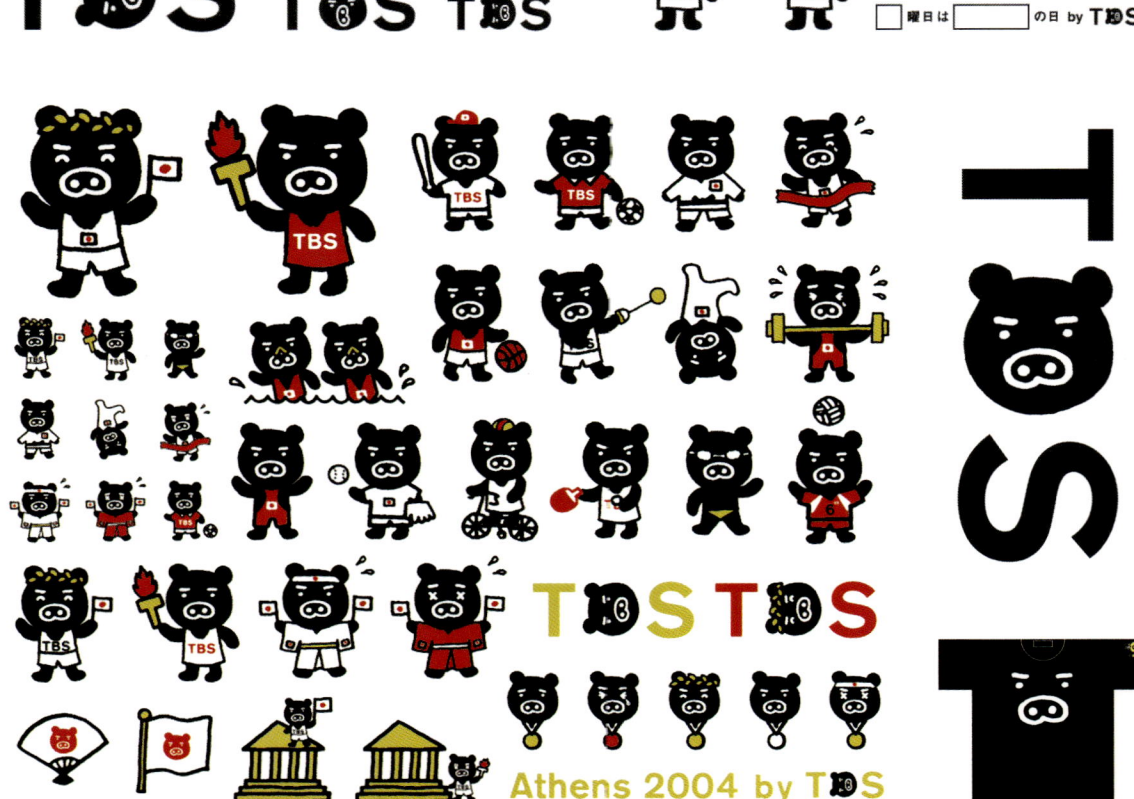

TBS TBS
Athens 2004 by TBS

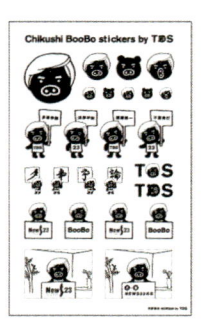

TBS
Promotion Items

Tokyo Broadcasting System's mascot pig character with the broadcast B nose poses in many different professions, side products and logos. Whatever the shape, size or disguise, the snout knows it's TBS time, but the public has since adopted a beloved familiar pet.

name:
TBS Promotion Items
art director:
Kenjiro Sano
designer:
Kenjiro Sano, Yuki Sugiyama
client:
Tokyo Broadcasting System

Copet © Seijiro Kubo/btf All Rights Reserved

Copet

Copet © Seijiro Kubo/btf All Rights Reserved

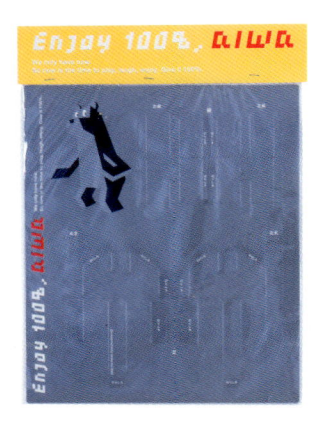

The simple, polygonal design of illustrator Seijiro Kubo's Copet characters can be easily applied to 3D images or paper crafts. The engaging figures were selected for AIWA ad campaigns and graced the cover of Java Press computer magazine. A children's game called "Pepa-robo" is in the works at Omron Entertainment Co., with Copet paper crafts as prizes. In the virtual world, Copet creatures are real animals living by the laws of the jungle, involved in stories full of action, romance and comedy.

name:
Copet
designer:
Seijiro Kubo/butterfly stroke Inc.
client:
butterfly stroke Inc.

178

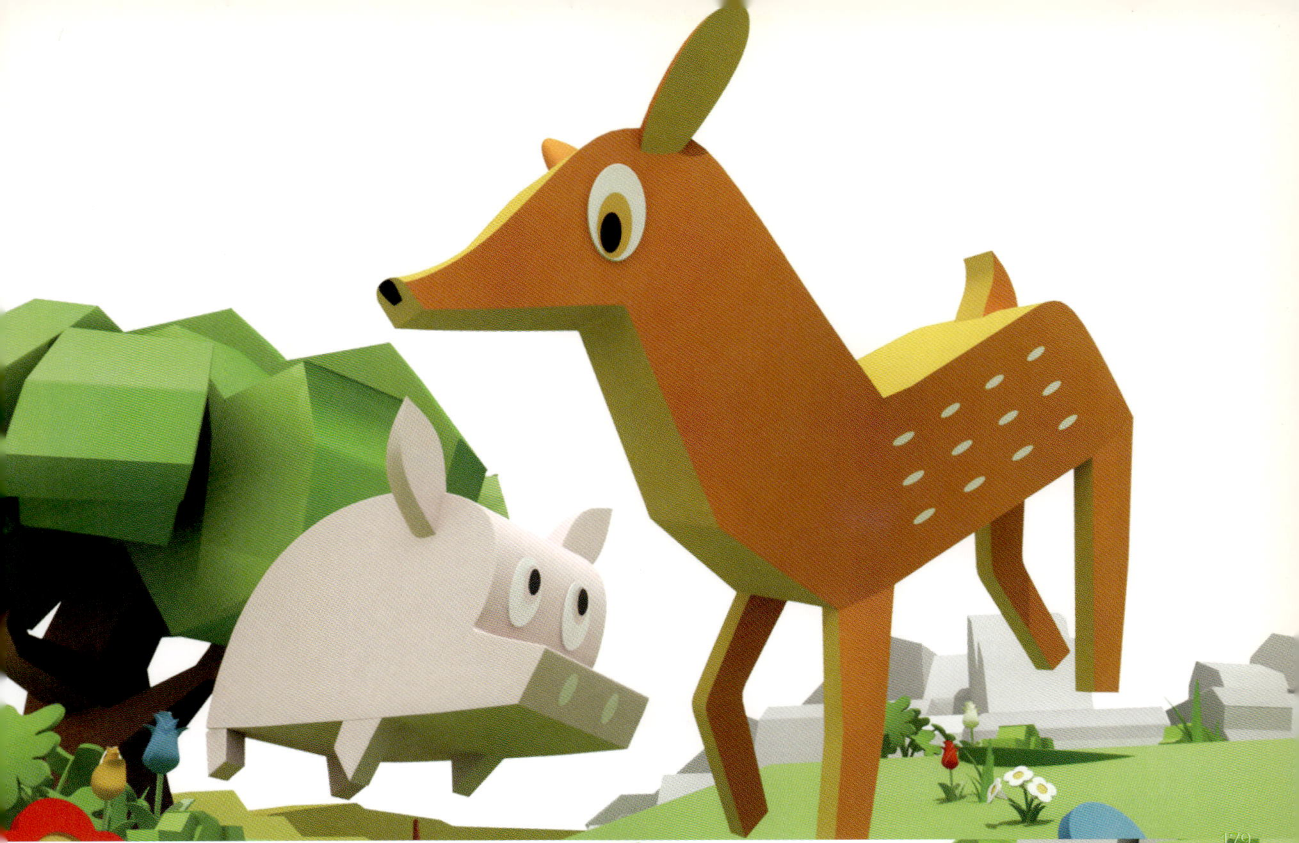

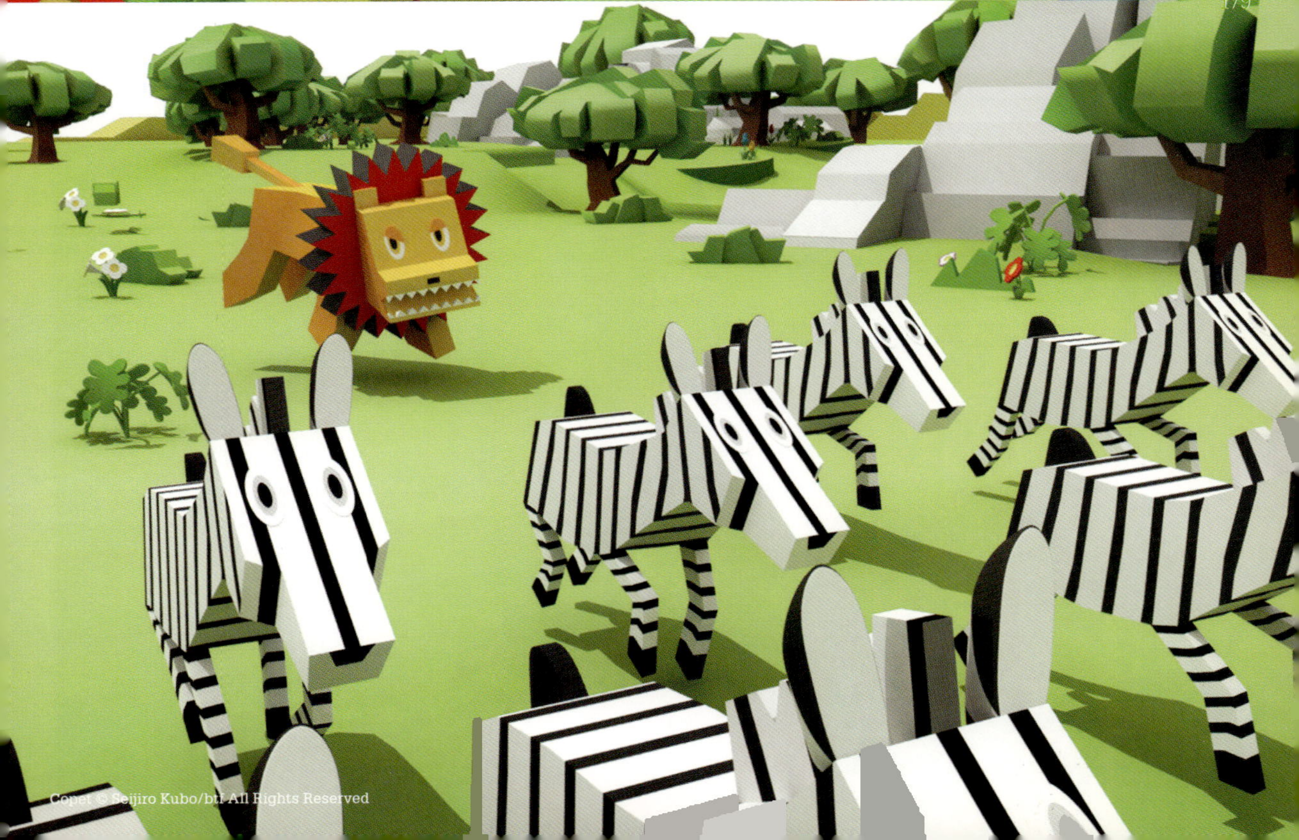

Kami-Robo

Kami-Robo © Tomohiro Yasui/btf All Rights Reserved

Kami-Robo are robot fighters made from paper, created by Tomohiro Yasui over the course of 23 years of play making over 200 wrestlers. The history of Kami-Robo professional wrestling is all about the battles within the ring in a valiant test of technique and character. Wrestlers come and go, friendships are forged and broken, trust is won and betrayed. Since Yasui's fighters went public, they have caught the attention of media both in Japan and beyond, as Kami-Robo CG images are now being created in preparation for broadcasting abroad. Kami-Robo wrestling figures will be released by Bandai Co. to coincide with the release of a Kami-Robo DVD and book.

name:
Kami-Robo
designer:
Tomohiro Yasui/butterfly stroke Inc.
client:
butterfly stroke Inc.

181

Kami-Robo © Tomohiro Yasui/btf All Rights Reserved

182

Kami-Robo © Tomohiro Yasui/btf All Rights Reserved
Opposite page: (from left to right, from top to bottom) Sword Man, Mont Blaer,
Shark Hawk, The Ole, Genie Jr., Fujiyama, Bird Man, Coconut Great

184

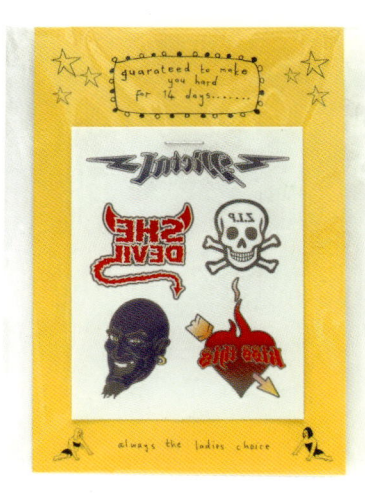

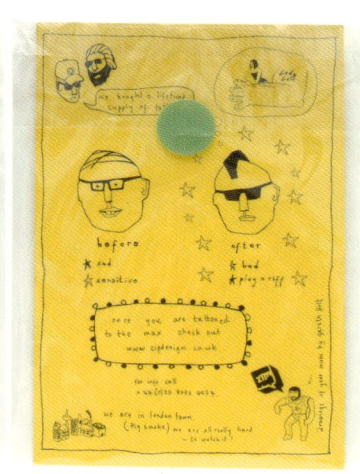

ZIP Promotional Mailer

How many times have you received a promotional mailer that was so dull it ended up straight in the bin? The best way to make a first lasting impression on an unsuspecting recipient is to make the person smile, or better yet, laugh. As simple as it sounds, the concept is to deliver an item that's both striking and humorous.

name:
ZIP Promotional Mailer
designer:
ZIP
client:
ZIP

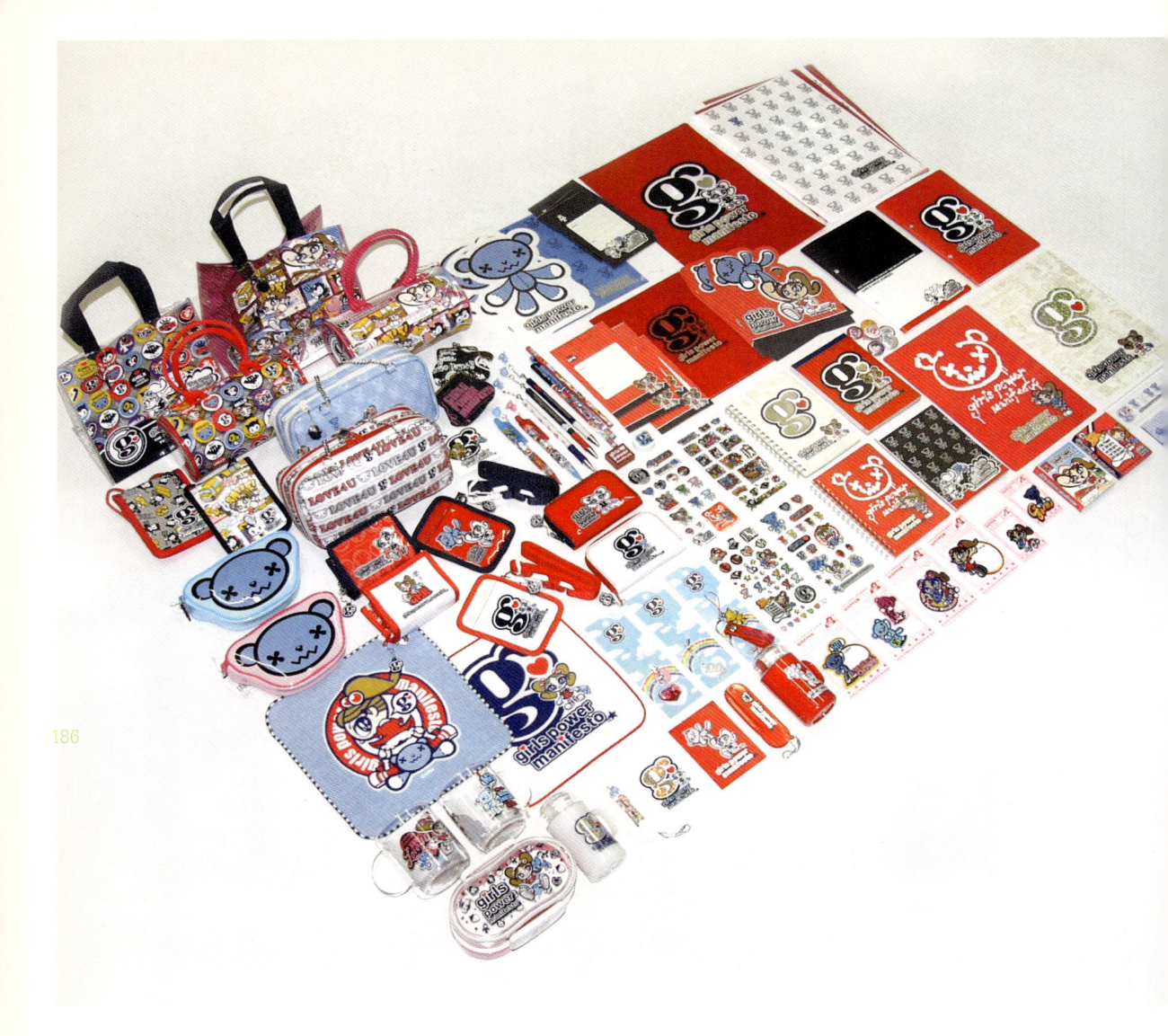

Girls Power Manifesto

Power girl Ginger and her stuffed bear Indigo with the crossed eyes were released on the market as stationery items and stuffed toys. While Ginger brands the notebooks with a giant lowercase 'g', Indigo comes in other colours and looks best in plush.

name:
Girls Power Manifesto
designer:
Furi Furi Company
client:
Furi Furi Company

girls power manifesto
INDIGO
KEYCHAIN
¥380-
LOVE4U

レモンインディゴ
http://www.girlspower.jp
¥380-
KEYCHAIN
girls power manifesto
LOVE4U

Coloured Collection
Colour Component Paper Goods

All stationery items are composed of geometric shapes in primary and pastel colours, folded at right angles with a clean cut and crease. Foregoing all flowery decoration and superfluous symbols, these forms are pure colour and composition.

name:
Coloured Collection
art director:
Katsu Kimura
designer:
Natsumi Akabane
client:
Zonart & Co., Ltd.

Box & Cox
Gift Box Set

Take a cardboard box and cut, fold and puncture it into geometrical shapes to make food-shaped paper goods. When circles become squares and ovals are triangles, cheese is hollow and bananas unpeel at right angles, all these non-edible foodstuffs can be folded out flat. This series of boxes is called the "Thing".

name:
Box & Cox
designer:
Katsu Kimura
client:
Katsu Kimura

Ecology/Recycling

Environmental responsibility for designers and manufacturers

Daniel Mason

As world population expands and our need to consume becomes ever greater, the waste generated not only in what is discarded but the energy needed to produce it is rapidly becoming a hazard.

Theorists have speculated that if this continues, we will physically disappear under the debris. In fact, there are areas of the world where islands have been created out of waste and are populated. We have become a victim of our own greed and it is our environment that has suffered.

We have to bear a global responsibility for this situation. As consumers it is our responsibility to demand that these products become more eco-friendly. For designers, the challenge is to educate themselves about these issues. As product manufacturers, there should be legislation demanding that these issues be considered first before any other.

This is a totally utopian vision of how the world should be, and in reality very few consumers consider their purchases from an environmental point of view. The consumption of products is a short-term fix to satiate the appetite of whatever emotion needs fulfilling. For the designer, research is too time consuming—besides, if there is a little logo or form of letters that can be placed somewhere (usually as small as possible) then they have done their duty. They are absolved of any further responsibility once their work is burnt to disc and sent to the printer. For the brand manufacturer nothing must stand in the way of the maximum profit for the lowest effort. The environment is too big. It looks after itself.

If packaging is looked at rationally, it divides into a number of areas: the material it is made from, the inks used to print it and the adhesive used to hold it together, coupled with the energy used by the factory producing the packaging. Come to think of it, what about the energy spent in powering the computers that were used to design it? Or the light and power from the building where it was presented to the client? The list goes on and on, spiralling out of control.

Today, more than any other time it is possible to engage in an ecological standpoint and, at least, make some rational decisions. Take for example the printing inks. Some larger factories now actively recycle waste ink to be used again. This has been common practice in the labelling industry for some years. There is a wide variety of adhesives available nowadays, but the problem with some is that they do not breakdown when they are buried in landfill sites or burnt. The choice has never been greater.

There are a number of choices when it comes to materials. If you want a very white cardboard, you cannot use a 100% recycled board. This is primarily because so much bleach is used that the board becomes non-environmentally friendly. Pulp board is more friendly but not as attractive and plastics have always been deemed as unfriendly. This is because they do not biodegrade when buried. However the plastics industry has tirelessly sought to make the process friendlier by recycling waste and energy at its plants, along with developing plastics that biodegrade when buried. It is regrettable that there are very little products we can use again. Not so long ago you could return glass bottles for a deposit. With the rise of canned drinks the glass industry has become worried and flooded the market with glass. The inheritance for the world today is a need to recycle glass when this could have been prevented.

No packaging can truly adapt to all the green issues that are placed before it. What you gain through one aspect you loose in another, and no amount of legislation is going to stem the tide. Product manufacturers should be encouraged to invest more money into the packaging component of their products and endeavour to avoid passing the cost onto the customer. Material and process suppliers should actively seek to educate the individuals, and designers should seek out this information. The process of discovery can lead to innovation in packaging, its effect being felt across all areas from fashion to electronics to cosmetics. Green packaging may not necessarily mean using brown cardboard and vegetable inks. It may mean making informed decisions about which components of the packaging itself are important and which are not. More environmental information should be placed on the box at the expense of telling the consumer what it would add to their lives. It is also possible to consider the notion that packaging should be more permanent with a view to intentionally designing it for re-use. For instance, the bag used to display a swimming costume in-store should be designed to function as a bag you use to visit the beach. A drinks bottle could be made so attractive that it can be used as a flower vase.

Chapter 4
Package Design?

The world of "packaging design" seems to cover a very wide range. Even the staff who took part in the collection and selection for this book had questions: "What is packaging design?" "Is this really a package design?" The general opinion was divided on the subject. In this chapter, we introduce a selection of work for which we couldn't quite reach a consensus on what exactly the package design was, but they are all very sophisticated, high-quality works.

Minä Perhonen shopping bag

This is a shopping bag with a godet bottom. The turn back at the opening features a slash, functioning as a muzzle. The bottom of the bag is printed in the same color as the shop floor, and is a representation of the reflection of the floor.

name: Minä Perhonen shopping bag
designer: Atsuki Kikuchi (blue mark)
client: Mina Co., Ltd.

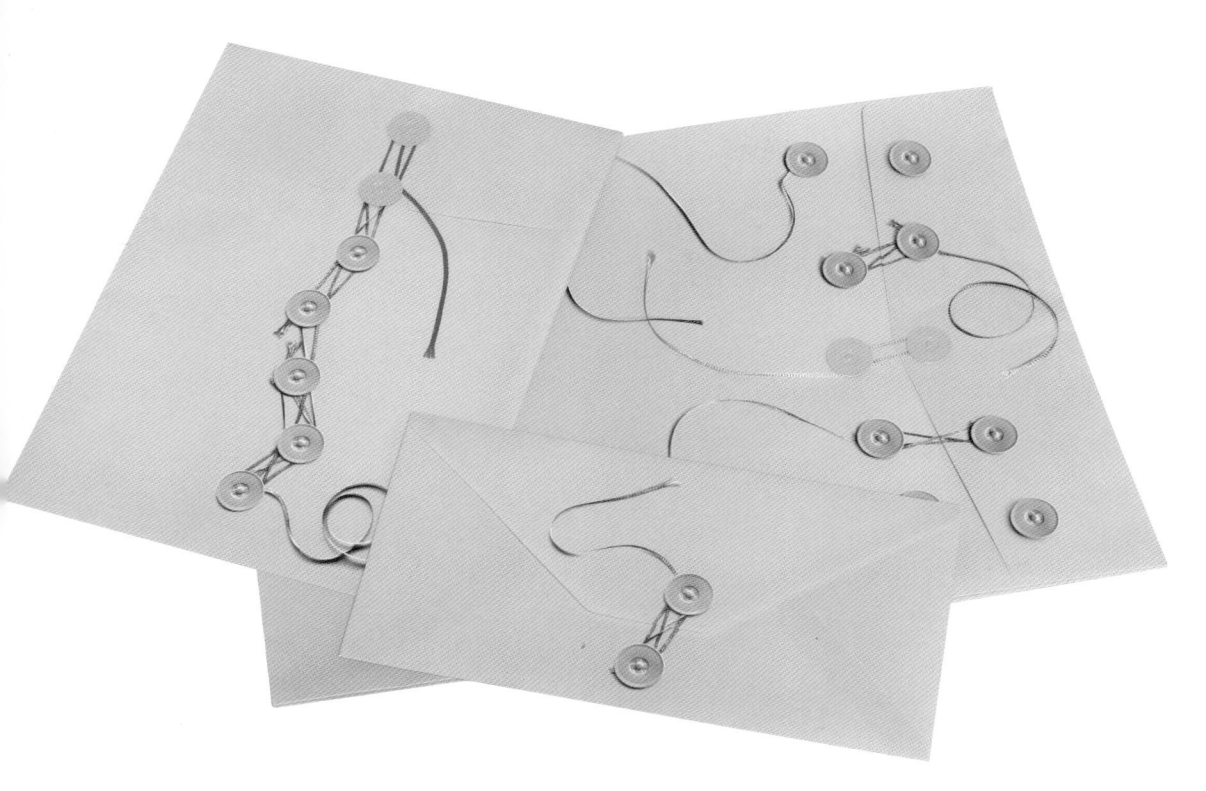

SOSU Mihara Yasuhiro envelope

This invitation envelope is designed with not only string and grommet closures, but also with printed imitations to create a visual illusion for the recipient. The design plays on its pointlessness.

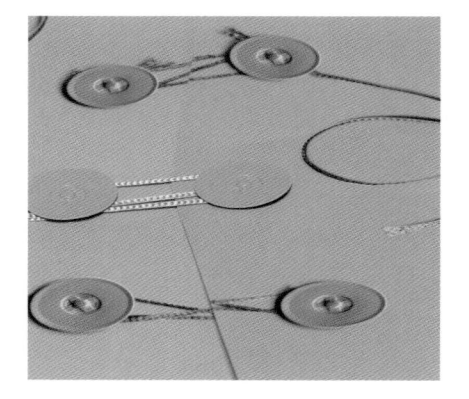

name: SOSU Mihara Yasuhiro envelope
art director: Ryosuke Uehara
designer: Ryosuke Uehara, Tatsuya Kawanishi
client: SOSU Co., Ltd.

Mirror Box

This gift packaging is available for sale at the store Accentual. Mirror Box is created to be an exquisite surprise when opened. One quarter of a flower printed on the interior is mirrored on the walls of the box, creating a full flower that spreads simultaneously as the box is opened.

name: Mirror Box
art director: Yoshie Watanabe
designer: Yoshie Watanabe
client: Vitras ink

Greeting Box Card

These split slipcase boxes are opened with a sliding action that mimics curtains being opened or a bow being untied. Sweet hand drawn characters are revealed inside, sending the recipient best wishes.

name: Greeting Box Card
art director: Yoshie Watanabe
creative director: Satoshi Miyata
client: D-BROS

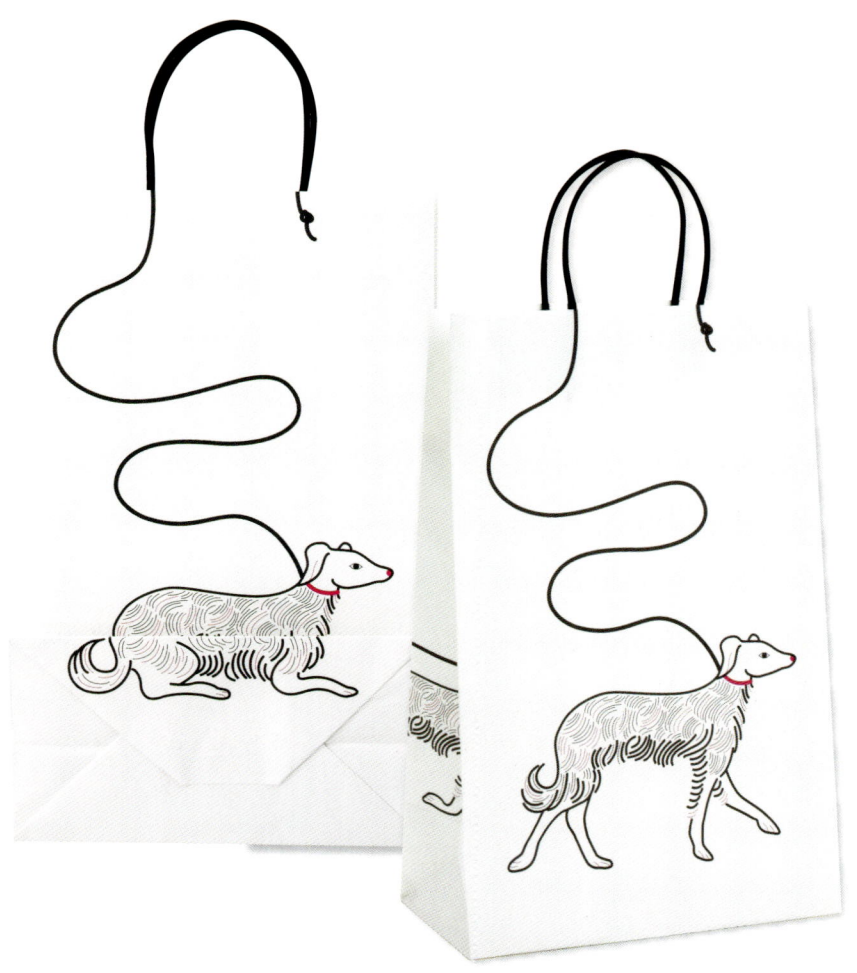

A Walk With a Dog

This packaging is designed for an underwear shop which develops their business along with the key words," a park". When the bag is folded flat, the dog printed on the bag is lying down, but when containing a product and unfolded, the dog appears upright and walking. As shoppers go home with their purchased items they, in fact, take a walk with a dog.

name: A Walk With a Dog
art director: Yoshie Watanabe, Ryosuke Uehara
designer: Yoshie Watanabe
client: Une Nana Cool Corp.

Birdcage

These soft semi-transparent gift-wrap sacks, available in various sizes, feature a birdcage print and are closed with ribbon by gathering the sack at the neck. When the sack is filled with a gift, it is carried in much the same way a birdcage is, grasping it at the top. The gift-wrap comes complete with a card in the shape of a bird, which can be slipped into an inside cavity between the lining and exterior of the bag. The overall effect gives the impression of a bird inside the cage.

name: Birdcage
art director: Yoshie Watanabe
illustrator: Yoshie Watanabe
designer: Akiko Sekimoto
client: Une Nana Cool Corp.

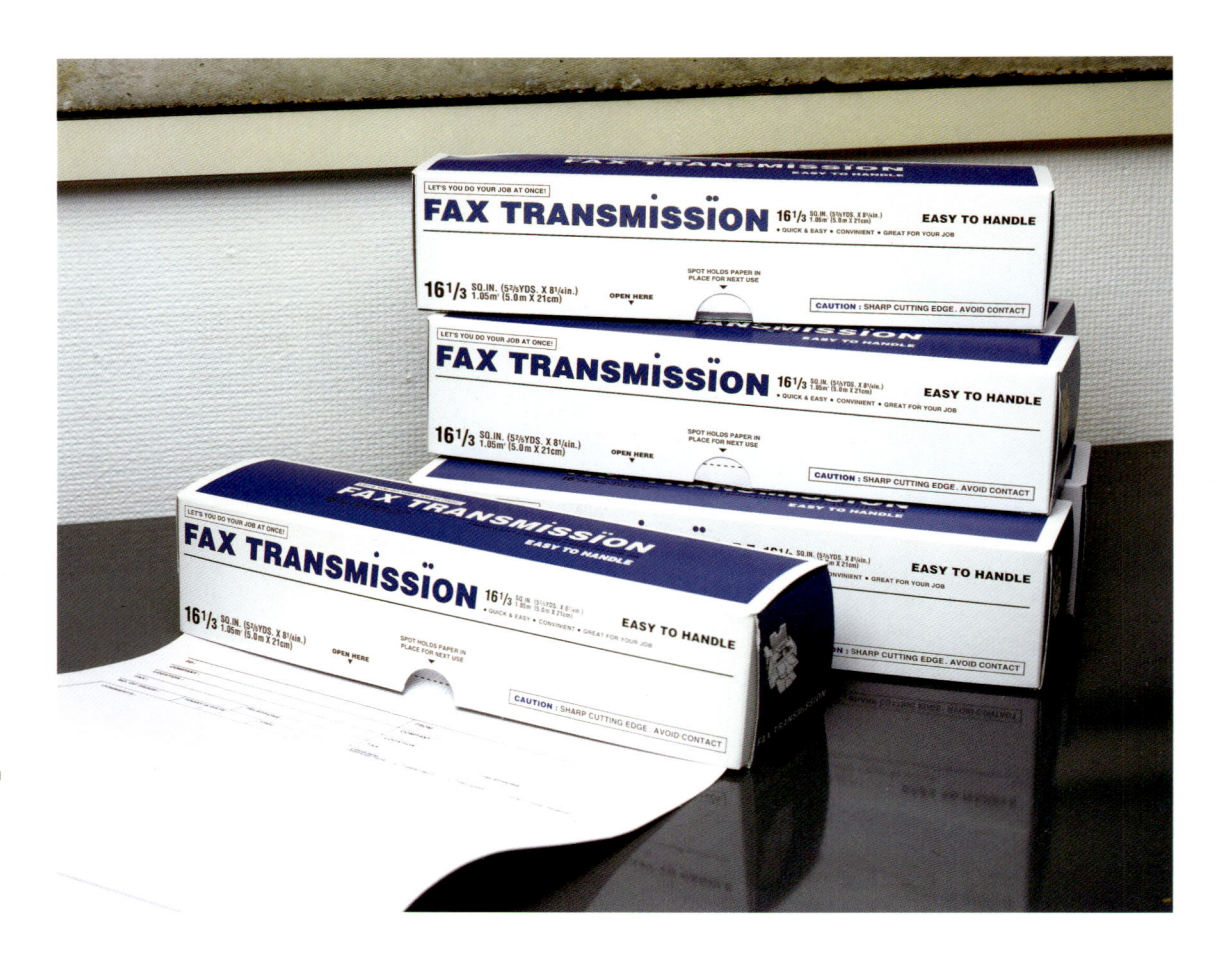

FAX TRANSMISSION

Fax transmission unrolled like a household sheet of aluminum foil or plastic wrap, entirely disposable and always easy to handle.

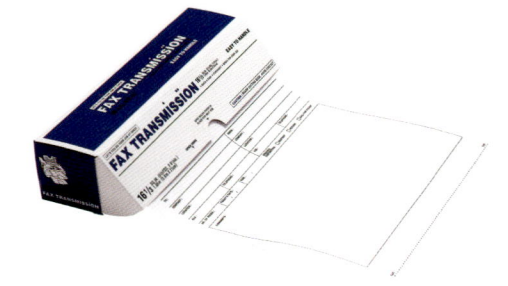

name: FAX TRANSMISSION
designer: Naomi Hirabayashi
client: Self Work

Warhol Gift Wrap

This winter season, have your holiday gifts hand-wrapped in original Andy Warhol screenprints. This gift wrap was introduced exclusively at Troy for winter 2002. $7,5-$25 per wrap. Selected prints made possible from Ronald Feldman Gallery, NYC. Originally conceived in 2000 for C.I.T.E Design, NYC.

name: Warhol Gift Wrap
designer: Tobias Wong
client: Troy, NYC

Box-File

Having heard the phrase "throw-away society" spoken so often, an analysis of domestic and office rubbish was undertaken to ascertain whether it would be possible to recover some useful life from that which is regarded as "useless". This led to the project 'Elevation of the Unwanted'. After office photocopier and printer paper is used, the cardboard storage boxes are normally discarded. This is a waste, especially when the very same offices often purchase new cardboard for filing and storage. This simple redesign of the 5-ream box allows it to be transformed into a box-file – quick and easy, requiring no glue, knives or scissors.

name:	Box-File
designer:	Edward Goodwin and Richard Hartshorn
photographer:	Goodwin Hartshorn
client:	Self-generated project

MeBox

MeBox is a new range of cardboard storage boxes with a unique labelling feature. The ends of each box have a grid of perforated discs – press them out to create initials, numbers, symbols and text. When assembled, the double-thickness construction presents your message against the contrasting liner colour of the box. They can be arranged in rows to create longer messages. MeBox comes flat-packed for easy self-assembly, in poly-bag with handle, and is available in a range of silk-screened colours and natural brown kraft finishes.

name: MeBox
designer: Graphic Thought Facility
photographer: Angela Moore
client: Graphic Thought Facility

'White Noise' Loudspeakers

The project was to develop a way of reusing the packaging that loudspeakers are sold in to give it a supplementary use. Following a period of investigation, it became clear that the packing material itself made excellent acoustic construction material, and as a result, the speaker enclosures were constructed from this. The speakers are a robust, low cost alternative to the usual veneered chipboard enclosures. Moreover, following acoustic and laser testing at a leading loudspeaker manufacturer's research facility, it has become apparent that the speakers perform better than the commercial speakers they were based on.

name: 'White Noise' Loudspeakers
designer: Edward Goodwin and Richard Hartshorn
photographer: Goodwin Hartshorn
client: Self-generated project

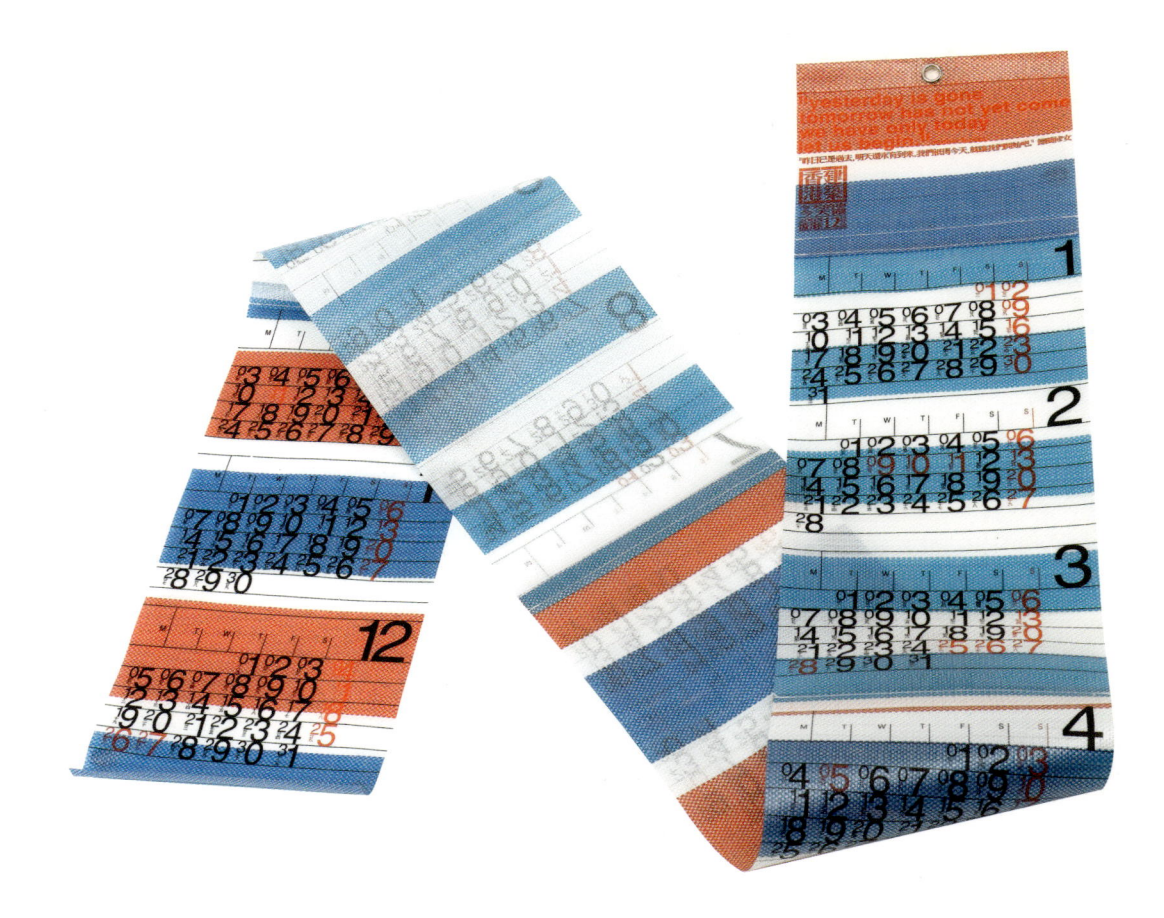

Building Hong Kong 12: Today's task done today

This '05 calendar is a continuous project from Building Hong Kong redwhiteblue to promote the positive spirit of Hong Kong. The calendar marks the relentless passage of time by recycling a suitably robust material – the heavy duty plastic weave usually reserved for hefty all-weather bags. All 12 months scroll through the year over red, white and blue stripes, simply indicated by big, bold, black numerals. Like a banner, the calendar can be hoisted outdoors as its weatherproof body stands the test of time. With a little help, it can even be flown as a dragon kite. Not to be outdone, the flag-like ribbon rolls up neatly into a portable scroll tied with a string.

name: Building Hong Kong 12: Today's task done today
designer: anothermountainman (Stanley Wong Ping Pui)
client: Building Hong Kong

Icon Umbrella

Whenever you find yourself walking under the weather, the Icon umbrella pops open to shine the spotlight on your stroll. White shapes on clear plastic make up a sturdy shelter from downpour to sprinkle, while happy, dancing, playful icons brighten all your rainy days.

name: Icon Umbrella
designer: AllRightsReserved
illustrator: Kimiyoshi Futori (Takora)
photographer: David Lo
client: Harbour City, Hong Kong

VAIO Cake Carrying Case

Life is a box of truffles every time you slice open the VAIO carrying cake case. Designed to fit the VAIO T and made of soft, lightweight acrylic with non-detachable parts, it incorporates two zippers to secure a safe enclosure of your computer in cake's clothing. Non-edible.

name:	VAIO Cake Carrying Case FOR VAIOIOI Project
designer:	Shibusawa Kenta
client:	Sony VAIO
producer:	AllRightsReserved

TO-FU OYAKO wooden case

TO-FU OYAKO © 2005 DEVILROBOTS
DEVILROBOTS x primitive+

The TO-FU OYAKO wooden case is made of maple wood, with a beautifully polished surface, just like TO-FU. Inside, TO-FU's white leather gently secures your VAIO notebook in place. A different TO-FU face is available for each day of the week.

name:	TO-FU OYAKO wooden case for VAIOIOI Project
designer:	DEVILROBOTS
client:	Sony VAIO, Hong Kong
producer:	AllRightsReserved

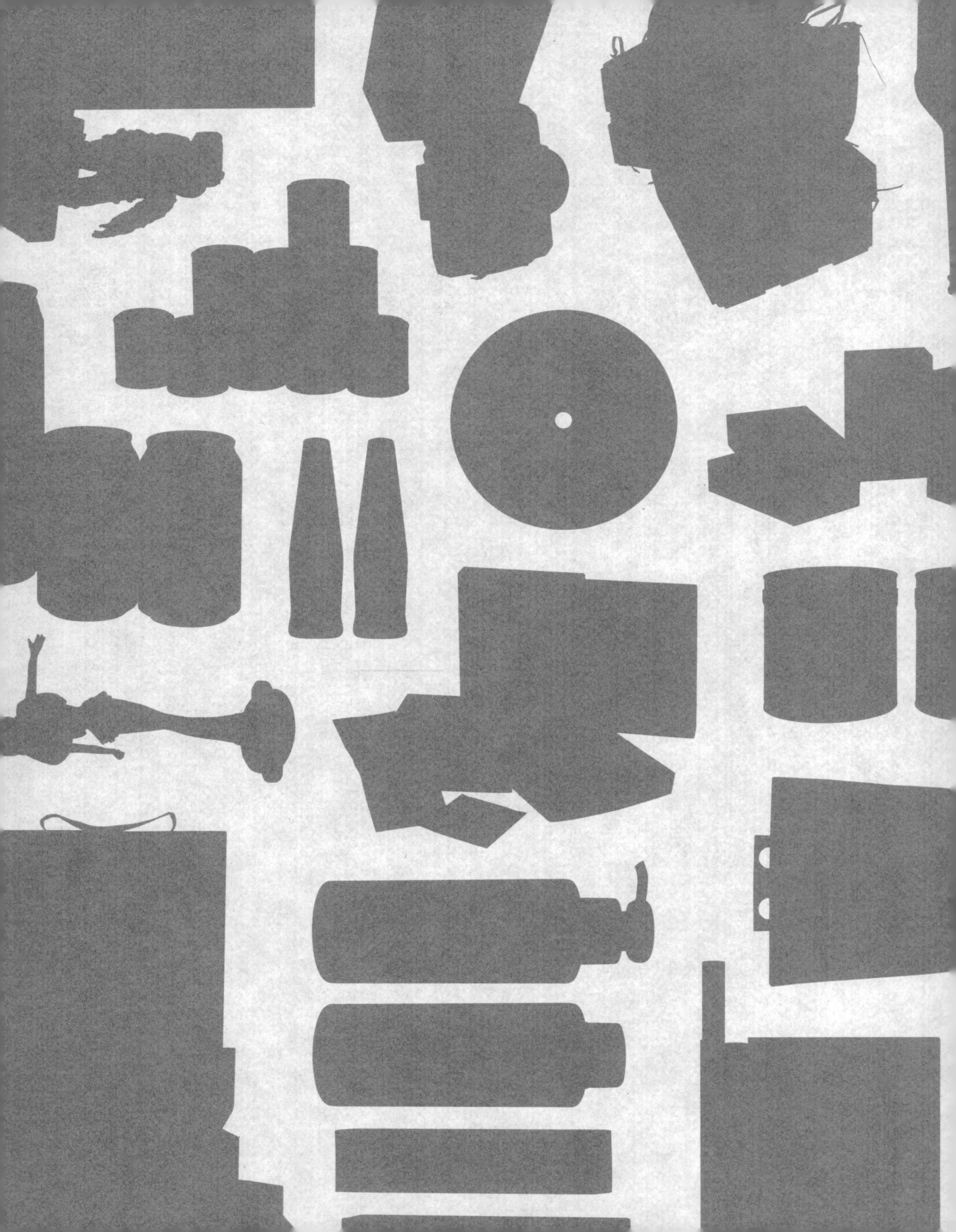

Contributors' Profiles

ASYL Design
www.asyl.co.jp

Founded by Naoki Sato, ASYL assumed the art direction of WIRED Japanese edition before producing a wide range of creative work committed to various media, undertaking projects from planning to direction and design.

Atsushi Kikuchi (Blue Mark)
www.bluemark.co.jp

Born in Tokyo in 1974, Kikuchi dropped out of Musashino Art University Sculpture Department in 1997. During 1997-98, he served as the director of Studio Diner, a modern alternative art space. He established Blue Mark Inc. in 2000 and worked as art director on the branding of fashion brands. Furthermore, he extends his efforts as an art producer in the non-profit organisation, Art Meeting Point, where he holds the title of administration officer.

CAMEL Pleasure Factory

A network for creativity which aims to reunite creators from various genres and exchange works freely. Launched in August 2003 and based in Kottodori in Aoyama, CAMEL Pleasure Factory has been producing various projects, such as performances and exhibitions by its members. Creators in the fields of music, graphics, fashion and art stimulate each other and encourage collaborations across all genres.

Clot

Clot is an independent lifestyle company. Our mission is to create. To bring into existence something new, done by a course of action and behavior. Our goal is to get into the minds of the youth generation and to turn on their engines about creating and evolving. Our course of action is simple, everyday we are creating and setting an example for those who want to do something for themselves. We love what we do because it has no boundaries. People never stop learning and with that we are always trying to create new platforms. As the world is getting smaller, a new type of thinking has evolved, known as the Hybrid thinking, taking bits and pieces from different cultures to create something new...

Communion W

Communion W was set up in 1998 with creative and graphic design as major strengths. Its understanding in the current market has resulted in a portfolio of memorable advertising campaigns and chic music packaging. Major clients include PCCW netvigator, now TV, Citibank I.T VISA, Canon, Towngas, Ztampz, Bread n Butter and Nike.

Design Bridge
www.designbridge.com

Design Bridge believes that brands are like people. They use their strategic and creative skills to unlock the potential in every brand, with over 15 years of experience in product and service branding. Their portfolio includes corporate and brand identity, promotional literature, three-dimensional expression of a brand, bespoke bottle, graphic packaging and digital media campaign.

DEVILROBOTS
www.devilrobots.com
info@devilrobots.com

A design team of six based in Tokyo, established in 1997. Main areas of work include planning/design/production of graphics, characters, illustrations, videos, web pages, music and wearable goods. The evil but cute, fun robot-like taste is their trademark. A wide array of characters exert their individualistic existence in various genres, creating a world that is "cute with a bit of poison".

Final Home

Final Home evolved from Issey Miyake Inc. and now exists as a brand synonymous with the concepts of survival, protection, functionality and recyclability. Final Home's manufacturing concept resembles an industrial manufacturing process. Products display particularities in their fabric and functionality designed to aid survival in various conditions of urban life, for example using industrial styles and supplies such as hunting garments, army coats and air-conditioning filters. Other manufactured lifestyle items include cardboard sofas, pocket sofa covers and chocolate candles.

fuseproject
www.fuseproject.com

Founded in 1999 by Yves Behar, fuseproject is an award-winning San Francisco-based industrial design and branding firm. In-house capabilities span industrial design, packaging, graphics and environmental design. fuseproject has developed innovative packaging and graphic solutions both as stand-alone efforts and in conjunction with industrial design projects. It has provided packaging and out-of-box experience solutions in fields such as technology, transportation, medical, beauty, fashion and home appliances.

GK Design
www.gkdesign.com

Glazer and Kalayjian, Inc. specialises in a broad range of integrated marketing and corporate communication projects. As a full-service communications design company with over 23 years of experience, it has worked with Fortune 500 companies across multiple industries in the US and around the world. Its areas of expertise cover all areas of marketing, strategic planning and branding strategy for all media, including print ads, brochures, direct mail to video, animation, CD-ROMs and websites.

Goodwin Hartshorn
www.goodwin-hartshorn.co.uk

Goodwin Hartshorn is a London-based industrial design consultancy. Co-founded by Edward Goodwin and Richard Hartshorn, they specialise in innovative product design across a range of consumer spheres. Core values include industrial design engineering, inclusive design and sustainable design. They have developed new packaging solutions, environmentally friendlier medical instruments and improved domestic appliances.

Graphic Thought Facility
www.mebox.co.uk
www.graphicthoughtfacility.com

Graphic Thought Facility is a graphic design consultancy working for public and private clients on a variety of national and international projects. It produces both print and three-dimensional graphics for publishing, marketing, press, exhibition, events, product development and brand applications.

Groovisions
www.groovisions.com

Groovisions is a design group led by Hiroshi Ito. Since 1991, Ito has been performing in a DJ unit called " groovequest" in Kyoto, until the group was renamed " Groovisions" by Yasuharu Konishi of Pizzicato Five, as Ito has been responsible for the art visuals of the Pizzicato Five World Tour. Today Groovisions is based in Tokyo and manages a wide range of projects including graphic design, promotional video, sound installation, fashion design and produces works for global companies such as Nike. Groovisions is also featured in international exhibitions including " Superflat", curated by Takashi Murakami and " JAM" in London, and a selection of its work is presented at Colette in Paris. Groovisions is also known for having produced the' Chappie" character. Its products are showcased in an original store in Tokyo.

Happypets
www.happypets.ch

Happypets is an experimental lab in creative, graphic design, image and illustration, based in Lausanne, Switzerland.

Hikaru Kawahara
(THE LINCOLN GRAPHIX FAMILY)
www.tlgf.com

Born in 1968. Graduated from Kuwasawa Design School. In 1997, founded The LINCOLN GRAPHIX FAMILY. Today, he wishes for his continuous happy life for graphic design and music in the world around us.

The Lincoln Graphix Family
#1401, Shibuya Homes, 2-1, Udagawa-cho
Shibuya-ku, Tokyo 150-0042 JPN

John C Jay
www.wk.com

John C Jay is a partner of Wieden + Kennedy with offices in Portland, New York, London, Amsterdam, Tokyo and Shanghai. Jay works around the world serving as Executive Creative Director and a member of the Global Management Team with special emphasis on Asia. He maintains an office in Portland and Tokyo where he continues his role as Co-Creative Director of the agency's independent music label, W+K Tokyo Lab. His creative work has appeared as a part of numerous shows in galleries and museums around the world. Jay's awards include creative work in graphic design, TV and print advertising, interior design, packaging design, short films, editorial design and marketing.

j-me
www.j-me.co.uk

j-me is a design studio based in London, specialising in the design and manufacture of contemporary design-led gifts and accessories for the home. The partnership was founded five years ago by brothers Jamie and Mark Antoniades, whose dynamic combination is the driving force behind j-me. The portfolio of designs started with the fle-sexi salt and pepper shaker, whose huge appeal inspired a generation of funky j-me products, with over 20 distributors worldwide.

Junkie Design

Junkie design is the streetwear label created by Godfrey Kwan in 2001. Kwan joined the Double X Workshop as an art director following graduation in 1993. His talent attracted the attention of Wing Shya who invited him to Shya-La-La Workshop in 1997, where he produced many award-winning album covers and advertisements. He is also responsible for most of the packaging and graphic design associated with renowned artist Michael Lau, creator of Gardener figures. Kwan now continues to implement his graphic influences in books, magazines, apparel, music videos, rave parties and packaging.

Kasia Korczak
www.kasia-korczak.com

Perhaps best known for his quadrifold cover, typographical art direction and overall design of Cross Magazine's identity, layout and website, Kasia Korczak has worked on a number of design projects over the past seven years, primarily in Paris and London. His professional art directing career began in 1997 at Barriedale Operahouse, a London performance arts company, where his work extended to both print output (ads, posters, promotional campaigns) and live performances (motion graphics, video, photography).

Kashiwa Sato (Samurai)

Creative Director/Art Director. Born in Tokyo in 1965, Sato graduated from Tama Art University with a graphic design degree, joined Hakuhodo Inc. and finally became independent in 2000. He established the creative art studio, Samurai, in May of the same year. His work encompasses product development, shop promotions, space usage and ad campaigns. His past work includes SMAP, Honda Step Wagon, Kirin Chibi Lemon, Taishitsusui, Kirin Gokunama, Namakuro, TBC, Parco, World OZOC, Shiseido La Beaut "TOKYO 02-03" in Paris, TSUTAYA TOKYO ROPPONGI, and INFOBAE of auby KDDI. Awards wo include Tokyo ADC Grand Prize, Asahi Advertising Award, Kamekura Yasaku Prize, JAGDA 2000 Best New Artist, Tokyo TDC Gold Prize and Japan Package Design Gold Prize.

Kenjiro Sano (Hakuhodo Design)

Born in Tokyo in 1972. Works at Hakuhodo Design as an art director. Has been working on TV commercials, posters, packages, character design and more: Vogue Nippon, the poster of the volleyball World Cup, Judo championship logo, posters for Japan Rugby Football etc. Awards to date include New York ADC Silver Prize, Distinctive Merit Awards and Merit Awards and Tokyo TDC Annual award. A judge of New York ADC in 2004.

Mark James
akamushi.com

Mark James is an illustrator, graphic designer and cardboard engineer based in London. He has worked mainly within the music industry for the past few years, designing cover art, identities, merchandise, etc. for artists. Influences range from early punk DIY imagery to Japanese youth culture and animation, a love of packaging and anything flat packed, and the idea of creating something 3D from a flat base. Mark recently signed to PlayBeast, the toy label set up by Pete Fowler, and has since created his own toy project, the flat-packed toy CardBoy.

Masayoshi Kodaira (FLAME)

Born in Osaka in 1970, Kodaira worked at Akita Design Kan from 1993 to 1996, and became an independent freelancer in 1997. He established FLAME in 2001. Awards won include JAGDA 2002 Best New Artist, New York ADC Special Award.

MEDICOM TOY CORPORATION
www.medicomtoy.co.jp
www.bearbrick.com
www.babekubcity.com

Since its establishment in 1996, MEDICOM TOY has been a Japanese toy company that continuously creates new trends with merchandise in the global toy market. Its principle is to value both product image and corporate image. Such effort has created many high-quality products, beginning with 12-inch action figures and eventually KUBRICK and BEARBRICK, which are now popular worldwide. Today MEDICOM TOY continues to evolve through self development, as well as through collaborations with various groups from street culture to global corporations.

Manabu Mizuno (good design company)
www.gooddesigncompany.com

Born in Tokyo in 1972 and raised in Chigasaki, Mizuno graduated from Tama Art University with an art design degree and joined Pablo Production in 1996. After experiencing a draft, he established good design company in January 1999. His main work includes all the creative production of advertising activities from product, concept and campaign development of ANA travel Smap, Toyota Synergy Research Institute and KIRIN903, as well as graphics for Rahmens and interior design for the beauty salon Stance. Mizuno won the JAGDA 2003 Best New Artist award.

Myeong-hee Lee
www.mattoct.jp

A Space Designer. Creates space which works as communication between reality and fantasy. Her principal works are "GAS SHOP", "JAM HOME MADE", "CAFE SIGN", "CAFE OFFICE", "BIT THINGS @ YCAM". Also joined a music label called "ATAK" as an art director.

Michael.Nash Associates

Stephanie Nash and Anthony Michael studied Graphic Design at St. Martins School of Art (1978-1981) before forming the partnership Michael.Nash Associates 18 years ago. Early work was based around the music industry as Stephanie Nash had worked at Island Records as an in-house designer, but the client base soon developed to include fashion labels. In 1993 the company was commissioned to design the brand food packaging for the London store Harvey Nichols, an association which continues and has included both the Fifth Floor and OXO restaurants.

Naomi Hirabayashi
naomi747@mac.com

Born in Tokyo. After graduation from Musashino Art University in 1992, she started working as an art director/graphic designer for Shiseido Co., Ltd. In 2002, she was granted an opportunity to work temporarily for the London design studio Made Thought. After returning to Japan, she worked freelance designing products, ads, packaging and book-binding.

NBStudio

NBStudio is a consultancy specialising in graphic design formed in 1997 by former Pentagram designers Alan Dye, Ben Stott and Nick Finney. Their approach to graphic design has always been multi-disciplinary, in the sense that they do not specialise in any particular niche. They believe they can apply their experience and working process to any graphic based project, approaching projects from a fresh perspective and producing results which are out of the ordinary.

Non-Format
www.non-format.com

Based in London, Non-Format has worked on a range of projects including music packaging for various record labels, illustration for fashion and advertising clients, as well as art direction for the monthly music magazine The Wire.

Norio Nakamura

Graphic Designer. Born in Kawasaki City in 1967, Nakamura graduated from Nihon University with an art degree in 1990. His main works include Meywa Denki graphic design, PlayStation software I.Q planning/art directing, Kokoku Hihyo covers in 1999, knockdown toy Ponchiki, i-mode site Motion-ID, 2000/2002 Tokyo Motor Show commercial vehicle, NHK Minna no Uta "Tetopettenson" and Magazine House relax serial "Katteni info".

Oliver Laric
www.ninjabuero.de

Oliver Laric was born in Caracas/Venezuela. He started aerobics at age five, winning several national aerobic and dance competitions in his early twenties. Oliver now runs the aerobic studio Runset Fitness in Malibu.

onedotzero
www.onedotzero.com

Founded in 1996, onedotzero is dedicated to commissioning, programming and producing the most cutting-edge work across all mediums of digital moving image. Since its inception it has collated and commissioned almost a hundred hours of original programming for the eponymous annual digital creativity festival and other projects. onedotzero currently tours its festival programming to over 60 world cities across Asia, Europe and the US, and launched the successful onedotzero DVD label in 2003.

Output
studio-output.com

Output was formed in August 2002 to create graphic communication which explores the possibilities of visual media. As well as retained work for major names in UK radio, it also works regularly with a range of clients in all areas of fashion, PR, music, leisure and the arts. Designers Rob Coke and Dan Moore were formerly the senior design team at twelve:ten in Nottingham. While the studio is based in Nottingham, client work has also been published beyond the UK in France, Germany, Ibiza, Malta, USA, Australia and Japan.

Pearlfisher
www.pearlfisher.com

Pearlfisher Creative Partner, Karen Welman, has won both a category award and the top "Best of Show" Award at the recent London International Design Award for her innovative, temperature regulating clothing range for babies: 37 Degrees. Karen also won Special Recognition Award at the GWIIN and Top 10 Woman Inventor/Innovator 2004 Award at the annual Global Female Invent & Innovate Awards 2004 in Singapore.

Red Design
www.red-design.co.uk

Red Design has been a key player in graphic design for the music industry since 1996. Red's 1999 sleeve for Fatboy Slim's seven million selling album "You've come a long way, baby" cemented Red's reputation within the music industry, which accounts for about 50 percent of Red's output. Other design projects range from fashion houses, book publishers, furniture designers, international hotels, company re-brands, educational projects, cultural sectors and worldwide exhibitions.

Ryosuke Uehara (D-Bros)
www.d-bros.jp

Born in Hokkaido in 1972. Entered Draft Co., Ltd. in 1997, an advertising and graphic design company in Tokyo. Since 1999, has joined the "D-Bros" project, which Draft Co., Ltd. launched as a new product line based on creating their original brand called "D-Bros". Awards include: JAGDA New Designer Award, Tokyo ADC Award with packing tapes and flower bases from D-Bros product line, graphics for "SOSU MIHARA YASUHIRO TOKYO", and New York ADC Gold Prize with the Calendar 2004 from D-Bros.

Sam Hurt and Jude Biddulph
www.suck.uk.com

SUCK UK was established in early 2000 and has grown from a two-man partnership to a brand-led design company. SUCK UK designs and distributes its own range of SUCK UK branded products as well as providing design consultancy services. The SUCK UK product range comprises contemporary lighting, furniture and personal accessory products, both desirable by the design elite and affordable to the man on the street.

Shibusawa Kenta

Shibusawa Kenta was born in Tokyo. After graduating from Tokyo Bunka Fashion College three years ago, he did work for Yohji Yamamoto, as well as styling for most major fashion magazines. He loves to travel, absorbing inspiration from new fashions around the world. In fact, it was in San Francisco that Shibusawa discovered his passion for fabricating chocolates and pastries, when he stumbled into a cake shop displaying an impressive array of colorful cakes. After tasting the beautiful pastries, he felt delighted and contented. In order to recreate this joyful experience, he decided to make his own imitation sweets, using his familiar fashion fabrics. Last year he was named Most Promising Artist by the Japanese fashion magazine So-En.

Shya-la-la
www.shyalala.com

Shya-la-la is an independent, visual communication agency with an eye for beauty and a heart for perfection. We understand the important relations between intriguing companies and their target consumers – building the bridge of communication, shortening the gap between the two.

Shuichi Ito
n110@cl.cilas.net

Born in Nagoya in 1970, Ito is a graphic designer who has hosted the annual baking, drinking, artifice event in a Nagoya general store, Manashila Haroguna, since 1999. Past awards include the outstanding performance award in the Seventh Yomiuri Advertising Agency Humor Advertisement in General Newspaper Advertisements.

Soup Design
www.d2.dion.ne.jp/~ohara34/soup

Established in 1999 by architect Nobuaki Doi and Satoshi Watanabe, graphic designer Fumikazu Ohara, product designer Yayoi Yamazaki and chef Rie Kuroiwa. Main activities involve designing magazines and books, producing advertisements, planning architecture/interior and producing/selling furniture. Representing work in graphics are R25, Neutral, Northern Europe Design Series, invitation, etc.

Stanley Wong Ping-Pui

Stanley Wong Ping-Pui, alias Anothermountainman, was born in Hong Kong in 1960. In July 2002, along with his partner, Stanley set up Threetwoone Film Production Limited, specialising in advertising film production. Stanley is also profoundly interested and deeply involved in fine arts and photography, focusing on human rights and social issues.

state
www.statedesign.com

Mark Hough and Philip O'Dwyer are state, a London-based design company. state work across all graphic media, having completed innovative projects in the fields of motion graphics, interactive media and print. Both are typographers, filmmakers and programmers, who also enjoy working closely with architects, musicians, sound designers, programmers and writers.

Studio Dror
www.studiodror.com

Studio Dror, a product design, interior architecture and creative consulting studio. is an extension of the designer Dror Benshetrit. With several years of combined art and design education from The Design Academy (Eindhoven, Holland) and The Center for Art Education at the Tel Aviv Museum of Art (Israel), Dror focuses on innovative uses of materials, technology and shapes, and thrives on the origin of movement. His creations reflect a certain way of living and well-being.

Takora / Kimiyoshi Futori
www4.famille.ne.jp/~takora

Futori produces pop visuals that are cute but aggressive, venturing far beyond national and disciplinary borders. In 2003, his first work, CHEAP POP, was released in the UK (available at pocko.com). In 2004, he spent the spring and summer working on textiles in collaboration with DRESS CAMP. His work was published in magazines and art books in Hong Kong and Singapore. He produced campaign goods for Hong Kong's fashion mall, Harbour City.

Templin Brink Design
www.tbd-sf.com

Since 1998, Templin Brink Design creates branding, packaging, corporate identity and advertising campaigns by combining the unique talents of its principals, Joel Templin and Gaby Brink. Joel is the down-to-earth Midwesterner with a taste for humour and Wisconsin cheddar. Gaby is the Swiss-born perfectionist with a photographer's eye and a preference for gruyere.

Tobias Wong
www.brokenoff.com

Originally from Vancouver, Canada, Tobias Wong creates in New York. Wong treats design as a medium rather than a discipline to show how it embraces the aesthetics traditionally relegated to the fine arts. He coined the term "paraconceptual" to describe his dismantling of the hierarchies between "art" and "design". Not merely conceptual, his work mocks its own consumption. Wong's readydesigneds (replacing the anonymous readymade objects with well recognised designer pieces) are simply refashioned.

Tsuyoshi Kusano

Born in Tokyo in 1973, Kusano formed Nendo Graphics in 1993, joined Ascii Co., Ltd.in 1995, and established the limited private company, Kusano Tsuyoshi Design Office, in 2003.

Tycoon Graphics
www.tygun.com

Founded in 1991 by Yuichi Miyaji and Naoyuki Suzuki. Participates actively in a wide range of design such as advertising, packaging, fashion, CD cover design and logo design. The motto is "Thick and chic". Started "TyGun" project and since 2002 has collaborated with a character by Takuya Nakadai.

Yoshie Watanabe (D-Bros)
www.d-bros.jp

Born in Yamaguchi in 1961. After graduating from Yamaguchi University, joined Draft Co., Ltd. and principally takes part in advertising and packaging design projects. Since 1996, she has been working on the planning and designing of products under the "D-Bros" project. She also undertakes Corporate Identity and Sales Promotion for underwear shop "Une Nana Cool" produced by Wacoal, and other advertising projects. In 2003 she collaborated with Makiko Minagawa (ISSAY MIYAKE textile designer) on "HAAT".

Yuki Sugiyama (Hakuhodo Design)

A graphic designer born in 1977. After graduating from Musashino Art University, Visual Communication Design course, she entered Hakuhodo Design. Her principal works include Tohato's 'Caramel Corn' and Kobunsha book series "Hon-no Mushi-kun (A bookworm)".

3KG
www.kgkgkg.com

Formed in 2001 in Sapporo, Japan, 3KG is a graphic design studio with a strong focus on graphic media. It works on a wide range of fields including advertising, corporate identity, brand development, custom publishing, web development and moving image. 3KG is Shin Sasaki, Hiroaki Shirai and Tomoko Takano.

AllRightsReserved
www.allrights-reserved.com
www.whats-good.com

AllRightsReserved is a young and aggressive company based in Hong Kong with a trustworthy reputation in the fields of creative, design, publishing and event management. Its mission is to provide a platform for creators to share experiences, exchange knowledge and resources with talented designers from around the globe. Its focus is on book design and publications, which include the monthly magazine Arts Link for the Hong Kong Arts Centre; Chris production collection There is a crack in everything and ClosetoChris. Graphic design books include LowFat Graphics, Fotomo, I Love Game Graphics and the latest creation, All You Need Is Sticker Graphics.

217

Publisher:
AllRightsReserved Ltd.

Concept:
AllRightsReserved Ltd.

Design:
3KG

Editor:
Kazutomo Ryuko

Contributing Editors:
Daniel Mason, Takako Narita, Naomi Hiyama

Translation:
Takako Narita, Naoko Ryuko

Proofreading:
Ann Asano, Cherise Fong

Photographer:
Nobutoshi Kurisu, David Lo (H.K)

First Published in 2005 by AllRightsReserved Ltd.
Tel (852) 2712 0873
Fax (852) 2712 6701
URL www.allrights-reserved.com

For General Enquires:
info@allrights-reserved.com

For Distribution:
garylau@allrights-reserved.com

For Editorial Submission & Collaboration:
editor@allrights-reserved.com

Copyright ©2005 by "AllRightsReserved Ltd." All rights reserved. No part of this publication may be reproduced, stored in a retrieval system or transmitted in any form or by any means, electronic or mechanical, including photocopying, recording or any information storage and retrieval systems, without the written permission of the publisher.
While every effort has been made to ensure the accuracy of captions and credits in this book, "AllRightsReserved Ltd." does not under any circumstances accept any responsibility for errors or omissions.

Special thanks to:
ASYL Design, Atsushi Kikuchi, CAMEL Pleasure Factory, Co Ito, Communion W, Design Bridge, DEVILROBOTS, Etsuko Sato, Final Home, fuseproject, GK Design, Goodwin Hartshorn, Graphic Thought Facility, Happypets, j-me, Junkie, Kasia Korczak, Kashiwa Sato, Kenjiro Sano, Mark James, Masayoshi Kodaira, Manabu Mizuno, Mitsugu Mizobata, Myeong-hee Lee, Michael. Nash Associates, Naomi Hirabayashi, NBStudio, Non-Format, Norio Nakamura, Oliver Laric, onedotzero, Output, Pearlfisher, Red Design, Ryosuke Uehara, Sam Hurt and Jude Biddulph, Shuichi Ito, Soup Design, Stanley Wong Ping-Pui, state, Studio Dror, Takora Kimiyoshi Futori , Templin Brink Design, TLFG, Tobias Wong, Tsuyoshi Kusano, Tycoon Graphics, Yoshie Watanabe, Yuki Sugiyama.

Printed in Hong Kong
ISBN 988-97054-8-6

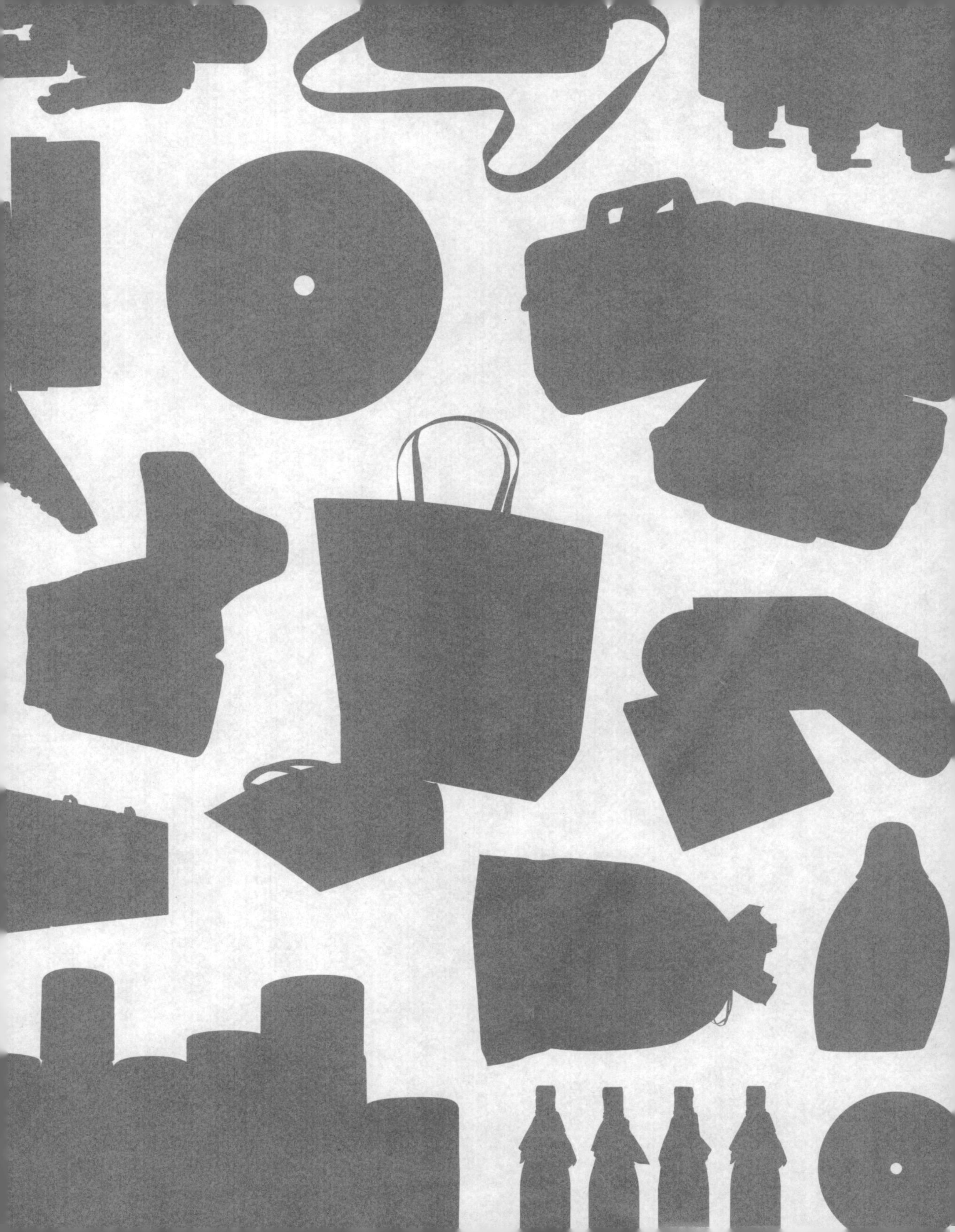